DEC 2011

No Animals Were Harmed

Also by Peter Laufer:

Forbidden Creatures
The Dangerous World of Butterflies
¡Calexico!
Hope Is a Tattered Flag (with Markos Kounalakis)
Mission Rejected
Wetback Nation
Exodus to Berlin
Highlights of a Lowlife (editor)
Shock and Awe
Made in Mexico (illustrated by Susan L. Roth)
Wireless Etiquette
Safety and Security for Women Who Travel
  (with Sheila Swan Laufer)
Inside Talk Radio
A Question of Consent
Neon Nevada (with Sheila Swan Laufer)
When Hollywood Was Fun (with Gene Lester)
Nightmare Aboard
Iron Curtain Rising

No Animals Were Harmed

The Controversial Line between Entertainment and Abuse

PETER LAUFER, PhD

LYONS PRESS
Guilford, Connecticut

An imprint of Globe Pequot Press

To buy books in quantity for corporate use
or incentives, call **(800) 962–0973**
or e-mail **premiums@GlobePequot.com.**

Lyons Press is an imprint of Globe Pequot Press.

"On the Roll" reprinted with permission by Leona Medlin and Richard Price.

Text design: Sheryl P. Kober
Project editor: Julie Marsh
Layout: Melissa Evarts

Library of Congress Cataloging-in-Publication Data is available on file.

ISBN 978-0-7627-6385-6

Printed in the United States of America

10 9 8 7 6 5 4 3 2 1

The author and publisher of this book do not have any relation to the American Humane Association, which operates the "No Animals Were Harmed"® certification program.

As The Shirelles doo-wopped:
This is dedicated to the one I love,
Sheila

The tank came in and pushed the wall over and you see what's in there. And all it is, is a bunch of chickens.
—Debra Ross, after watching Maricopa County sheriff's deputies raid her neighbor's house, arrest him on suspicion of cockfighting, and euthanize over a hundred of his birds.

CONTENTS

Contents

PROLOGUE

Imagine sitting in the audience at SeaWorld—or some other animal show—and watching the skillful choreography between man and beast collapse into a sudden explosion of mayhem and death. What would your reaction be? Horror, probably. Or perhaps you'd be secretly thrilled. No doubt you would tell the story over and over again to friends and family.

Just as my book about the world of exotic pets, *Forbidden Creatures*, was going to press, Dawn Brancheau was killed by Tilikum, an orca she shared the SeaWorld stage with in Orlando, Florida. The sparse journalese of an Associated Press dispatch set the scene: "The killer whale snatched the 40-year-old trainer from a poolside platform in its jaws and thrashed her around underwater, killing her in front of a horrified audience."[1]

The path from the Romans cheering as lions and Christians were forced to battle each other seems to lead directly to our contemporary human fascination with animals as entertainment. None of us is immune to seeking diversion from an animal show, whether we insist our dog rolls over for a treat or we ogle danger from the bleachers at a SeaWorld-like event. (I for one remember well going to Marine World in Vallejo, California, with my wife and our then-young son to watch the trapped dolphins execute tricks.)

Where is the line that separates animal use from abuse? Those dolphins, we human animals now know, experience emotions. Exploiting them and other animals for our own pleasure is selfish. And what about the human participants when animals are used and abused? Plenty of the people involved face the conundrum themselves. Certainly Tilikum's trainer Dawn Brancheau was more a victim of human fascination with animal antics than was the orca. (She died of drowning and blunt-force trauma to her head, neck, and torso, according to the autopsy.) Some cases are obvious. When professional football player Michael Vick was caught beating dogs to death, there was no question that the perverse entertainment value he reaped from his hobby constituted abuse. He became a proverbial poster child for animal rights activists, serving a prison sentence before returning to sports stardom. Not that his notoriety stopped dog abuse among celebrities. Rapper DMX (Earl Simmons), who features bull terrier photographs on some of his CD covers, was locked up in the notorious Maricopa County tent jail in Arizona for ninety days,[2] convicted of animal cruelty after police located emaciated and dead dogs at his home in Cave Creek on the north side of Phoenix.[3] His songs' lyrics and album liner notes suggest he, too, is a dogfighter.

Yet animals also serve as entertainers in circumstances sometimes arguably privileged. Travis, the chimpanzee that went on a brutal rampage in suburban Connecticut, was served wine in stemmed glasses and imported chocolates. The more I thought about the point where use and abuse converge, the more intrigued I became with studying the nuances involved. I started to list those places where we gawk at animals: zoos and circuses, rodeos, bullfights and cockfights. One of my neighbors years ago in Nevada fought cocks. These fights are now illegal in all fifty states yet still embraced aboveground in the U.S. territories of Puerto Rico and Guam, and in plenty of other places around the world. Lanny, my Nevada neighbor, would line his various knives and gaffs on the counter of Bonnie's cafe in Dayton and tell me love stories about his chickens and their fights. In Portugal I encountered a brutal rural bullfight. High in the Michoacán mountains I walked out of a roadside circus; it was too difficult to watch the scarred and scrawny show cats being whipped, poked, and prodded. I remembered meeting Dutchess, a retired racing greyhound, now living a life of luxury greeting tourists at the Greyhound Hall of Fame in Abilene, Kansas.

Step right up, ladies and gentlemen, as the circus barker would say: What's okay and what's not okay?

Homing pigeons? Sled dogs? Fox hunting? Dancing bears on the streets of India? Elephant polo in Sri Lanka? Alligator wrestling on the Miccosukee Indian reservation in Florida? In Harris County, Texas, near Houston, a man was arrested, I learned, for fornicating with his neighbor's goat,[4] presumably for entertainment purposes. How about canned hunts, the challenge of paying money to shoot an animal confined on private property?

In the center ring, ladies and gentlemen, is Exhibit A, an infamous politician! It was on a canned hunt for quail in Texas that then–Vice President Dick Cheney infamously shot Harry Whittington, his friend and contributor to his political campaigns, in the face.

My friend and primary contact at the Fish and Wildlife Service, Ed Newcomer (the special agent who introduced me to his dangerous world of butterflies when he arrested the World's Most Wanted Butterfly Smuggler), helped me realize the codependent relationships among roadside zoos, circuses, and canned hunts. There are cases, he alerted me, of animals from failing roadside zoo businesses and animals no longer of value to circuses being sold to entrepreneurs who pen these exotics in places with lax animal control laws, such as Texas, and then sell the opportunity for "hunters" to come bag a trophy. Humorist Carl Hiaasen uses a Florida canned hunt as a backdrop for a bittersweet look at animal abuse in his book *Sick Puppy* (spoiler alert: the rhino prevails).

I surprised Agent Newcomer with tales of fighting crickets. They're not defined as "wildlife" by his agency, but he was unaware that the ancient tradition of dueling crickets is experiencing a resurgence amongst the newly moneyed classes in China. What really shocked him were the stories of handlers doping their crickets: fueling the fighters with compounds to increase their stamina and ferocity.

Ladies and gentlemen, it really is a circus out there! I learned of wild pig hunting in rural northern California and black bear hunts in the foothills of the Sierra Nevada. Over a cup of morning coffee in a cafe not far from my Bodega Bay home, newspaper columnist Chris Smith told me, "Up the road ambles this big black pig." He was recounting an unfortunate event that marred one of the wild pig hunts he enjoys each year on a ranch in Mendocino County with a group of buddies. "I'm expecting the pig to bolt, and the pig doesn't. Rifles are chambered and one guy takes the shot. It was a clean shot. Head shot. The pig falls over." It was a two-hundred-pound porker. Trouble was it was no wild pig. It was a neighbor's pet pig; the guys had wandered across the property line. The neighbor's wife and daughters cried over the loss, and the pig killer paid a $500 consolation prize. "It's a boys' weekend," Smith explained about shooting at pigs for entertainment. And for several years no pigs were brought down, the fellows just clambered around in the wild. "It's recreational. Nobody feels bad about it because the wild pigs are non-native, destructive, and they taste good." Who knew pigs could qualify as entertainment?

As I was researching the topic of animal use and abuse, a new term was added to my lexicon: crush videos. These are the animal equivalent of snuff films in which stiletto-heeled women crush the skulls of small animals under their feet. I first heard of them just before the U.S. Supreme Court ruled that trafficking in such moving pictures is protected by the First Amendment, even though the images portrayed may be pictures of illegal animal abuse. But ladies and gentlemen, how do those crush videos compare with the work of the Algerian artist Adel Abdessemed, specifically his piece "Don't Trust Me," which caused controversy when it was shown at the San Francisco Institute of Art, its images of animals being killed with a sledgehammer closed to the public after a few days on exhibit?

"I'm not a pimp. I'm not a malcontent," Paul Huln told me when I called him to arrange a meeting in rural Louisiana to talk cockfighting with an expert. He agreed to see me as long as I agreed to tell his side of the cockfighting story. That's why I wanted to talk with him. "I started fighting chickens in 1941," he said on the phone, as he remembered that in the mid-1950s a colleague told him that eventually cockfighting would be illegal in Louisiana—something that seemed farfetched to him back then. "Anything is possible," he mused to me from the vantage point of the year 2010, trying to make his point clear by adding, "We have a Muslim president." He confirmed our date and continued in the same laconic tone of voice, "God bless you, brother."

I considered catch-and-release fishing. Cruel and unusual? I thought about falconers, the Kentucky Derby, and greased pig chases at county fairs. I wandered down the street to the Tides restaurant in Bodega Bay (made famous by Alfred Hitchcock as a locale in his film *The Birds*) for lunch. There, adjacent to the snack bar, was a row of video games, and a couple of young boys were lingering over one equipped with two mock rifles. They were beseeching their mother for spare change. "Can we have a quarter?" "Trophy Hunting Bear and Moose," the game was called. After she denied them and they departed, I dropped a quarter in the slot and watched computer-generated images of bears move right to left across a forest scene. I aimed my rifle and squeezed the trigger. The bears on the screen sped up. I shot again and watched as one of them fell to the ground. The game flashed my accrued points on the screen near the warning sticker, ANIMATED VIOLENCE MILD. Is this just a game, or another example of how we instill in ourselves that animals are our playthings?

Before long I had pages of notes, a stack of pertinent books, a growing list of appointments, and a new assignment. The characters were revealing themselves, from the grotesque to the absurd. Absurd like Hans Kurt Kubus, the German tourist in New Zealand who attempted to fly home with forty-four geckos and skinks stuffed down his underwear—over $25,000 worth of endangered wildlife. Herr Kubus seems like a circus act himself; like clowns coming out of the midget car, the geckos and skinks were pulled from his pants.

The more I read, the more I observed, the more animals—human and nonhuman—I met, the more it seemed to me that a possum was pointing me toward my conclusion. "We have met the enemy," Pogo taught us, "and he is us." Even the one thing I wanted to promise the reader as I embarked on this project—that no animals were harmed by me during the writing of this book—proved an impossible task.

CHAPTER ONE
Swim with Dolphins!

IT WAS MOTHER'S DAY AND THE RADIO STATION WHERE I WAS WORK-ing provided us with free tickets to what was then called Marine World, an amusement park alongside Interstate 80 on the edge of the San Francisco metropolis in Vallejo. Our youngest son was in grammar school, and my wife, Sheila, and I took him and a friend to see what was billed as the killer whale show. The bleachers around the pool were packed, and the announcer asked two mothers to volunteer to participate in the act.

"You do it!" We all encouraged Sheila, and she joined another woman poolside. Volunteering to join the show is not out of character for her. Up at Lake Tahoe, for another example, she answered Dick Clark's call from the stage one evening to sing with the Shirelles. She's a good sport (and sings quite well!).

The Marine World barker announced that the other woman was the wife of the local 7 Up bottling company owner and that she would be the first mother to do a trick. Mrs. 7 Up was told to make specific hand gestures and that the killer whale would swoop up out of the water and plant a kiss on her. Indeed it did just that. Or almost. It rose from the pool and made a kiss-like maneuver close to her face. She swooned, the audience cheered, and the announcer moved over to the opposite side of the pool where he had stationed Sheila.

"I thought, 'That's pretty fun and it will entertain the kids,'" Sheila remembered later, as the trainer showed her what gesture he wanted her to make to the killer whale waiting in the water. "I assumed the same thing would happen, that I would get to kiss the whale. They put me by the edge of the pool and told me to make the gesture, which obviously was a signal to the orca." But this gesture differed from the one made by Mrs. 7 Up.

1

The killer whale again rose up out of the pool, but just far enough to use its pectoral fins to splash Sheila. "I was completely doused with water. I was drenched, and the audience laughed and clapped." It was a warm day. No harm done. Immediately after the splash Sheila saw trainers throwing fish for the orca's reward. Sheila's reward was a button that read I SURVIVED THE KILLER WHALE AT MARINE WORLD.

She was her typical good sport about the affair, but she did not appreciate being the butt of the joke. "I was a little miffed. I felt cheated. I figured it was fun for the kids, although it would have been much better if I had gotten the kiss."

We talked about that Marine World experience after the SeaWorld killer whale trainer was killed. "I would never do it again," she said. "It was immense. It scared me. I felt a bundle of emotions when I was splashed—fear because of the size of the creature, along with a feeling of being somewhat humiliated and used." She reminded me how tiny—especially in comparison to the animal—the pool looked to us, and how we hoped the orca lived in a much larger enclosure when it was not performing. "They have no business taking it from its natural environment and trapping it," she said these years later. "I suppose at the time I anthropomorphized the whale. I guess I saw him as happy, having a good time, pleasing the trainer."

Pleasing his trainer is not what was on the mind of Tilikum at Orlando's SeaWorld when he yanked her into the water and killed her early in 2010. Amateur video of the attack is difficult to watch as the orca repeatedly and violently grabs at Dawn Brancheau and in minutes leaves her lifeless. SeaWorld staff escorted the audience away as quickly as possible, but not before the crowd watched the attack.

Just prior to the attack, Brancheau was rubbing the six-ton marine mammal from poolside, as usual. Suddenly it grabbed her ponytail and flipped her into the water.

2

"You can't put yourself in the water unless you trust them and they trust you," Brancheau told the *Orlando Sun* in 2006.[5] And trust them she did. Dramatic footage from a 2000 television interview shows Brancheau being lifted out of the water on the snout of another killer whale. "I'm actually sitting on the nose of the killer whale and she's blasting me up out of the water," she tells the WESH TV interviewer.[6] It is an exquisite sight, Brancheau standing on the whale and then diving off into the pool they share. "We're accentuating the power and the strength of the killer whales," she explained about her act. The interviewer is enthralled, as were audiences. "That's the fun stuff," Brancheau said about the stunts she performed with the animals.

After the attack SeaWorld kept Tilikum out of performances and sequestered him in a pool at the park. But the company refused to announce his retirement, despite the fact that in British Columbia he was one of three orcas in a pool when another trainer had been killed in 1991. He attacked a man who broke into Sea-World in 1999 after hours and was found, dead, sprawled on top of the whale. Nonetheless, Dawn Brancheau's older sister, Diane Gross, hoped SeaWorld would not punish Tilikum and announced that her family considered the killing an accident. "She loved the whales like her children, she loved all of them," she said of her sister. "They all had personalities, good days and bad days."[7]

Tilikum was captured in the waters off Iceland in 1983, at an age estimated at two years. Because of his youth when he was seized, handlers doubted he could survive in the wild were he released after his years in captivity: He never learned how to take care of himself. He is the largest killer whale in captivity, so big and unpredictable that trainers no longer swim with him. His value to SeaWorld is not only as a performer; he is also a prodigious captive breeder with at least thirteen offspring to his credit,[8] one of which, named Ky, seemingly tried to drown a SeaWorld trainer in San Antonio.[9]

The attack in Orlando did not surprise independent researchers—those who weren't working for commercial marine mammal amusement parks. "I'm sure it was a high stress situation," was the observation of Nancy Black about Tilikum's lifestyle. Black is the lead marine biologist at and owner of California's Monterey Bay Whale Watch, a company that offers excursions in the Pacific to observe whales in the wild. That he was born wild made life in small tanks especially frustrating, she told Husna Haq, a *Christian Science Monitor* reporter. "I'm sure he had a hard life, kept in a holding pen, not getting a lot of exercise." She theorized that his frequent breeding activities—Tilikum was trained to engage in artificial insemination—could have contributed to his aggressive behavior. "Maybe he was stressed out, maybe he had frustration," she said after the attack. "So he grabbed the closest thing to him to take out his frustration and high energy level. These animals are too big for tanks. They're wild, intelligent animals with a big social structure. They're really not an appropriate animal to keep in captivity."

"It's an unfortunate way to experience nature: to see animals turned into Disneyland animatronic puppets for the entertainment of people," was the response of Richard Ellis, a marine conservationist at the American Museum of Natural History in New York. "I would rather they weren't, but this is where we are in entertainment and education right now, so I don't think this is the end of it."[10]

Marine World in Vallejo is known as Six Flags Discovery Kingdom these days. The audience participation continues, and it's not limited to getting kissed (or splashed) by killer whales. You can opt for the Swim with Dolphins ticket. "Get in the water with our Atlantic bottlenose dolphins where you will spend quality time swimming with these marine mammals in a rare hands-on learning session," is a tempting offer from the park. The deluxe experience will cost you $149, and includes your admission. That means "wild and gut-wrenching" hi-tech roller coasters, plenty of food to buy inside, and an array of souvenirs—in addition to bobbing around with marine mammals.

CHAPTER TWO

Whale as Sushi

JUST AFTER I BEGAN WRITING THIS BOOK, THE DOCUMENTARY FILM *The Cove* stunned audiences and earned an Academy Award for its dramatic investigation into and exposé of dolphin slaughters in a national park in Taiji, Japan. Japanese fishermen—and it's difficult to use the title *fishermen* when *murderers* seems more accurate—are shown corralling and then harpooning dolphins in the waters of a dead-end cove that turns red with the blood of the dead and dying cetaceans. The abuses are multiple. Some dolphins are harvested alive to be sold to amusement parks like Marine World. Those killed are packaged for sale as meat for human consumption. Pollution in the seas around Japan and the fact that dolphins eat at the top of the food chain mean that the meat is laden with toxic levels of mercury.

The Cove is an important and sobering film, even for me, a longtime quasi-vegetarian. Up until this point, I'd made an exception for fish, but the night Sheila and I watched the film, I left my fish dinner on the plate, went into the kitchen, and made myself a peanut butter sandwich.

Most of us know dolphins are not fish. Fish are cold-blooded and secure their needed oxygen out of the water. They're not known for their smarts: As pets they can't fetch the paper or keep rats out of the kitchen. Dolphins are warm-blooded. They're mammals and, like us, breathe air, give birth to live young, and, at places like Marine World, interact with humans in what often is interpreted to be peer-to-peer relationships.

I woke up the next morning still disturbed by the information and images presented by filmmaker Louie Psihoyos. In the film Psihoyos explains to the audience how he feels driven—because of his love of oceans and ocean life—to draw attention to abuses such as what he witnessed in Taiji, and to do what he can to stop horrific human behavior directed against marine life.

Activist journalism is powerful stuff, and I decided that next morning that my fish-eating days had come to an end. It wasn't just the dolphins that Louie Psihoyos and his daring crew, who risked their lives to obtain the incriminating footage, convinced me to avoid. I realized that there was no reason to continue eating any animal, and a long list of reasons to quit killing and consuming all animals, even mindless bottom-feeding farmed catfish. From selfish concerns about my own health, to worries about the deteriorating environment, to the inequities of wasting resources raising animals for food, to the moral ambiguities—I realized that I'd finally drunk the full-vegan Kool-Aid.

Not that Louie Psihoyos is necessarily one of my heroes, however. Before I saw the film and a few days before the Oscars, one of my sources in the law enforcement community encountered Psihoyos displaying what the cop called "an interfering dose of personal opportunism." Psihoyos tipped off agents at the National Oceanic and Atmospheric Administration (NOAA) (the federal agency that enforces laws protecting marine mammals and regulates commercial fishing) that a trendy Santa Monica restaurant was offering certain customers whale sushi. Psihoyos made a deal with NOAA: He would trade his insider information for the liberty to record informants and undercover agents being served whale in the restaurant—stuff that he thought would make dramatic footage for another movie. The deal with NOAA was a win-win. Psihoyos would wire his sophisticated equipment to a couple of shills (or "confidential informants" in police lingo). If all worked as planned, these informants would hang out at the sushi bar, chat up the sushi chef, and before the evening ended they would solicit an order of whale. They then would secrete a sample of the whale into a concealed doggie bag as evidence. Louie Psihoyos's crew would turn over copies of everything recorded to NOAA investigators and hold off publicizing the encounter until the investigation was completed. That embargo was critical to the deal from the point of view of the NOAA agents. They didn't just want to close down a Santa Monica restaurant. They wanted the initial encounter to lead them to whomever was supplying the whale meat, a trail that could result in shutting down other illicit sushi joints and putting at least one wholesale whale meat supplier out of business.

The informants first ordered traditional sushi fare: tuna, halibut, and the like. As the night wore on, they were served more exotic variations that included raw beef and horsemeat. It was a dinner of *omakase*—the chef's specialties. Next off the sushi chef's knife was blowfish—*fugu* in Japanese—the pufferfish that can kill the diner if the chef makes a mistake while carving around the poisonous parts. Around closing time the informants made their move and ordered whale. The chef slipped out a side door for a few minutes and came back with a plastic bag. He laid it on his cutting board, cut open the bag, and started slicing the contents.

"What's that?" a woman at the bar asked.

The chef said nothing. The informants, the undercover agents, and the innocent bystander customers, including the inquisitive woman, chatted among themselves, speculating. More horse? Different tuna?

After a few more guesses the chef leaned over to the woman and whispered in a voice loud enough for Psihoyos's equipment to record, "Whale."

"Whale?" she repeated in a loud voice, surprised. When no one at the counter objected to the illicit fare, the chef relaxed. My source present at the scene seized the opportunity to ask the chef about the dish he was preparing. As he created the sashimi, he reiterated that it was whale, that it was fresh, and that the restaurant sold so much of it it had to reorder every few days.

Mission accomplished, the informants pocketed the sample, paid the $600 tab, and called it a night. They headed home with plans to continue the investigation.

Louie Psihoyos thought otherwise. He wanted an immediate raid on the sushi bar. Reneging on his promise not to interfere with the investigation, he leaked the ongoing story to the *New York Times* and Fox News, according to my source, in hopes that inquiries to investigators from the newspaper and television reporters would force NOAA to move on the restaurant before reporters tipped the chef off that he was in jeopardy. Prosecutors tried to convince Fox and the *Times* to hold the story, but they feared Fox would not honor their request. The result was a decision to abandon the wide dragnet and just take down the one Santa Monica restaurant.

Two nights before the 2010 Academy Awards, a posse of agents hit The Hump (described by the *Los Angeles Times* as "a hip hangout") for illegal possession and selling of whale meat. It was jammed with customers when agents flashed their badges and ordered the sushi chef to put down his knife and stick up his hands. Diners were asked to pay their bills and leave the restaurant, which was officially closed for the night.

From the point of view of the law enforcement agents, director Louie Psihoyos manipulated events to serve his short-term gain. "We recorded surreptitiously using all the same gear that we used to make the movie *The Cove*, except we're using it on American soil this time at a sushi restaurant," Psihoyos primped to reporters who were anxious to hear him tell about his own derring-do. The news was flashed around the world. "It was actually more exciting busting this restaurant than winning the Oscar," he said with Hollywood panache,[11] seemingly unconcerned that reneging on the deal he made with the NOAA agents might mean sushi restaurants on American soil would continue to serve whale procured from the same sources that supplied The Hump.

Don't get me wrong. *The Cove* is an amazing movie. But I was disappointed to learn about the apparent behind-the-scenes frailties of a fine filmmaker.

Nothing wrong with breaking the story, was Louie Psihoyos's vehement response when I reached him at his studio in Boulder, Colorado. He reminded me that the law only knew about the whale sushi on the under-the-counter menu because of him. His beef, so to speak, with the agents came when they refused to share critical information about their operation with him and his crew. He was not, he said, informed about the specifics of when the authorities planned to move in and arrest all the whale sushi purveyors.

"That wasn't the deal at all," Psihoyos said about his arrangement with NOAA. "At the point where I felt like we were being ostracized from our own sting, I felt they were not living up to their agreement, so we released it on our own time frame." Psihoyos also told me his company paid the restaurant tab for the undercover agents, provided the surveillance equipment, and considered themselves partners in the operation. "They were just treating us like any other news media," he complained. "We didn't need them. Our goal was to broadcast this over the largest possible network so that it would instill the fear of God into anybody who was selling whale meat around the country. And that's what it did," he said with satisfaction months later, expressing the belief that up and down the Atlantic and Pacific coasts "there was whale meat being dumped in Dumpsters because they didn't want to be caught."

I asked Psihoyos about the charge that because he broke the story on his timetable he jeopardized the investigation beyond The Hump. Did suppliers and other distributors escape NOAA's net because he talked before the cops wanted him to talk?

Not important, was his response. "What we wanted to do was send a shock wave up to the Japanese government, and that's what we did by making it international news." The law enforcement officers were more interested in their own careers, he said, than in saving the animals. "My interest was in trying to save the species." He's convinced that The Hump's sister restaurant in

Japan was the supplier, a supplier protected by Japanese law from any American prosecution. "It's just different motives. They were interested in busting mid-level people. We were interested in giving a black eye to the Japanese government, which is complicit in allowing endangered animals to be hunted in a marine sanctuary. That, to me, is just unconscionable. I think they," he said about the law, "had their sights set too low."

What about the charge that Louie Psihoyos was self-serving about his news release, that it was timed to augment the publicity surrounding his Oscar win?

Nonsense, was the director's reply. "Virtually nobody went to see the film, compared to a feature film," he said with an ironic laugh. "We just broke even on the film yesterday." (He and I talked just before Thanksgiving, 2010.) "In terms of enlarging our pocket? That's almost laughable in terms of documentary. When you do a documentary, it's not about trying to make money. It's about trying to solve an issue. That's what I'm trying to do, solve the issue. Sometimes what you do is outside-the-box thinking. When it comes to outside-the-box thinking, I don't really care about human laws. Human laws are really kind of laughable. The Japanese government says it's fine to kill endangered whales in a marine sanctuary. That's a law." He's speaking at a faster and faster pace, clearly agitated. "I would say trying to bust a mid-level whale meat salesman is self-serving as well." Psihoyos said his ultimate goal is to mobilize public opinion to force an end to whale hunts. "To that end, we're achieving what we set out to achieve."

As for The Hump, it never reopened. Its owners published a mea culpa, apologizing for their illegal behavior and announcing they would make a "substantial" contribution to organizations working to preserve endangered species. "The Hump hopes that by closing its doors, it will help bring awareness to the detrimental effect that illegal whaling has on the preservation of our ocean ecosystems and species," said their farewell message.[12]

CHAPTER THREE

Ted Nugent Is My Blood Brother

WEEKS LATER I MEET WITH RICHARD ELLIS, ONE OF AMERICA'S LEAD-
ing marine conservationists, in Manhattan, at Punch Restaurant
in the Flatiron District. It is a hot late spring day and the breeze
feels good coming through the open front of the eatery. Ellis
is anxious to talk porpoises, but he's a regular here who hasn't
been in for dinner lately; the beginnings of our chat keep being
interrupted as one after another of the pretty waitresses stop by
our table to greet him with New York air kisses. Enjoying the
attention, he offers a weak excuse—"This is the only restaurant
in New York where this happens"—and punctuates the disclaimer
with a contented smile. Ellis is the author of a shelf full of books
on marine life, and he is a prolific artist, drawing and painting
animals that live in the water for magazines and museums. When
the initial flurry finally abates, he gives the matter at hand his full
attention, his brow furrowing with an intensity that is augmented
by the austere look of his gold wire-rimmed eyeglasses.

"People have a very poor understanding of wild animal motivations. They think that because they can get a dolphin to jump
through a hoop," he says in a soft voice that competes with the
restaurant clatter, "that they become the masters of that domin-
ion. More often than not terrible mistakes are made in misunder-
estimating," he laughs as he uses what he calls George W. Bush's
favorite word, "the capabilities of these animals."

Ellis is convinced no one will ever know what motivated Tilikum to pull his trainer into the pool to her death, but he is ready
with a theory. "There is the possibility that this was the whale's
idea of play." Killer whales come equipped with the second-largest
brain of any animal on Earth today, second only to sperm whales.
Yet Ellis is not prepared to indict the whale in question for bad

behavior. "A whale, no matter how big its brain, cannot know a human being will drown if you keep it underwater." The fact that trainer Dawn Brancheau is the second person drowned by Tilikum might make it easy for some to presume that the whale is trying to kill its trainers, but Ellis does not believe that is what occurred. He subscribes to the theory that her death can be ascribed to an unfortunate accident.

The bigger puzzle for Richard Ellis is why killer whales allow themselves to be kept captive.

"What would the alternative be?" I ask him. The killer whales that perform at marine shows either are caught and placed in pools with no exit to the ocean or they are captive bred and lodged in such pools. "How could one of these whales prevent such a fate?"

His answer is easy and influenced by human emotion. "Bash its head against the wall until it died. It surprises me that these animals allow themselves to be kept in captivity." But then he reconsiders. "They're smart enough to realize that they can't get out. So they might as well relax and enjoy it."

"Deal with it," I offer.

"Deal with it," he agrees. "It's anthropomorphizing in a big way to say that it's a silly life for the world's largest predator to be jumping through hoops and playing basketball. But they can't know, especially the ones born in captivity, that they would have a better life out in the wild."

Using animals such as killer whales, lions and tigers, and other apex predators for our own entertainment satisfies some atavistic need we fall prey to, Ellis suggests as we talk. We want to exert control over animals, animals that used to have control over us back when human beings were their prey.

As we chat I recount the story of an old high school friend. He and his wife went swimming with dolphins in the Pacific off the coast of Mexico during their honeymoon, an experience they continue to talk about dreamily these many years later. There is nothing necessarily wrong with enjoying interaction with any animal. "The abuse comes the moment you put them in a pen," Ellis believes. "These are free-ranging wild animals," he says about dolphins and porpoises. Yet the marine mammals caught for amusement parks (or captive bred in such parks) often seem to live well enough. They're fed a healthy diet, they play with their trainers, and they make babies. They're free from great white shark attacks, Japanese fishermen, or tuna nets. Perhaps they're just as happy in the parks' tanks as they would be in the open ocean, and they serve humanity because of the educational value offered by up-close-and-personal encounters with them.

But such talk, Ellis believes, is now an antiquated idea. Now that technology and photojournalists provide intimate sightings of wild beasts engaged in all their daily activities, from eating to breeding to hatching or giving birth, from fighting to hunting to sleeping and dying, there is no educational rationale for locking them up in cages and tanks and putting them on public display, no matter how large, cozy, and luxurious the enclosures.

Moral issues, including the point at which animal use becomes abuse, cannot be legislated, Richard Ellis suggests. How can an animal lover expect governments in Orlando to buck the power of SeaWorld and its adjacent amusement parks with all their political power and financial influence? But he feels confident such moral issues can be taught and explained.

Not that the conservationist isn't susceptible to objectifying animals himself. Ellis and his wife keep a parrot in their Manhattan apartment, a parrot with clipped wings ("It kept crashing into the window," he says). He claims that the parrot, captive bred in Texas, is happy and runs his household. It says, "Wants some more," when it demands to be fed, and his wife salutes and comes running with food.

"But how was it treated where it was bred in Texas?" I ask. "Should it have come up from Texas to live in hyper-urban New York City? Should it have had its wings clipped? Why is it living in Manhattan?"

Ellis interrupts me with a smile and says, "Because it's having a really, really good time."

"You're making the same judgment the Japanese fisherman does when he decides it's fair and reasonable to kill dolphins en masse and hunt whales," I charge, although keeping a pet bird in Manhattan differs from slaughtering countless fish for a dining novelty.

"Of course I am," he readily agrees. He takes a drink of water. "It's easier to make a blanket statement if your hands are clean."

"I would wager that if a cockroach shows up in your New York apartment, you're going to stomp it." Our amiable conversation enters the world of moral relativism.

"You bet I am," he says about the ubiquitous urban pest. "Absolutely. Do I think about cockroach rights when I do that? No," he answers his own question in a quiet voice. "There is a scale. You're not going to stomp on a chimpanzee that wanders into your kitchen. For one thing, it will kill you if you tried." He can rationalize stomping the cockroach because as human beings we've put ourselves at the top of the *scala naturae* and cockroaches figure down near the bottom. "I'm not saying we should stomp 'em," he quickly adds.

"That scale is created from our human-centric point of view," I remind Ellis.

"Yeah," he agrees with amiable diffidence, "but whose point of view are we going to use? An octopus's point of view?"

Richard Ellis defines for me what he considers the most egregious example of human beings abusing other animals: big game fishing and hunting. "It doesn't get more abusive than killing an animal minding its own business, whether it's a marlin or a swordfish or a kudu."

I start to imagine trophy kills, and envision the taxidermied animals I've seen adorning saloon walls in Nevada, California, and Oregon. The storied Rancho Nicasio in Marin County is just an hour south along the coast from Bodega Bay and it's home to a herd of stuffed game heads looming over the bar in poses that would be ominous if the animals were still alive. "Or a moose," I add.

"Moose," Ellis agrees and continues with his litany. "Or a whitetail deer. Yet there is an enormous subculture—or perhaps it's a superculture—that thinks this is necessary."

Maybe not necessary, but there is a huge cohort that considers big game hunting perfectly appropriate behavior, behavior that's part of the American frontier mythos and is popularized in the current era by a trend-setting minor rock 'n' roll star, Ted Nugent. Nugent distances himself from the peace-and-love rock 'n' rollers with his trademark camouflage let's-go-hunting clothing and the hunting trips he organizes for fans. Spring and fall, for example, Nugent travels to New Brunswick for bear hunts. The $3,500 fee (plus $150 for the license) includes meals, accommodations, and "bear trophy prep" to ensure that the bear's head will be as good as the game adorning the walls at Rancho Nicasio. Buffalo on a private ranch in Michigan are the target of another opportunity: For $4,500 a hunter can hire guitarist Nugent as his hunting partner and guide. The promotional literature promises that "unlike most buffalo hunts at other ranches, the hunters at Sunrize Acres get to keep all meat, hide, horns and everything."[13] Skip Mr. Nugent as guide and the price drops a thousand dollars for a bull buffalo, and bagging a cow buffalo goes for a bargain $1,800.

Sunrize Acres is Nugent's Jackson County, Michigan, ranch where he also offers special Father's Day hunts for trophy wild hogs and rams. "Bring your camera to capture these magical family moments and the wildlife," reads the brochure, illustrated with the picture of a happy father and son, alongside a freshly killed hog. "Kick back by the rustic lodge and enjoy the fresh Michigan air!"[14]

Ted Nugent was on my list of potential interviewees for this book. As Richard Ellis and I talk at Punch, I'm negotiating with

Nugent's personal assistant, Linda Peterson, about a meeting with the man known to his fans as "the Nuge." After my first query letter to her, she sent a nice note back headlined, "Greetings from Tedquarters." She indicated that Mr. Nugent's schedule was full, that he was preparing for an upcoming series of concerts gently named the "Trample the Dead, Hurdle the Weak" tour. I told her I was patient. Meanwhile, I signed up for Nugent's newsletter and received a warm welcome.

"Dear Blood Brother," Nugent's website called to me over his name. "Welcome! The American Dream is not supposed to be a spectator sport. It must be a participatory duty—and we celebrate that in every way right here at TedNugent.com." I was told the newsletter would keep me posted on upcoming hunts, like the opportunity to spend $1,500 on a hog hunt (branded "Porkslam") for two days, one of which would be graced by the Nuge himself. My note ended with this reminder from Nugent: "Call it ego, call it bragging, call it whatever you want, but there's only one alpha male and that's me."

While I was waiting to hear back from Ms. Peterson, I learned that Nugent violated the game laws in my home state, California, and was found out because he broadcast his illegal hunting on his own television hunting show, *Spirit of the Wild*. California Fish and Game wardens who were watching the show say they saw him killing a deer too young to be hunted legally, and that the macho man lured the deer to his gun with a bait known by the trade name "C'mere Deer."[15] Nugent's lawyer showed up in court for him and entered his no contest plea to deer baiting (baiting wildlife is illegal in California) and to irregularities with his hunting license. The Nuge was fined $1,750 for both misdemeanors.[16] The Yuba County district attorney accepted a plea bargain that included dropping the charge against Nugent for killing an immature buck.[17] In a note on his website, Nugent's comments were limited to a terse few lines. "I should have been better informed, more aware," read the posting, "and I take full responsibility. The honorable hunting lifestyle is my deepest passion."[18] Honorable? Shooting fawns? Deer baiting?

Conservationist Ellis laughs when I tell him about my talks with the Nuge's office.

"I'm laughing," he explains to me, "because Ted Nugent will shoot you if he doesn't like what you're saying."

"Oh, pshaw."

But Ellis acts serious. "He will come to your interview with a 30.06 across his knees, because he likes shooting things." Then he laughs again. "And I suspect he would like shooting people if he could." Ellis believes that hunting is an anachronism, even if it is for meat, not trophy. "Ted Nugent, I am sure, will argue that he doesn't kill anything he's not going to eat. But it's mostly a hairy-chested thing to do—greatly atavistic. Guy walked out of the cave, 'Me bring food back. Me hit mammoth over the head with big stick. We eat.' And so everybody said, 'My hero. You kill mammoth with stick. We all love you. We make you king.'" We're talking just a few days after Ellis sent his latest manuscript, a book about sperm whales, off to his publisher. Predation by humans is on his mind. "Hunting and fishing is so unfair," he muses. "Hunting is craziness. Sneaking up on a bear? Where is the glory proving you're smarter than a fish, fercrissakes. I've never liked hunting or fishing. I've never done it. I'm on the moral high ground here."

"Or perhaps Ted Nugent would call you a lily-livered pansy," I suggest.

"Yeah, well let him say that to me!"

I crossed the Nuge off my list of interviewees, not because I feared a 30.06 in his rock 'n' roll hands, but because I decided any "hunter" who uses C'mere Deer in his quest to bag Bambi's relatives defines animal abuse.

Months later one Thomas Gilbert wrote a letter to my local newspaper, a letter that caught my attention because of the headline: HUNTERS ARE JUST "HIDERS" NOW. He referred to recent articles about hunting and called them "a reminder that not all of us have evolved out of the blood-lust most of our species was driven by a few thousand years ago." Gilbert wrote about those who call hunting a sport: "They are not hunters, they are hiders. They prey upon weak animals." He cited duck hunters in particular and compared hiding in a duck blind with the wars in Afghanistan and Iraq. "Our nation is at war, not with ducks, but with fellow humans. I learned many years ago that hunting humans is the ultimate game." Gilbert challenged hunters "to man up and do something 'positive' with their blood-lust."[19]

Ted Nugent failed Thomas Gilbert's test when he was presented with the military option to exercise his love affair with guns and hunting. In a July 15, 1990, *Detroit Free Press* interview, Nugent described how he dodged the Vietnam War–era draft, saying he arrived at the induction center in excrement-caked and urine-stained pants, but claimed, "If I would have gone over there, I'd have been killed, or I'd have killed all the hippies in the foxholes. I would have killed everybody."

CHAPTER FOUR
Searching for a Louisiana Cockfight

COCKFIGHTING IS NO RELIC OF DAYS GONE BY, NOR IS IT AN ARTI-fact of strange and exotic cultures. It's alive and well throughout contemporary America. Louisiana politicians play well with words. When Louisiana joined the rest of the states and outlawed cockfighting in 2007, Opelousas representative (now state senator) Elbert Lee Guillory refused to join his fellow legislators. He voted against the law and made an intriguing argument for his decision.

"The cockfighting industry in St. Landry County is a $12 million industry, in a place where there are very few industries and it's very difficult for people to make a living," Guillory said at the time. He expressed frustration at what he called society's hypocritical embracement of chickens, a sentiment that could be summed up: fried, okay, but fighting, not okay. "We eat billions of chickens every day. What we're talking about is putting the interest of chickens over the interests of people." Those chickens destined to be cooked, said the lawmaker, can be adjudicated much worse off than their fighting brethren. The fryers live in "hellish conditions, in stench and chemicals." Guillory joined a chorus of cockers and other observers who insisted, "If you come out to look at where a fighting chicken is raised, it's a totally different life. It's the difference between being in prison and being free."[20]

Just because Louisiana passed a law against cockfighting hardly means there are no cockfights to be found in Louisiana. Louisiana, after all, is where the former governor Edwin Edwards—still serving time in federal prison on multiple corruption charges as of this writing—gloated with typical glee on the eve of one of his campaigns that the only thing that could prevent his victory would be "if I get caught in bed with a dead girl or a live boy."[21] And that's just one example in the long colorful history of Louisiana outlaws. The political atmosphere combined with the wilds of Cajun country means if you want a cockfight, you sure won't be stopped by legislation passed in Baton Rouge. I decided to book a trip south to poke around.

Not that it's necessary to single out Louisiana. In March 2010 in Murray County, Georgia, Sheriff Howard Ensley announced that his deputies rounded up over sixty cockers in a Saturday raid. The local paper listed the names and addresses of those arrested; "gambling" and "cruelty to animals" were the charges.[22] Two years before the Georgia raid, authorities in Washington and Oregon swooped down on more than two dozen houses and farms and collected more than sixty West Coast cockers, charging them with violating the 2007 Animal Fighting Prohibition Enforcement Act. Later, in 2008, sheriff's deputies in Humboldt County, California (famous for its not-so-underground marijuana economy) raided a McKinleyville farm and took away 1,387 roosters, along with a wide assortment of cockfighting paraphernalia: Thirteen pairs of gaffs and seventy-two knives were confiscated, all designed to fit on gamecocks' legs for combat.[23] Cockfighting has been illegal in California since the late nineteenth century, but it remains only a misdemeanor—many other states consider cockers felons.

As I started to learn about the current status of cockfighting, some Louisiana legislators were working on a new bill designed to thwart cockers. It was now illegal to stage a cockfight and illegal to bet on a cockfight. The pending legislation would make it illegal to attend a cockfight. I searched my virtual Rolodex for Louisiana contacts and reconnected with Su Garfield; we'd worked together years ago at a California radio station before she relocated to New Orleans and a new career as a cabaret impresario.

"Louisianans just hate being pushed into anything," Su wrote to me in an attempt to explain the state's reticence to outlaw the fights. "Maybe it's that French history; maybe the carpetbaggers." She suggested Washington bullied Louisiana into the prohibition, holding out federal aid for victims of Hurricane Katrina as bait for the new laws. "But the games go on in back-buildings all over Louisiana," she wrote. "The cocks, the dogs, and the men continue to fight because people will pay to watch 'em, and the threat of a misdemeanor charge never stopped nuttin'." Right she is.

She introduced me to Danny Martiny, the state senator who drafted the bill against audience participation at the fights. The senator and I talked on the telephone, and after he enticed me with more Louisiana lore, we agreed to meet when I came to Louisiana. Of all the work he's performed in Louisiana, he said, only his effort against cockfighting resulted in a personal threat against him.

I contacted another old acquaintance, a woman who lives in Cajun country along the Mississippi River. She left a message on my voice mail, the romance of the swamps and bayous enhanced by her soft and lilting accent. "I have some information for you," she offered in response to my query about illegal cockfights. "I spoke with my weekend neighbor here in the country, and he has friends who do this. I'm sure you know that it's now illegal here in Louisiana. But it's," she paused, and lilted, "*about.* This family does horses and cocks. Call me back."

Call her back of course I did, and she connected me with the neighbor, John Hebert, an acupuncturist in Lafayette. Weeks later we met at his downtown office, Camelia House, a gracious white colonnaded relict of the Old South. He took a few minutes out from his work schedule to brief me on his memories of growing up in Acadiana during a time when cockfights were legal and common, before sending me south to Abbeville to meet with an old friend of his, a friend with employees who fought cocks, at least until cockfighting was outlawed.

John Hebert's medical training included two years in China, and while in Asia he took a break from his studies in the mid-1990s to vacation in Bali. He rented a room in a family-owned guest-house in Ubud and relaxed. Among the local events he witnessed were cockfights, but he didn't pay particular attention to them since they were commonplace events back home in Louisiana. "It wasn't that foreign a thing to me. It didn't even raise an eyebrow. It was just like, okay, they cockfight over here."

But one day a cockfight came to his guesthouse, a cockfight unlike what he was used to back home.

Hebert's rest and relaxation were disrupted by tragedy: A woman in residence in one of the rooms was killed. Flame from a candle in her quarters lit the drapes on fire. She woke up choking on smoke, ran out of the room, and fell down stone steps trying to escape the burning house. The fall killed her. It was the third unexpected death in the house within a short period of time. "The assumption was," Hebert told me in his soft Louisiana voice, "that the house needed a cleansing." Enter the roosters.

The family secured a Hindu priest for the cleansing ceremony. Ornate decorations festooned the house. Elaborate spreads of enticing food were prepared. Musicians were hired. Herbert was invited to watch as the priest recited words designed to rid the house of what plagued it. "And then," Hebert says with a laugh at the memory, "the priest says something and there is a cock-fight, right in the middle of this formality." In Bali as in Lafayette, the winning chicken killed the loser. "He picks up the bird that lost the fight," Hebert tells me, still surprised at what he witnessed well over a dozen years before, "and he walked around the premises with the bird, sprinkling blood."

Once the blood was distributed, the festivities began. "Every-thing was okay. There was an immediate release of tensions. We had a great day. Everyone felt all things had been righted." The cockfight (and the blood sprinkling) was the punctuation that ended the formal grieving period and gave the guesthouse a fresh start. "Those images are burned into my mind," Hebert muses. How could they not be: He watched a bloody rooster exorcism.

Cockfights figure in Balinese purification rituals, not just at family homes, but also at Hindu temples. The hope is that the blood spilled appeases evil demons.

Anthropologist Clifford Geertz attended a Balinese cockfight in 1958, when he was engaged in fieldwork in Indonesia. He published "Deep Play: Notes on the Balinese Cockfight" in 1972, a paper about his experiences at the match—a paper that popularized cockfighting in academia and led to a bookshelf of other scholarly works on cockfights—some disagreeing with Geertz's conclusions about the importance of cockfights' "commentaries on status hierarchy and self-regard in Bali." The fight Geertz attended with his wife was not part of a religious ceremony presided over by a priest. Rather it was an illegal match that was raided by the police. Geertz and his wife escaped the dragnet "bewildered but relieved to have survived and stayed out of jail."[24]

CHAPTER FIVE
Cockfighting as Sport

SOUTH FROM LAFAYETTE U.S. 90 CUTS A CONCRETE SWATH THROUGH Cajun country toward New Iberia. I was heading for Paul Huln's place, a spread south of the Queen City of the Bayou Teche that was once teeming with gamecocks. "If you see Jeff's Upholstery you've passed us," Huln's wife, Sherry, told me when I called for directions. I turn into their packed dirt driveway and park in front of what turns out to be Huln's workshop. He's inside at his workbench, fashioning and sharpening the steel gaffs that he sells to cockers for $90 a pair. Sixty-nine years old (he tells me repeatedly) and still big in physical stature but not in the best of health (he complains often), he's nursing a Diet Coke. A red grease-stained apron covers his ample belly, and there's a patch of grease on his forehead. From a slightly receding hairline a crop of silver hair rises—and the more we talk about chickens the more that shock of white hair on his head looks to me like a rooster's comb. After years of companionship, it's said that some dogs and their people start to look like each other. After a lifetime of raising and fighting cocks, Paul Huln looks a tad like a rooster, and I'll bet if he read this, he'd laugh and agree.

Rooster combs, I learned later, offer us relief from some of what ails us. The fancy poultry hats are mined for hyaluronan, a molecule that is used to reduce arthritic inflammation, retard the development of scar tissue after surgery, and smooth wrinkles. There's no shortage of the combs for medicinal use; they're a byproduct of the slaughterhouses. Hyaluronan is injected into the knees of racehorses, it is used to protect the cornea during cataract surgery, and it competes with Botox as a wrinkle eraser. The pharmaceutical giant Pfizer isolates the compound from roosters it specifically breeds for bountiful combs, just as Paul Huln bred his roosters for combat. The bigger the comb, the more hyaluronan per rooster—up to a point. "We stopped getting it bigger and bigger because all of a sudden the rooster couldn't keep his head up," Dr. Rolf Bergman told the *New York Times*. Bergman is a physical chemistry professor at Uppsala University who works rooster-breeding duty for Pfizer.[25] Cockfighting is illegal in Louisiana, but raising cocks for their genetically modified inflated combs to harvest hyaluronan is legal—hyaluronan that's used to offset the aches and pains of horses suffering after grueling races. Use versus abuse. The distinction at times seems vague.

"Louisiana has lost its culture," Huln told me, "and it has become politically correct." It's the pat argument he and other Cajun cockers make when asked to explain why their state joined the other forty-nine to outlaw what they call a sport. He blames lobbying by the Humane Society. "They want to abolish all animal use," he says, convinced that animal rights advocates don't just want cockfights abolished, they want to close butcher shops. "I won my first derby in 1948," he tells me. "That's a long time ago. I've been fighting chickens all this time, from 1948 until last year, legally. Last year I became a criminal. My agenda was fighting chickens, not wining and dining politicians. They spent a gazillion dollars stopping cockfighting in Louisiana." He cites a specific figure: $94 million.

"Nonsense," the Humane Society's Julia Breaux tells me a few days later, pointing out that the cockfighters hired the best lobbyist in the state. "We didn't spend a dime," was her response to the charge that her organization spread money around the Huey Long Capitol Building in Baton Rouge. "I certainly wasn't wining and dining legislators." The Humane Society hired a lobbyist and she called their efforts "grassroots." But "there's no shoving money in the pockets of legislators, definitely not!"

Paul Huln thinks Louisiana lawmakers ought to weigh concerns about dead and dying fighting cocks against the tax money the state could make if it regulated the fights instead of outlawing them. "Last weekend they fought a fight," he reports, "and I'm not going to say where, I'm just going to say it was not here. They had 117 entries at $500 an entry fee. Do you know how much money that is?"

"That's a lot of money," I agreed and made the calculation: just shy of sixty grand.

"If they had taken 10 percent of that for taxes, the politicians would have been patting us on the back." The mistake cockers made was not deciding to define rooster fighting as a sport, he is convinced. Their mistake was not demanding that Baton Rouge license and tax the cockpits. As a Californian, his logic makes me think about the marijuana growing north of my Bodega Bay home, up in Humboldt County. With the fishing and timber industries shattered along the northern California coast, illegal marijuana has been the leading cash crop for years—profiting outlaws while denying Sacramento critically needed tax revenue. Multiply that $60,000 in cash by a couple of dozen derbies every Louisiana weekend from November through August, Huln says, and consider the tax value. He is getting exercised, his voice gets louder, and he punctuates his math with self-criticism. "We were stupid."

"It's okay to get an abortion and kill a child," Sherry chimes in, "but you can't kill a chicken." Of course you can kill chickens. Were Paul and Sherry raising chickens for fryers, they could kill as many as they could eat. What's illegal—because it's been deemed by lawmakers to be cruel—is pitting roosters against each other in a fight.

"We're too politically correct," Paul says in a tone of voice both wounded and disgusted. When I ask him why he thinks cockfighting should be legal, he falls back on the Bible for his argument and launches into a self-righteous soliloquy.

"It's a blood sport. I don't fight dogs. But if a man takes care of his dogs, and raises them and breeds them, he should have a right to fight his dogs. I don't fight 'em—don't like 'em. But I don't have the right to tell you not to do that, because God gave us the whole deal. He said, 'You have authority over the animals.' I have fought chickens all my life. Do you know how hard it is to keep chickens fighting good? Cutting. Drivin' the spur. Being game, with the intestinal fortitude to take all that beating. And still be competitive. And I'm competitive worldwide. I'm not talkin' about just in the backyard. I'm talkin' about: You name it, I've been there. I've done it, I've won it." His speech is becoming rhythmic; he almost sounds like a gospel preacher. "I've done it with my family of chickens. It's a genetic thing."

Cockfighters who raise their own gamecocks consider the breeding work they do an integral aspect of their sport. I suggest to Huln that when he protests laws against cockfighting because they threaten his Cajun culture, he's invoking his own genetic makeup.

"Sure. It's my breeding," he readily agrees. "I'm a coon-ass. My father, my great-grandfather, they all fought chickens."

"You're a coon-ass?"

"I'm a coon-ass," he affirms, his tone now quiet, assertive, and contemplative all at the same time. "I'm a real coon-ass. I was born and bred down here. Do you honestly believe that they can make me quit raisin' chickens?"

"No," I say without hesitation. "After knowing you for just twenty minutes, I have no doubt that if you want to keep raising chickens and fighting chickens you'll figure out how to take your act underground." Huln strikes me as not just full of bluster. He sincerely believes there's nothing wrong with cockfighting, and the only reason he would end his lifelong role as a cocker would be to stay out of jail.

"Get real. Get a life." He's addressing authority now, not me. "There's no way they're going to make me stop owning chickens." In the next breath he covers his coon-ass, making it clear for the record that he's not violating the letter of the law. "I can't fight 'em anymore because I can't train 'em like I used to because of my health. I have diabetes real bad."

Coon-ass is both a derogatory term for Cajuns and an expression of Cajun pride. As is so often the case with such slang, who is saying what to whom determines the meaning. One of the experts on the use of *coon-ass* is Cajun historian Shane Bernard, whose doctoral dissertation was a study of his own culture. According to his research, the origin of the term is unclear, but it seems to derive from one of two contexts: Cajuns eating raccoon and/or the inference that a Cajun's social status is lower than that of a black person.[26] Bernard lives in New Iberia and serves as historian and curator to the McIlhenny Company, the makers—since 1868—of Tabasco sauce. Company headquarters is on Avery Island, just a few miles from where Paul Huln raised his fighting cocks. And there is a direct cockfighting connection to Tabasco. Cockfighting lore includes the tales of a technique for jump-starting a bird that's not showing adequate aggression in the cockpit: an application of Tabasco up the chicken's anus.

Historian Bernard earned his PhD at Texas A&M, and the Aggies are the butt of a Cajun joke that has made the rounds since Louisiana outlawed cockfighting. A character named Boudreaux is cast in the joke as the best undercover detective in the Louisiana State Police. He is reporting to his sergeant after investigating illegal cockfights.

Boudreaux say, "Dere is tree main group in dis cockfightin' bidness."

"Who are dey?" his sergeant ax.

Boudreaux reply, "De Aggies, de Cajuns, an de Mafia."

"How you know?" axed da sergeant.

"Well," says Boudreaux, "I done seen da cockfight, cher. I knowed da Aggies was involved when a duck was entered in de cockfight."

"What about da others?" question da sergeant.

"Well, I knowed da Cajuns was involve wen sumbody bet on da duck. You know dem Cajuns, dey drink too much an say 'Aw, what da hell?', an dey'll do anyting crazy."

"Mais, Boudreaux," axed da sergeant, "How cum you know da Mafia's involve too?"

Boudreaux say, "Da duck won."[27]

Cocker Paul Huln is a complex study. As he speaks, he code shifts. When he is analyzing the potential value to his state if cockfights were taxed, his language is precise and without a noticeable accent. When he spins yarns about his favorite chickens—cockers use the terms chickens and roosters interchangeably for their fighting cocks—and talks about the good old days of legal Louisiana cockfighting, he drops his g's and adopts the sing-song cadence of the Cajun drawl. The coops on Huln's land are quiet—all but empty. He and Sherry insist they no longer fight cocks, but make their money selling paraphernalia: He sells the weapons and she sells the T-shirts.

"It's a lost art," he says about cockfighting gaffs and knives. Craftsmen now face fines and imprisonment for shipping cockfighting weapons across state lines. Overnight their marketplace collapsed. Huln says the law caused his sales to drop to a fraction of the 1,500 pairs of gaffs a year he was accustomed to peddling. "I'm a po' boy," he insists with an intense and serious look on his unshaven face. "I'm a sick man. I can't go work. I can do this," he points to his workbench and a gaff under construction, "because I'm sitting down all the time. So they cut me out of $130,000 a year in sales." On a good day he says he cranks out eight pairs.

The drawl returns. "You see, that's where the rub comes. Can't sell no chickens no more." It's illegal to sell a rooster destined for the cockpit. "The way you can get around that is by not cutting the comb on a rooster, not trimming it." The trimmed combs lighten the birds' load during a fight, preventing the head from being weighed down when the birds make leaping attacks.

I study the gaffs, vicious-looking curved spears a few inches long that could penetrate deep into a challenging rooster. The workmanship is complex. The spear is attached to a steel collar that fits over the roosters' natural spurs, appendages just above the feet that are amputated by the cockers to make a place for the weapons. A strap affixed to the steel collar wraps around the legs and once it is secured, the chicken is ready for the fighting pit.

The craftsman takes a swig of his Diet Coke.

"Later this week I'm scheduled to meet with Julia Breaux, the top dog in Louisiana for the Humane Society," I tell Huln. I pause as I realize I just used an animal metaphor to describe her. We often attribute human traits to animals, especially pets. And we're quick to explain ourselves using other animals. Quiet as a mouse. Strong as an ox. Busy as a bee. "What do you think I should ask her?"

Paul Huln's voice turns hushed as he uses another animal metaphor. "I know the bitch."

"What should I ask her?" I repeat.

"If she'd like to go play in the traffic," he suggests, and laughs, but it's not a fun laugh, it's a bitter and resentful laugh.

"Be serious," cajoles Sherry.

He sighs.

"What would you ask her?" I say.

"Me? The first thing I'd ask her is, 'Why did you want to take my sport away from me?'" He's both pleading and antagonistic as the words march out of his mouth. "I'm a veteran. I went overseas. Everybody ran into Canada to avoid the draft. I stayed and I fought for their right to do that. Here it is, fifty years later, they've all come back from Canada. They're all vegetarians and they want to take my sport away from me." His point is obvious, even if his numbers are off. Only some fifty thousand Americans—compared with close to three million who shipped out to the war—went north to protest the war or to avoid service in Vietnam. Most of those fifty thousand exiles stayed in Canada after the war, and well over 90 percent of them eat meat.[28] "They want to take my sport away from me," his voice gets louder, as he casts himself as a victim. "Why? What have I done to you? I pay my taxes. None of my children are on welfare. What have we done to you? This is not the America that I signed on for. This is not what I went over there for. This is not what I shot at them guys for. I don't deserve to be treated like this. I'm a citizen. I'm a human being. And no one, no one, takes better care of their chickens than me. I guarantee that because I could not be a winner if I didn't."

Despite the piles of money that change hands at cockfights, Paul and Sherry claim it's the competition that thrills them, not the cash.

"It's not about the money," he insists. "We fought for $380,000 one time, and we had a shot at it. It didn't even enter my mind," he says about the cash. "It was just the winning."

It's hard for me to imagine not thinking about so much loot.

"When you win, it's like a high that's so unbelievable," she tries to explain to me.

"If dope users get like that," he says, "I can see why they do dope. It's such an adrenaline rush to see your rooster duck and dodge and hit. Did you ever box when you was younger?" He smiles at his own street fighting memories. "It felt good when you whupped someone. That's how it is when you're fighting them chickens." He sounds almost romantic about his chickens as he tells me it's impossible for me to understand the attachment he feels for them after mating their "mom and daddy," hatching the egg, raising and training the rooster for a couple of years, catering to its needs en route to the derbies ("make sure Continental Airlines didn't bang him around too much"), and then the fight.

It's time for my moral relevancy query. Paul Huln and I make a list of animals that humans pit against one another for blood sport—from crickets to roosters, from dogs to mongooses to bulls. Is there a difference one animal to another? Not to him, as long as the animal is well taken care of—until the fight, to have it kill or be killed.

"To have it whup somebody," is his perspective. He prefers his roosters fight with a gaff instead of a knife because puncture wounds, he claims, can heal well enough to allow the losing chicken the chance to fight again. Knife cuts, he says, inflict so much muscle damage the loser rarely survives.

Huln is proud of his backyard breeding history—the care he takes matching mates in an attempt to produce tough and aggressive fighters. "The respect I have for my roosters is beyond imagination." Yet those that fail to meet his standards he discards without mercy. "If he does some wrong like bite me or hit me or kick me, I will kill him." He turns from proud to pragmatic and cold. "I will destroy him because I don't want that in my gene pool. I spent too much of my life getting a perfect animal to abide by that."

What strikes me as bizarre is that Louisiana law does not care if Huln wrings the necks of roosters he believes won't serve him well in the cockpit. He can kill them to eat them. He can kill them because he doesn't like their personalities. He can kill them because he just feels like killing them. But if he pits one against another in a cockfight, he's breaking the law even if they both live through the match.

"Isn't it odd that it's perfectly legal for you to kill them, but you're violating the law if you fight them?"

He's contemplative for a second, and then smiles. "I never thought about that," he admits.

"You should have hired me as your lobbyist," I say. Cockers contracted with Randy Haynie to work the legislature for them in their vain attempt to keep cockfighting legal. "He's the most powerful lobbyist in Louisiana," the Humane Society's Julia Breaux would tell me when we met in New Orleans. Haynie's motto is "No one gets the job done better" and his client list is a who's who of Louisiana businesses, including Pfizer—whose Swedish branch is busy breeding rooster combs for their pharmaceutical value.[29]

When Paul Huln smiles his eyes twinkle like a Norman Rockwell Santa Claus. He's laughing now and smiling at the thought of me lobbying the Louisiana legislature on behalf of cockfighters. It seems an ideal time to seek entrée to what's become an underground world.

"What do you suppose are the chances," I say smiling back at him, "of an outsider reporter from California coming into Louisiana and finding a fight to see."

He sighs and turns serious. "It's going to be hard in Louisiana," he says. "Let me tell you what the problem is. If they catch you fighting, they confiscate the property. You could lose your home. So we go to Alabama. Every Saturday we go to Alabama."

He looks over at Sherry and asks her in Cajun what she thinks about taking me to Alabama. She doesn't look thrilled with the idea.

He shrugs. "What could he do? He can't do shit."

"I can't do shit," I readily agree. "And I wouldn't want to do shit. But think about it. Don't decide right now. Think about it. And let me leave my butterfly book with you so you can get an idea of how I work."

"I think you should go to Alabama," Paul says with authority. "You could ride with Sherry. How long are you here?"

"Until you and Sherry take me to Alabama."

"Saturday," he says. "Saturday."

"First of all," says Sherry, "there's no cameras."

"Secondly," Paul instructs me, "you can't be taking notes and you can't tell them you're a reporter."

"I've got no problem with that," I say.

"They will tar and feather you if they find out you are a reporter," says Sherry.

"And me, too," says Paul. It's unclear if he means that the derby participants will tar and feather him along with me or that he will also tar and feather me after the Alabama boys do their job. A rooster crows from the Huln's yard. The upcoming derby, they say, is a big one. It's Cinco de Mayo. They expect as many as 150 entries at $500 each. That's $75,000 before the betting starts.

In Alabama, cockfighting is treated much like an expired parking meter. Cockers risk only a misdemeanor conviction and a fine no greater than $50. The law does not forbid raising fighting cocks, possessing knives and gaffs, or showing up at a cockfight as a spectator.[30]

"There's women and children there," says Sherry. "It's a family derby. We don't shy our children or grandchildren from rooster fighting because we don't see anything wrong with it."

They show off a picture of a grandson with a rooster.

"He's not going to turn out to be a drug addict and a murderer," says Sherry.

"The kid's a straight A student," says the proud grandpa.

"He's been honor roll since he started school," Sherry says.

They're trading lines like a vaudeville act.

"Do you know what his goal is now?" Paul asks. "He wanted to be a paleontologist, but he don't want to be that anymore. He wants to be governor of Louisiana. 'How come, Bud?' I ask him. 'So I can make chicken fightin' legal again!' he says."

We're all laughing. But the two of them quickly turn serious as they recount a raid at the Little Bayou Club.

"About thirty cops in full SWAT garb with machine guns were screaming for everybody to hit the ground," says Sherry. "They put that gun in that boy's face."

"An AK-47," says Paul. It's just a detail, but it's not likely that the Louisiana State Police use the Soviet-designed AK-47s.

"He's seven years old," says Sherry. "Do you think he was traumatized over the rooster fighting or the gun in his face?"

The Little Bayou Club raid took place on March 14, 2009, the initial raid following passage of the ban. Police confiscated 635 fighting cocks at the cockpit in Sulphur, Louisiana. The Humane Society's Julia Breaux was on the scene and told reporters, "Cockfighting is a cruel and barbaric practice, and there can be no doubt that every cockfighting enthusiast knows that it's a crime to participate in these staged fights." After surveying the blood and feathers, she announced, "We are grateful to the Louisiana State Police for cracking down on this form of animal cruelty."[31] Most of the confiscated roosters were killed by the authorities: Their claim is it's difficult to find foster homes for fighting cocks—foster homes don't want the roosters because of their prowess in the cockpit. The worry is that they'll fight other fowl at the home. The idea of killing the roosters to save them from the cockpit makes me think of the famous line war correspondent Peter Arnett attributed to an unnamed U.S. Army major after a battle at the Vietnamese provincial capital of Bén Tre: "It became necessary to destroy the town to save it."[32]

The Huln family survived the Little Bayou Club raid. State police only issued misdemeanor citations.[33]

"They can't do nothin' to me. They can't afford my medicine," Paul laughs. "Before I met Sherry I chased every skirt in town, drank a quart of whiskey a day, and smoked three packs of cigarettes." We're walking out to his chicken house; he's about to show me the birds he still keeps on the property. "Now I take $600 worth of medicine just to keep going. This clean life is killing me." It's a glib line that sounds well practiced, especially when Sherry makes it clear that they've been married twenty-seven years. He says it again: "This clean life is killing me."

There are few roosters left in the chicken house. Huln culled his flock after the cockfighting law was passed, and he says most of what was left he lost to thieves. But a few prize fowl are still squawking as we tour the feather-littered coop. "He's dandy ain't he? Look at this guy!" Huln points to a tough-looking bird, grabs it, and thrusts it into my arms. "Feel the body and the breast," says Sherry as I cradle him. "That's some muscle, huh brother?" exudes Paul.

The rooster—a black-breasted red—clucks. He's docile and he seems to like me. It feels good to hold him. His feathers are soft to pet and his muscles hard as Paul's probably were when he was first chasing Sherry. He's a gorgeous animal; his vibrant coloring glistens. Holding him, strange as it may seem, feels much like holding a fat cat.

"What's his name?" I ask.

"When you've got five hundred of 'em, you don't name 'em," Huln says, while insisting that the lack of name does not reflect negatively on his relationship with his birds. "My chickens treat me better than most people do. They'll come to me and they respect me. And I just love 'em. Love 'em, love 'em, love 'em!"

We walk back to the shop as roosters make cartoon-like cock-a-doodle-doo calls after us. "We're not malcontents," he offers along with his good-bye, "we're just misunderstood."

Sherry follows me out to my car and hands me a jar of pickled quail eggs. She and Paul raise the quail and she pickles the eggs. "A product of certified Cajun Louisiana," announces the label, which features pictures of quail and Acadiana swamplands along with a list of the ingredients: quail eggs, vinegar, xanthan gum, pepper, and garlic powder.

Prior appointments in California mandated a quick trip back to San Francisco before the Alabama derby Sherry promised to take me to see. At the New Orleans Louis Armstrong Airport, a blue-shirted TSA officer stops me as I pass through the security checkpoint. He points to my satchel, which had caught his eye on the monitor as it passed through his x-ray machine.

"What have you got in there?"

"Quail eggs," I confess. I had been worried that the vinegar would trigger the alarm now that no more than four ounces of liquid is allowed in a carry-on bag. Twenty quail eggs require more than four ounces of pickling.

"Quail eggs?" he repeats. "I love quail eggs." He pulled them out of my bag. "You'll have to check them."

I wasn't about to check Sherry's quail eggs. I travel light: carry-ons only.

"You take them," I say to the officer. "You love them."

He looks conflicted. "I can't eat 'em. High blood pressure. I bought some just last week and my doctor says I can't eat 'em."

"Then give them to someone who will like them," I say. "Just don't throw them out." I start to collect my bags as the TSA guy heads toward a garbage can. I say again, "Don't throw them away!" But he's not. He opens the jar, pours out the liquid, and hands the jar full of eggs back to me, grinning.

"Just fill it with vinegar and hot sauce when you get home," he orders. "They'll be fine."

I love Louisiana.

CHAPTER SIX

Destroying the Village to Save It

JULIA BREAUX REMINDS ME OF WHAT A SOUTHERN DEBUTANTE IS supposed to look like, and where we meet probably helps reinforce the image. She joins me poolside at my New Orleans French Quarter hotel on Bourbon Street on a sparkling spring morning. Lively Dixieland jazz is on the outdoor speakers, and Ms. Breaux is all cautious smiles as we shake hands and face each other over a tea table that's probably seen more whiskey glasses than teacups. She's no stranger to politics. Her father was a U.S. senator representing Louisiana, the protégé of Governor Edwin Edwards (of the famous dead-girl-or-live-boy-in-bed fame).

"Why do you consider cockfights animal abuse?" I ask the Louisiana director of the Humane Society. She looks like an all-American cover girl with her sweet smile and shoulder length blonde hair. Before she has a chance to answer, I ask her if she's ever been to a cockfight.

"Have you ever been to a cockfight?" she counters.

"Not yet," I tell her, "but I intend to. Have *you* ever been to a cockfight?" I ask her again.

"I have," she allows, but quickly adds, "I want to know where *you're* going to a cockfight." The Humane Society seeks out scheduled cockfights, shares their intelligence with police forces, and joins the cops on raids, providing technical support ranging from identifying evidence such as weapons and other fighting paraphernalia to destroying seized birds. "Are you going to one in Louisiana?"

"I'll tell you afterwards," I say. My job is not to do hers for her, and I'm certainly not going to burn my sources.

"Okay," she agrees, and point by point she recounts the Little Bayou Club raid from her perspective. "It was very gruesome, not just because of the abuse of the birds. It was very bloody and very nasty. But in addition to that there also were a lot of drugs involved. There's some sort of seemingly underground prostitution going on. It's very strange," she says, her proper and refined presentation a stark contrast to what she is describing.

How did she know drugs and prostitution were augmenting the chicken fights?

"We found a lot of marijuana in the trailers."

And the prostitution? Our conversation is oddly punctuated by a bawdy-sounding blues tune on the poolside speakers.

"I'm not 100 percent sure," she acknowledges with a nervous laugh. "That's what the State Police reported to us because they found a couple of women in trailers, left behind and locked inside the trailers as their partners fled."

Was she there for the fights?

"We got in right as the fights were ending, right as the police broke it up. There were still birds in the ring. One was already dead and one was still alive, slashing [at the other]. Lots of blood, lots of birds in trash cans—half alive and half dead." Her job was to mark the abandoned birds as evidence, a nasty task. "A lot of them had been shoved in the trash cans with slashes across their chests and open wounds. Other wounded birds were back in their cages. She saw "a lot of bleeding, missing eyes, that's the part where you go . . . ," and she makes a guttural sound. "It's just horrible to look at that."

Hundreds of birds. Some dead. Some injured, some not. All confiscated. What happened to them next?

"The ones that were severely injured were euthanized on site, about a hundred of them. More than six hundred others went to the Calcasleu Parish animal control headquarters until the district attorney deemed them contraband. Then those birds too were destroyed."

"Help me understand what the difference is between a bird being killed by parish animal control officers and a bird that is killed in the cockpit," I ask. "They're both dead, and the one in the pit in theory enjoyed a fighting chance at survival."

She clears her throat. "Humane euthanasia done with lethal injection is completely different than sticking knives and gaffs on a bird's feet and watching it fight to the death for your own pleasure. Intracardiac euthanasia, when done correctly, is very humane. It's a very peaceful way for the animal to go." Her voice is so quiet I find it necessary more than once to ask her to speak louder. "It's not them fighting for their life for someone else's pleasure. It's completely different."

Allowing animals to suffer and die for the pleasure of spectators defines what opponents of blood sports—cockfights and dogfights, bullfights and foxhunts, even cricket fights—find offensive. As my research continued I found plenty of hunters and meat eaters who could not abide blood "sports."

"But they're still dead," I protest about the mass euthanasia of the captured fowl. "You guys killed the birds instead of the cockers."

"In the end it's the same," she agrees. "Yes, the bird's dead. It's the manner in which the bird died." She pauses and quickly adds, "I didn't kill the bird. Calcasleu Parish animal control did." But it's not just the chickens she's worried about. She reiterates her concerns about drugs and weapons and "all that criminal element that you're bringing into your community unnecessarily. For what? To watch two birds kill each other. To me it's really senseless."

"Do you eat meat?"

"I do eat meat, yes."

"Isn't that in conflict with your sense of what is right and wrong for us to do with animals?"

"I try to eat meat that has not been factory farmed," is her studied response. "Organic. I don't eat a lot of meat." She says she was on a strict chicken-free diet for a spell after the Little Bayou Club raid.

I quote Paul Huln to Julia Breaux, his brandishing of Cajun culture and the assault he feels from Baton Rouge. She rails at the suggestion that Huln and company define Cajun culture. Her voice is no longer quiet, and her attitude turns combative as she announces, "I'm from Lafayette, Louisiana." Lafayette is the heart of Cajun country, just north up Highway 90 from the Huln place. "My dad's from Crowley." That's just west of Lafayette. "My mom's from Lafayette. I've got roots there." She cites her name: Breaux. "I'm *not* not Cajun. It's a little offensive to me when people tell me this is part of our heritage. My grandparents never went to cockfights. I've asked them, I've grilled them. My grandfather said, 'It's horrible. It's disgusting.' I don't think it's necessarily part of Cajun heritage. It might be what some people did, but it's certainly not what all people did. Not that I'm the Cajun heritage expert, but I have street cred," she says with understandable authority.

~~~

A few days later I'm on the phone with Sherry Huln, to arrange my trip to the cockfight in Alabama. She's apologetic.

"I talked to the guy who owns the place and he's not too hot on you coming. He said, 'Sherry, do you know him?' I said, 'I don't *know him* know him.' I told him you're a writer and that you seem okay. He said, 'There is too much heat on us. What if he is from the Humane Society?' They lie to get in and take undercover pictures. I don't want to go against him because he is the owner of the place. He's just being cautious and I can understand that."

I leaf back through my notebook, checking my other cockfighting contacts. If I don't witness the phenomenon with Sherry in Alabama, I'll find another. Kentucky looks like a likely locale; it's another slap-on-the-wrist state. And there's always Puerto Rico.

~~~

Whose version of Cajun culture is correct? Paul Huln proudly holds up a rooster as an example of what makes Cajuns unique while demure Julia Breaux quotes her grandfather—who hails from just a few miles northwest of Huln's coops—who calls the fights Huln loves "disgusting."

Yale professor and poet J. D. McClatchy is an expert on one of the icons of Cajun culture that both Breaux and Huln undoubtedly hold dear: the Longfellow epic "Evangeline." I checked in with him to try to make some sense of self-proclaimed Cajun exceptionalism with an analysis of the Henry Wadsworth Longfellow poem, a poem that was studied by most American schoolchildren until the mid-twentieth century when it and Longfellow, McClatchy explained to me, fell out of fashion. "The tides of fashion ebb and flow," he observed, although the story of Evangeline keeps the eponymous poem, and hence Longfellow's name, always in vogue in Louisiana.

"Let me tell you a little bit about how the poem came about." Professor McClatchy is an engaging storyteller, and clearly loves the lore surrounding "Evangeline."

"In 1840 Longfellow had a dinner party with some friends. One of those friends was the novelist Nathaniel Hawthorne. Hawthorne brought along with him from Salem an Episcopal priest friend of his who told the story of what the Acadians called *le Grand Dérangement*, when the English expelled them from their homeland in Nova Scotia in 1755. It happened on the wedding day of the most beautiful couple in the village of Grand-Pré: Evangeline Bellefontaine and Gabriel Lajeunesse. In swept the English and threw everyone out, and even on their wedding day."

Many of the displaced Acadians, after rigorous wandering across North America, resettled in French Louisiana; their descendants are today's Cajuns. Longfellow fictionalized the exodus of Bellefontaine and Lajeunesse, from their tragic forced separation to the day they found each other again. "Even though," noted

McClatchy, "there are no records that Evangeline ever existed, she seems so real." Lajeunesse dies in her arms.

Professor McClatchy sees lessons for our era in Longfellow's classic. "In scary ways it's a poem that, written in 1847, anticipates so much of the ethnic cleansing that's going on, where the powers that be decide that you're not like us, pick you up and bodily remove you, if they don't murder you. It's a poem about that." As the epic draws to a close, Longfellow reminds his readers that Evangeline and her people were uprooted from their homeland: "Still stands the forest primeval; but under the shade of its branches/Dwells another race, with other customs and language." The "Evangeline" mythology is embraced by Cajuns today intent on preserving their unique language and customs—customs that for some include cockfighting.

CHAPTER SEVEN
The Charge of an Animal Rights Brigade

"IS THERE USE OF ANIMALS THAT IS NOT ABUSE?" I ASK DR. ELLIOT Katz in his Marin County office. Katz is a veterinarian who founded In Defense of Animals (IDA)—one of the most radical of activist animal rights groups—more than a generation ago.

"It's a fine line," he answers. The view is of the San Francisco Bay shoreline off in the distance, although the office park locale is hardly bucolic. It's a blustery spring morning, and Katz, despite his gray hair and beard, approaches my questions with the enthusiasm of a youngster; he smiles often, adding to his cherubic look—a façade that may, at least initially, disarm some of his adversaries. His organization's mission statement is simply that it's "dedicated to ending institutionalized abuse of animals by defending their rights, welfare and habitat." But that dedication, often personified by Dr. Katz, extends to civil disobedience and direct action. IDA literature is littered with images of Katz in various stages of arrest as he and his supporters work their pet projects. The group is proud to announce that its operative went underwater to sever nets and free trapped dolphins in Japan, that it forced a research lab to stop experimenting with chimpanzees, that it rescued greyhounds from U.S. Army researchers who wanted to break the dogs' bones to test ideas for treating human osteopathic problems. The list continues: cats saved from cocaine addiction studies, puppy mills closed, dogfighting matches shut down. From its modest headquarters in Marin, the organization's reach is global.

Animals as entertainers, Katz tells me, should be looked at from the point of view of humans as entertainers. "It's a reverse of the days of the Roman Empire when they threw the Christians to the lions." The trademark smile appears on his face as he says,

44

"Now we tend to throw the lions to the Christians." Some types of people seek danger as a pastime; he lists skydiving, mountain climbing, and boxing as examples—those things that excite and titillate participants and observers at least in part because participants risk injury, or death. Animals, he points out, are used to amuse audiences seeking similar kinds of vicarious thrills. "Obviously it's been exploitative for animals, as it's been exploitative for people," he says about zoos and circuses, rodeos, racing, and fights. "It's part of society's general exploitation of who can be exploited, and animals are the most vulnerable now."

Charlie lopes across the office and licks me again. He's a terrier of some sort—he looks like what's often referred to as a pit bull, golden fur and somewhat sorry-looking eyes. He's a rescue dog, in residence at the IDA offices for about six months.

"Did you meet my dog?" Dr. Katz had asked me when we shook hands that morning. Charlie, in fact, had introduced himself, greeting me at the front door of the office suite with his soggy tongue.

"He bit me to death," I said.

"Yeah," countered Katz, "he licked you to death."

It's obvious that Katz likes the dog, that the dog entertains the office staff and their visitors.

"Is he being exploited?" I ask.

Katz says Charlie's life—of course—no longer fits his working definition of an abused entertainer. "Before we got him, he had been chained up in somebody's backyard for three years, 'entertaining' that person, but on a whole different level. The person did not give him any love, didn't give him any sense of freedom. He was a possession, a piece of property. He kept being confiscated by the Marin Humane Society." Charlie was sentenced to death when Katz and his staff adopted him.

"It's obviously very subjective," Elliot Katz says about the line that separates animals used as entertainers and those abused as entertainers. To define an acceptable relationship, Katz seeks to ascertain that there is a mutual benefit—species to species—and he changes the language that describes such cross-species interactions. "I want us to move away from 'pet,' which is demeaning, and use 'animal companion,'" which may not be demeaning but is certainly more clunky. A dog lover should respect his dog's needs, he insists, be its guardian. Exploitation can start with breeding, he points out, and he cites dachshunds that suffer back trouble because they were "designed" to develop long backs to entertain their owners with their hot dog looks.

He stretches to come up with an answer when I ask what kind of animal act he might approve of. "Little poodles, dancing around?" he suggests, and smiles. "As long as they're not put in a cage and they are living with a family."

But most training for shows, he's convinced, involves physical domination at the expense of the animal's well-being. "Most animals in zoos and circuses are there to titillate the public," a role Katz rejects. "It's like the old days of the freak shows with the fattest man and the fattest woman on display for people to stare at." In his soft, slow, and reserved voice, he lashes out at circus trainers and muses about what must go on in the minds of the audience. "Look at this trainer in the middle of this cage, snapping his whip. These dangerous lions, are they going to attack him?"

I tell him about an upcoming research trip I've planned to Budapest to watch the Hungarian State Circus, where the Ukrainian big cat trainer Vladislav Goncharov adopts the famous cliché circus pose and places his own head inside a lion's mouth at the climax of his act. If I can get some time with this madman, I question Katz, what should I ask Goncharov?

"He raised that cat from a baby," theorizes Katz about why the act works, "and if you give it love, it's going to love you back." He suggests I ask what the lion does and where it lives when it's not performing, and what will happen to the lion once he becomes too old or too dangerous ever to perform again. What would the trainer do with the lion were it to hurt him or others? One thing

Katz feels sure about is that Goncharov's motive for creating the act is money. As for the crowd, it buys tickets because the show "is exciting and titillating for the audience. That's why they go to the circus." He pauses; there's another factor. "They're wondering when is he going to get his head smashed." Katz laughs, and it's a laugh at human nature. "A lot of people are not necessarily hoping to see him get hurt, but to watch his courage. Even though for him there's probably not that much courage involved because he's raised that cat, it's like a kitten to him."

It was not long before Elliot Katz and I met that Dawn Brancheau had been killed by the orca at SeaWorld. Given his caustic, "when is he going to get his head smashed" remark, I wondered if he thought witnessing the attack by the orca was added entertainment value for the audience.

"No," he says quickly and emphatically. "People want to see the danger, but they don't want to see the hurt. When you watch the NASCAR running around you're thrilled because you know there could be a crash, but if somebody is really hurt, that's devastating. No one wants to see the trainer killed. They just want to be titillated."

What should happen to Tilikum, the orca that killed Brancheau? From his perspective as an animal rights activist, Katz lobbies for relocation to a protected cove, even if he must be fed fish for the rest of his life because he no longer is able to hunt for himself. "I think the orca would enjoy a much more natural life, guaranteed it would be a better life." Katz and other animal rights activists lobby for the release of all dolphins and orcas held in amusement parks such as SeaWorld.

"Hi, Charlie," I say to the terrier, who strolls over to me for some more licks.

Dr. Katz softly instructs the dog to lie down and roll over.

"That's okay?" I ask. "It's okay for you to tell him to lie down and to roll over? Aren't you making him entertain you for your amusement?"

"But you see how gently I said it," Katz explains, and laughs. "Look at the tail going. He loves to have his belly rubbed. But at the same time, you can see there's fear. So the chances are he was abused."

"How do you see there's fear?" I ask.

"Just look at him. You can see he's frightened. There's a certain fear in his eyes that he doesn't know what's going to happen to him."

"He's not relaxed looking?"

"No, I don't think so." Katz turns to Charlie. "You want some food?" He adds some kibble to the dog's dish and orders, "Eat." Charlie eats and Katz says with approval, "He's so loving."

CHAPTER EIGHT

The Cowardice of Canned Hunts

DR. KATZ INTRODUCED ME TO SOMETHING THAT'S KNOWN IN THE animal rights business as "canned hunts." These provide entertainment for gun-toting wannabe hunters who pay a fee to slaughter animals in enclosed spaces. Investigators often trace the victims of such canned hunts back to tawdry roadside zoos and circuses that sell animals no longer of value to exhibit because they are old, sick, or injured. When he was a Fish and Wildlife Service special agent, Jim Stinebaugh busted a canned hunt operator—a veterinarian gone bad—along with a client, one Sonny Milstead, a California doctor who apparently forgot the Hippocratic Oath "to do no harm"[34] and instead paid for the opportunity to kill defenseless animals.

It is gruesome and painful to watch Dr. Milstead exercise his hobby. Not only did he lust after shooting caged cats, he chose to document his actions, ordering that videotapes be made as he bagged his trapped trophies. On one tape he kills an endangered Bengal tiger and a lion.

On a flight from San Francisco to Dallas, I slipped a DVD of the encounter into my laptop, pleased that the woman in 36A was dozing. I would not have wanted her to think that the images flashing across the screen were my choice for entertainment. The picture is not crystal clear—probably the result of multiple duplications, and in it a male lion is walking in some sort of grassland. Behind the animal is a row of trees, and behind the trees is a high mesh metal fence. The lion walks a few paces and the film cuts to the back of a man in shirtsleeves and slacks. He's equipped with a rifle. The lion is in the background, and metal fencing is no longer in view.

"Sonny, if you want to," says an off-camera voice belonging to the veterinarian, "move to my right so you can get a broadside shot of him."

The rifleman moves right.

"Just remember where the truck is," advises the voice. Why? To keep it out of the picture so the scene looks wild? The voice then asks, "You got a good shot? Do you want to get on higher ground? Or are you okay there?" No concern is expressed about danger from the lion.

The man shoots. The lion jumps in response. Is he hit or is it just the sound of the gunshot that makes it start?

"Aim again, Sonny," coaches the voice.

Another shot. The caged animal is obviously hit this time, and it collapses to the ground. It gets up and moves in a limping circle, apparently looking for where it's been hit.

"Right in the shoulder," urges the voice, and there is a third shot.

Sonny is shown walking up to the lion, his rifle pointed at the body now lying in the grass, motionless.

A second show opens with a majestic tiger lying under a grand tree. The tiger is calm and looks directly at the camera from a distance close enough that the cameraman might be in danger if the declawed old cat was actually a threat.

The same "hunter" approaches after a distinct edit, a cut that changes the camera angle to a position above and behind the shooter. The impression is that the shooter is much farther from the tiger than the camera operator was for the introductory picture—seemingly stalking the passive animal.

"I wouldn't go any further than that," advises the "guide"— perhaps to ensure that the video makes the "chase" look sporting.

He shoots. The tiger starts, and runs. He shoots again, and it is out of the camera's view behind another tree. The next image is of the shooter full faced, looking at the camera, holding the rifle with one hand while offering a hearty thumbs up with the other. He approaches the killed beast, squats, and holds its head up so that the two of them can be captured on videotape. He then places the tiger's head back on the grass and pats the dead tiger's side.

———

Now enjoying his retirement on a Texas spread out near the Hill Country between San Antonio and Del Rio, Jim Stinebaugh is well respected by his peers. His résumé includes the U.S. Marine Corps, the Border Patrol, law enforcement work with Texas Parks and Wildlife, twenty-seven years as a Fish and Wildlife Service special agent, and even a short venture with the Exotic Wildlife Association as their executive director. The Exotic Wildlife Association is the trade organization that represents private landowners who raise hoofstock for—among other things—the pleasure of hunters. He didn't hesitate for a moment when I explained to him that I was seeking to define the transition point where use of animals becomes abuse.

"Hunting is one of the biggest money-making things in this state. Deer are worth more than cattle," he told me in his hospitable Texas drawl. "People get all upset if you starting talking about it being abuse of animals to hunt, and I don't think hunting is abuse of animals. Legal hunting of animals is just a wildlife tool, simply as that. You don't allow any livestock to over populate. If you can turn an animal out in a pasture where he can live a decent and a good life," Stinebaugh told me, he sees nothing wrong with hunters paying for the opportunity to stalk hoofstock. "I don't see ethical hunting as much different than if an animal was in Africa or India or wherever and he would very possibly get eaten by a lion or a tiger or a leopard, or he would die in the drought. But there's a departure point and it would be interesting to me to see where you think that is." I accept his challenge as we talk.

After chasing animal abusers most of his career, Jim Stinebaugh knows where he defines the abuse/use shift. "There're no two sides to holding something inside a cage and shooting it. That's wrong. I don't even like anybody to keep predators. Nothing good is ever going to happen to that animal, and even worse is when they're propagating them. When an animal is born in a cage in Texas, California, or anywhere else, anywhere but a scientific type program, nothing good ever is going to happen to it and there's no excuse for propagating them. That's my opinion. They sell them to rock stars, and all kinds of strange people. Dope dealers are infamous for having these kinds of things. It's just miserable for the animals. That's why I don't think anybody who's not involved in scientific work should own these types of things."

Stinebaugh's work on the Texas-Mexican border makes him acutely aware of how much trafficking goes on in just the type of animals he's convinced should not be in private hands. "The truck that says Buttercrust Bread might be full of skinny lions and a tiger." He mused about a haul he and fellow agents pulled over. "We stopped a truck one night that came across the border from Mexico at Eagle Pass with two bears and a tiger in it, in terrible shape." They took those animals to the San Antonio Zoo, but finding decent homes for seized live contraband is problematic. "Most zoos and legitimate organizations have more of those kinds of things than they need."

What is the mentality of somebody who would engage in a canned hunt? Years after arresting Sonny Milstead and working to see him successfully prosecuted, Stinebaugh still cannot answer the question.

"I've tried to make sense of it and the only thing I can see is that some people who are trophy hunters want to add a Bengal tiger or an African lion to their trophy rooms, and this is the way to get it done." But there are also bragging rights, a desire to show off to friends and neighbors, and to pretend that the canned hunt was a wild safari. Why else would the stage-managed and edited video be created to document the sorry event? The video of Sonny Milstead's "hunts" is designed to make it appear as if there were challenges for the misguided doctor. "They were trying to make them look exciting and not show that they were done on a one-acre trap," Stinebaugh informs me.

I imagined that after he busted bad guys like Milstead, the agent must have made them talk and explain themselves. I was wrong.

"I never got any of them to sit down and explain themselves, ever. I literally had to drag everybody in. Everybody did the standard lie to me, deny it and get attorneys." Despite their lawyers and denials, prosecutors secured convictions. The criminals still kept quiet. "I never had anybody say, 'You know, this is sickening. I don't know why I did it and I'm never going to do it again.' Nope, that never happened. As far as they were concerned, the only thing wrong with this whole thing was that this federal agent messed it all up." Lawman Stinebaugh calls the canned hunters he caught violating the law "illegal and immoral." Not that they suffered much. Dr. Milstead, for example, paid several thousand dollars in fines and spent no time behind bars.

Stinebaugh has doubts that canned hunts will end anytime soon. "As long as there is money involved and someone is willing to do it, someone will find the animal and offer the opportunity. There gets to be big money involved. It's out there somewhere."

⸻

Dr. Sonny Milstead is not alone in his perverse hobby. In late October 2010, after a court battle, the U.S. Fish & Wildlife Service released video images to the animal rights organization Showing Animals Respect and Kindness (SHARK) that depict the country music star Troy Gentry, of the duo Montgomery Gentry, killing a tame bear (Fish & Wildlife claimed they feared the evidence would constitute a privacy invasion were it seen by the public; a judge disagreed). Gentry bought the black bear—named Cubby—from its owner, Lee Marvin Greenly, a Minnesota entrepreneur who maintains a menagerie of animals at a Sandstone business he calls Minnesota Wildlife Connection. Cubby was suffering dental problems, and according to federal investigators, Greenly decided to sell the bear to Gentry for $4,600 instead of fixing Cubby's teeth.

With Cubby in an acre-sized enclosure secured with electrified fencing, Troy Gentry is shown on the video—shot as a souvenir for the "hunter"—using a crossbow at close range to injure Cubby, who wanders off to bleed to death.

Gentry looks at the camera, smiles a show business smile, and says, "Wow. What an experience. This is awesome. Great black bear hunting up here in north Minnesota."

In 2006 Troy Gentry negotiated a deal with prosecutors. He pleaded guilty only to the false registration of Cubby as wild. The penalty was a $15,000 fine and three months probation. In addition, Gentry was forced to forfeit his Cubby trophy and the bow that killed the bear. The singer's enabler, Lee Marvin Greenly, pleaded guilty to aiding a hunter to illegally kill a bear. His penalty was only probation.[35] Late in 2010 Gentry posted a handwritten public apology note on his business website. "There is none who feels as badly about this as I do," he wrote after SHARK released his staged hunt video on YouTube. "I have beaten myself up about this over the years. I made a mistake, a bad decision and it has been an embarrassment to both me and my family. I have learned my lesson and have paid a huge price both personally and professionally."[36]

He wrote plenty about himself—"I am a different and better person"—but not a word about Cubby. And in the song "Something to Be Proud Of," Troy Gentry sings about doing the best you can, which is good enough for him.

I grab the local newspaper, the *Newport Miner* ("the Voice of Pend Oreille County Since 1901"), when I'm passing through Newport, Idaho, and the lead on the sports page captures my attention. It's another animal story. They're everywhere these days. The headline cautions, WEARING BRIGHT COLORS COULD SAVE YOUR LIFE. Bear season is about to open and the article retells a story from the year before. A hunter mistook a hiker for a black bear and killed the hiker. Wear bright colors, the *Miner* urges its readers. "Do not wear brown, tan, or light colored clothing that blends in with the landscape. Making noises, talking, singing, or whistling can alert hunters of your presence."[37] So, a nice, quiet stroll in the Idaho countryside could prove deadly.

Black bears are not just hunters' quarries; they're also fancied as pets. Father and son Rocky and Jonathan Perkett raised a cub they found while logging at their homestead near Coos Bay, Oregon. Windfall, they named her, and the three lived together until game wardens heard about her and confiscated her in late 2005; the Perketts had run afoul of laws that restrict taking wildlife, laws they claimed were news to them. Windfall was two when the law arrived, 150 pounds, and eating, sleeping, and showering with the Perketts, who said they loved her like a daughter and fed her pizza and Dr Pepper. She was resettled at the Applegate Park Zoo in Merced, California, where she was weaned of her Dr Pepper and pizza habits and provided with a bear cage mate named Missy.[38] "At first she was scared to death of Missy," according to zookeeper Donna McDowell. "She'd never been around another bear before. Now they sleep together and play together. They're as happy as can be."

Not so sanguine is Rocky Perkett, who can't bring himself to visit because "it would be too big a heartbreak. Being used to having her free and us running around in the woods with her, to see her in a cage would be rough. At least we know she's happy and well cared for. That's the most important thing."[39]

A few days after I watched Sonny's canned hunt, I was eating dinner on the Austin, Texas, patio of Matt's Famous El Rancho ("Best Mexican Food in the World Since 1952") with some friends and colleagues. The subject of this book came up and the fellow sitting next to me told me about a pastime he enjoyed as a boy in Austin. He and his pals would catch common red wasps. "We snipped off their stingers and tied thread around . . ." He paused and thought for a moment. "What is the waist of a wasp called?" No one at the table responded to his query (while wasp-waisted is the term used to describe a tightly corseted woman, the wasp body part in question here is the petiole). The Austin boys tied thread around the waists of the wasps they caught and, said my dinner companion, "We'd fly 'em around." The wasps were now harmless, their stingers rendered impotent. The boys would play with their tethered insects until they tired of the game and "then we'd let 'em go."

These antics with Austin wasps seemed harmless to my table partner as he looked back on them, especially in contrast with what he told me he did when his family moved to Hawaii. He recalled orange and black centipedes—"aggressive sons-of-bitches"—that he and his Hawaiian friends would cut the heads off of. Their stinging apparatus was lopped off with the heads. They would then put the remainder of the insect on their arms and it would flail about, looking dangerous, the missing head (and stinger) not obvious, and they would attempt to impress the little girls in the neighborhood. Another dinner companion offered his thoughts on the use and abuse of animals for entertainment. "I can connect you with some good old boys who shoot feral pigs from helicopters," he volunteered. South Texas, he told me, was the venue for the whirlybird pig hunts. He wasn't sure if it was sheer amusement the hunters were after, or if they rationalized their antics with the need to cull the invasive pigs—animals prone to damage crops and livestock. Texans in choppers with rifles pointed at pigs and little boys with wasps on leashes. Just two more examples of a phenomenon I discovered: Most everyone is quick to share stories they've experienced or heard regarding humans using other animals for diversion.

CHAPTER NINE

Infiltrating Cockfights

RAY JONES DOES UNDERCOVER WORK FOR ELLIOT KATZ'S IN DEFENSE of Animals organization, other animal rights groups, and for law enforcement agencies investigating animal abuse charges. (Jones asked me to shroud his real name, the name he uses when he infiltrates cockfights.) His family was one of those—like Paul Huln's—who believed that there is a constitutional guarantee allowing Americans to fight animals because animals are private property. Jones followed family tradition and as a young man started fighting cocks in Virginia and the Carolinas. As he remembers it, he won about $6,000 at his first fight. After other early successes he wandered west to Louisiana, Oklahoma, and California and, to use his jargon, "fought birds." He added Guam and Guatemala to his scorecard and started selling his fighting roosters for $1,000 each. The eggs he was breeding went for $300 a dozen. Life seemed good: Money, travel, and adventure were his until a Virginia derby in 2005, which Jones calculates as his epiphany.

"There was a boy, he couldn't have been more than seven or eight, and his dad had given him a rooster," he remembers, telling the story to me in his melodic Carolinas accent, a story he's obviously told often since that day. "That boy's rooster was my opponent. And I killed that kid's rooster. That little boy carried that dead rooster around all day. He'd been out in the dirt so there were tear stains down his face." That was the end of cockfighting for Ray Jones. "I just could not do that anymore, I just couldn't be a part of that. I called my wife and told her, 'Honey, I can't do this anymore.'"

The crying boy cradling the dead bird may have been the catalyst for Jones to change sides in the cockfight wars, but he claims he never felt comfortable with hurting animals, whether it was hunting in the Carolina countryside, slaughtering a farmyard pig for food, or fighting roosters. Abuses he witnessed at cockpits troubled him. Watching cockers dispatch birds that failed to show adequate "gameness" scarred him, he tells me. "A bird can't help what its mom and dad is, what its bloodline is, no more than we can help who we are." He offers another example of what repulsed him about the cockfight scene. "I've seen a bird fight a really good fight for a guy for an hour and get pecked last, so he got counted out. He fought a really good fight. He tried really hard." Nonetheless, the owner killed the rooster because it lacked gameness, the trainer "took 'em out and just wrapped its head around a tree and said, 'That sorry motherfucker wasn't game, wasn't no good.'"

Ray Jones figured he was an ideal undercover agent: He knew the cockfighting business and he knew the players. He traded the thrills of cockfighting for the intrigue of espionage, and the satisfaction of feeling that he was working for a worthy cause— the tear-stained boy's face was both a motivator and a powerful image when he wanted to explain his changed lifestyle. Yet he goes to cockfights in order to help develop evidence, and he still keeps roosters (a legal activity). His flock (comprised of "hundreds and hundreds of birds"), he claims, provides credibility for his undercover informer status. "If you go by my house, you'd think I was a cockfighter."

Jones says he goes to the fights, and there he socializes with his peers while he bets the government's money in order to help the cops build cases against those involved not only in animal abuse but also in illegal gambling.

"Do you have any sympathy for these colleagues you're setting up for a felony fall?" I ask him. The owners and operators of cockpits face time behind bars, fines, and confiscation of their property.

He says he sure does, that "they're very friendly people. They're just doing something I don't agree with."

"Why not leave them be to do what they want to do?" I ask him. "You decided it's not what you want to do, but why chase after them?"

"Because I think it needs to stop." He cites the money spent gambling by those who cannot afford to lose. "They dream of winning big. They neglect their families. They spend money on these birds when they don't have groceries at home. Cockfighting really affects human lives as well as animals in a negative way, and I want to make that stop." He's convinced that with it illegal in all fifty states most cockfighting in America is just informal backyard matches, and that the bulk of the sophisticated cockpits—with packed bleachers and concessions stands selling souvenirs and refreshments, with hundreds of birds lined up to fight and piles of cash changing hands—now are a not-so-distant memory.

Kentucky remains one of the exceptions to the improved scenario he sketches. There, as of this writing, fighting cocks and operating a pit are (at worst) both misdemeanors with the potential of being only a little more expensive than the Alabama experience. The maximum penalty? A year in jail and a $500 fine.[40] As is the case in Alabama, possessing the killer roosters, the gaffs and knives, or being a spectator at a fight is not forbidden in the Bluegrass State.

Ray Jones cites Pikeville, Kentucky, as a locale with all but wide-open cockfighting. And just days after Jones and I talked, reporter Russ Cassady wrote a feature story for the *Appalachian News Express* ("The Conscience of Eastern Kentucky") detailing the escapades of Pike County cockfighters. He quotes the owner of a cockpit (who requested anonymity) who dismisses the anti-cockfight efforts of Jones and organizations like the Humane Society. "I ain't a damn bit scared of those people," the entrepreneur told the reporter. "We've run it 21 years, and we've had only one little boxing match here in the parking lot," he said. "We got it stopped in about five minutes. [And it was] over a girl. It wasn't over the chickens." In fact, whether the fighting is illegal at all is questionable because the germane Kentucky statute refers to a "four-legged animal."[41]

That "four-legged animal" clause does not rule out prosecuting a chicken fighter; it simply makes it highly unlikely. And, believe it or not (as Ripley would say), the odd four-legged chicken has existed. Henrietta, for example, was hatched at Brendle Farms in Somerset, Pennsylvania. "It's as healthy as the rest," Mark Brendle said about his chicken. The bird was equipped with two normal front legs and dragged the two extras.[42] Henrietta was not alone. Now and again a four-legged chicken hatches. But, mutants aside, the Pikeville cockpit owner stands by his definitions. "It ain't an animal," he explained to reporter Cassady, defining fighting cocks. "We're fighting chickens," he said. "We're not fighting no animals. Anything that flies is a fowl," he insisted. "You can't say a fowl is an animal." Of course you can. Any of us living things classified in the Animalia kingdom are, ipso facto, animals—in my favorite Oxford English Dictionary and in Pike County, Kentucky.

"Cockfights are common in Pikeville, eh?" I say to Ray Jones. "So if I were to go to Pikeville, Kentucky, I could just walk into a cockfight."

"Well, no," he rejects the idea. "If they don't know you, you're not gettin' in there. I wouldn't advise that."

"Why not?"

"Because if they thought you had something to do with caring for animals, you might get your ass whupped?"

"My ass whupped?" Tarred and feathered in Alabama, ass whupped in Kentucky.

"I don't know any other way to say it," says Jones, "but they'd probably beat you. Basically, it's not a good idea."

Makes me want to witness a cockfight, see the crowd, meet the fighters even more.

CHAPTER TEN
Art as Animal Abuse

THE SCENE IS A NOISY BREAKFAST AND LUNCH RESTAURANT ACROSS the street from the College of Marin, a fine two-year public college in my neighborhood where I've studied Spanish and German over the years. Its bucolic campus lazes just a few miles north of the Golden Gate Bridge, in the shadow of Mount Tamalpais. This is where art historian John Rapko is teaching after losing his tenured professorship at the venerable San Francisco Institute of Art. His former employer says his job was the victim of budget cuts, but Professor Rapko is convinced he was kicked out of the art school because of his critiques of an exhibit installed there by the Algerian-French artist Adel Abdessemed. "I felt like prey, like an animal hunted down," is how he characterizes the affair. Titled "Don't Trust Me," the video presentation is art or an animal snuff film, depending on the audience's point of view. The images presented are of animals beaten to death. For Rapko "Don't Trust Me" is without a doubt a snuff film.

"I didn't publicly object to it when I first saw it," Rapko tells me. "I turned away from it and said, 'This isn't something that I want to spend any time with.'"

Days later, he decided to object to the video from the standpoint of an art critic.

"I read an e-mail from the artist's publicist that said there was a lot of controversy around this work and that the people who were objecting to it were mostly poorly informed people." Professor Rapko is an art scholar and considers himself plenty well informed. "The hint that there was going to be an official story that if you objected to this work or were repulsed by it was a sign that you were naïve or uninformed sent me into a rage."

The school closed the exhibit within days, citing fears about the response to it from animal rights advocates. "We've gotten dozens of threatening phone calls that targeted specific staff people with death threats, threats of violence, and threats of sexual assaults," was the explanation from the Institute's president, Chris Bratton. "We remain committed to freedom of speech as fundamental to this institution, but we have to take people's safety very seriously."[43]

He's not arguing against free speech, says critic Rapko. His objection to "Don't Trust Me" is that the work lacks artistic merit. "It is perverse to aim to cause suffering. Corrupt art is art with an aim to cause suffering." In the case of the video of the animals in question—beaten to death with a sledgehammer—such suffering occurs, he says, "perhaps in the animal and/or perhaps in the viewers. Then the question is: Is the suffering in the viewer meritorious suffering?" After a couple of years considering the work, Rapko's opinion remains unchanged. "There's no artistic merit in having undergone the experience of the Abdessemed piece."

Elliot Katz and his In Defense of Animals group created a news media barrage designed to draw negative attention to the "Don't Trust Me" exhibit. "It was an animal snuff film," Katz tells me without hesitation. "To shoot video in a slaughterhouse, that's not illegal," Katz acknowledges, "because that's actually happening. But to kill animals purposely for the video, that should be illegal because that's animal cruelty. That's abuse."

The impact of the sledgehammers was looped, exposing the audience over and over to the assaults and the flailing responses of the animals. The Art Institute's Walter and McBean Galleries' announcement of the show is written in typical artspeak double talk: "'Don't Trust Me' portrays six animals—a sheep, a horse, an ox, a pig, a goat, and a doe—being struck and killed by a hammer. Each killing occurs so quickly that it's difficult to determine definitively what has happened. Do these incidents represent slaughter or sacrifice? What are their social, cultural, moral, and political implications? Or are such questions now verging on irrelevance, as if something else altogether were taking place (or about to), something wholly other, unforeseen, unexpected?"[44] Huh? Read that catalog excerpt again, I propose, and it will make no more sense than it did the first time.

Before the show was shuttered, Okwui Enwezor, a dean and spokesman at the San Francisco Institute of Art, insisted that the controversy revolved around a simple question: "Is this gratuitous violence, or is it the image of violence? These are two different things."[45] Is that statement analysis or is it artworld-speak?

After the controversy, Adel Abdessemed was not an easy man to reach for his side of the story. I spent months beseeching the gallery that represents him to arrange an interview. First they told me that he felt uncomfortable engaging in an English-language interview; I said it was not a problem to conduct the exchange in French. Then they suggested he just did not want to discuss the incident or "Don't Trust Me" with me (he didn't trust me?). Finally, I managed to find the artist at the Ontario College of Art & Design in Toronto, where he was engaged as an artist-in-residence. The curator of his show there graciously forwarded to his guest the questions I wanted Abdessemed to answer, and a few weeks later I received his responses via e-mail, along with a rather snippy note from his gallery representative demanding, "Adel doesn't allow any of his words to be changed, neither the questions."[46] Well, the questions are mine, and as to his answers, they came in French. Here is our exchange translated into English. As I do with any interviewee I quote, I've made the best effort to keep my reporting true to his meaning.

I first asked Abdessemed if the decision to close his show could be interpreted by him to mean his "Don't Trust Me" was a success in San Francisco because of the controversy it generated.

"I think I understand what you mean" was his response. "It's a rather sad state of affairs. That sort of question," he continued, "assumes that there's such a thing as 'scandal art.' But I have nothing to do with that. That's the interpretation of other people, not mine," he said about the outcry from Katz and other animal rights activists, and about the shuttering of the show. "They're entitled to it, even if most of these agitators haven't seen the work. For me what's most important is that the work rings true, but the reactions and the scandal don't interest me."

Nonetheless, animal rights activists such as Katz became art critics when they protested the show. "How do you relate to their outrage and their efforts to censor your work?" I asked.

"Animal rights advocates have their ideology, their feelings," he told me. "My goal is different. As an artist I am not looking for sensationalism because violence is repugnant to me. There is always friction between the individual work of art, the democratic setting, and the politically correct milieu. Let's try to move forward without pronouncing who is right and who is wrong. But let's talk about fear: economic collapse, poverty, epidemics, food, global warming and its consequences. That kind of fear is set in front of us at the dinner table every day. We are fed on fear."

I referenced Professor Rapko's label: that "Don't Trust Me" is dangerous and without artistic merit. "How do you define art?" I asked Abdessemed.

"Art is always dangerous, but not perverse. It's not neutral. It's not about design," was his explanation. "As you know I detest neutrality. I always take a position. And we are all at the scene of the crime."

I left him with the question that is at the heart of my quest. "What, for you, differentiates animal use from animal abuse?"

"What about Wikileaks?" he answered with a question of his own. "Do they use or abuse information? If we look at the question seriously, I don't see any difference. Using and abusing is the same thing. When you eat a steak, you're not going to ask yourself if you're using or abusing a cow, are you? And I imagine you continue to eat it with a knife and fork."

Not me. I haven't eaten a steak since Ronald Reagan defeated Jimmy Carter. Or to put it into a French context, since Mitterrand was elected the first Socialist president of the Fifth Republic. But I take his point: It is worth considering if there is any difference between the use and abuse of animals. And my friend and colleague Jeff Kamen, the proud companion of monsters like Newfoundlands, dislikes the word "use" for his relationship with his dogs. "What you and I do with dogs isn't using," he insisted when we chatted about my search, "it's sharing life."

Images of attacks on animals presented as art are as old as cave paintings. In our own era, in 1968, the Destruction in Art Symposium came to New York City's Judson Memorial Church featuring Hermann Nitsch's so-called assemblage in which animal brains, lungs, and blood were spewed over surfaces covered with white tablecloths. Rafael Montañez Ortiz (known in the 1960s as Ralph Ortiz) announced his intention to tear black and white chickens apart (a statement on American race relations) at the event, but audience members freed the poultry before they were wrought into art. "Art is the symbolic artistic realization of all the hostile destructive urges that have placed mankind in crises since the beginning," Ortiz explained at the time.[47] The year before, his *The Life and Death of Henny Penny* consisted of the artist swinging a live chicken out over his audience. Next he cut off the chicken's head and whacked the body against a guitar until both the guitar and the chicken were in ruins.[48]

What differentiates the Adel Abdessemed piece from crush videos? Context? Hipster art gallery opening versus lurking around YouTube in the middle of the night in a dark room? Crush videos prove that if you can imagine it, somebody somewhere probably wants to do it or at least see it. A typical crush video shows a woman—usually barefoot or wearing stiletto heels—crushing small animals by repeatedly stomping them. Congress passed a law in 1999 banning crush video trafficking, but the Supreme Court, in an 8 to 1 decision, ruled the ban unconstitutional in 2010, saying it violated First Amendment free speech guarantees. It seemed at first glance an odd ruling, since the animal abuse depicted during the production of such videos is illegal. But the Court's complaint was that the wording of the 1999 law was too broad, and could be interpreted as including images of activities like legal hunting. It forbade the creation, sale, or possession of "a depiction of animal cruelty" for profit, and defined a depiction of cruelty as a document that shows "a living animal intentionally maimed, mutilated, tortured, wounded, or killed." Congress rewrote the law—which had never been used to prosecute a crush video peddler—months later, in an attempt to address the Supreme Court's objections.

"Animal torture videos are barbaric and have no place in a civilized society," explained Michigan congressman Gary Peters, one of the bill's sponsors. "By promising to lock up the people who produce and distribute these videos we can work to put a halt to this horrendous practice."[49] When the rewritten law was waiting for President Obama's signature, I spent a few Internet minutes searching for crush videos. The images were available, but they were not easy to find.

While researching this book I stayed a week in Yorkshire, England, in the borrowed Victorian flat of my colleague Lance Pettitt. Professor Pettitt teaches cultural studies at Leeds Metropolitan University, and his bookshelves are lined with titles that analyze post-colonial Britain. *Ornamentalism: How the British Saw Their Empire* immediately caught my eye. On the front cover is a dapper Anglo gentleman wearing a quite formal suit: a long dark topcoat with covered buttons, a white double-breasted vest, and a high-collared shirt all accented with a neatly knotted tie and a handkerchief peeking out of the coat pocket.

His hands are resting on his walking stick and his left foot, clad in shoes showing off a high shine, is resting on the rump of the tiger he just killed. The Great White Hunter's lips are pursed. To me they make him look both uncomfortable and arrogant. His eyes are cast down at the beast; its eyes stare lifelessly—with a look of resignation—at the camera. The left side of the photograph decorates the book's back cover. There, striking a similar pose, sporting his own formal attire—a headdress and an ankle-length robe—with his conquering foot on another tiger's ribs, a stately Indian gentleman looks into the camera, his eyes suggesting much the same attitude as the tiger's, as if he were saying, "This is my fate. This is what I do."

The caption is simple. "Lord Curzon, with the Maharaja of Gwalior, 1899." Author David Cannadine refers to such hunts in the text as examples of the duties representatives of the British Empire performed as they traveled their lands reinforcing their control. They shot tigers, he writes, "for recreation."[50]

CHAPTER ELEVEN
Who Would Abuse a Swan?

"STAINES," SAID THE UK IMMIGRATION OFFICER QUIZZICALLY WHEN I answered her question about where in England I was going. "Staines?" she repeated incredulously, pronouncing the city's name sty-nzz, like the pigsty she was suggesting it must be.

"What's wrong with Staines?" I asked her.

She reverted to her official role and refused further comment, but she was rolling her eyes with her entire face.

The hotel I booked is well past its prime—threadbare, chipped paint—but directly on the river, with a view of the swans I'm in England to check on. (Ending the preceding sentence with a preposition seems appropriate for England. Winston Churchill is often quoted as responding to criticism about such usage as saying something along the lines of, "That is criticism up with which I will not put!")

I'm sitting on my balcony at the Staines Thames Lodge. It's about seven miles upriver from London and just minutes from Heathrow. Departing airliners periodically disrupt the bucolic scene. Lilypads dot the river. Narrow canal barges—converted into touring houseboats—putt-putt by, decorated with boxes of flowers atop the living quarters. Trains to London pass frequently over the bridge that's close enough to my room that their clatter wakes me in the night.

Swans bring me here. A pair is floating past me as I write this. One moment they look graceful and archetypal: the gentle curve of their necks and the fluffy white sweep of their back feathers. But the next moment they look silly and undignified as they dunk their heads and necks into the river, upending themselves. They're upside down foraging for food, leaving nothing but their tail feathers and their scrawny legs and wide feet exposed to my view from above the water.

Sleepy Staines was once a manufacturing center and made its mark on the world because this is where linoleum was invented. A characterless shopping mall sits on the site of the original lino factory, but just a few blocks from my balcony, on High Street, the Staines legacy is enshrined by a bronze sculpture of two heroic linoleum workers carrying a roll of lino. "On the Roll" is an ode to the ubiquitous floor covering, written by local poets Leona Medlin and Richard Price:

Roll out the lino
From Staines to the world!
Release every pattern
From chessboard to twirl!
In every hopeful kitchen
Let life unfurl,
Bathrooms are artrooms
From soapsuds to swirl!
Roll out the lino
From Staines to the world!

A few miles from the shrine to linoleum I find the Swan Sanctuary—land along the Thames secured by swan fancier Dorothy Beeson as a place to nurse abused swans back to health. This is a large-scale facility, complete with a clinic equipped for complex operations and its own swan ambulance, a van outfitted to provide emergency care en route back to the sanctuary. The ambulance brings a new patient just before I sit down to talk to Beeson.

"We had a call about a mother swan in Staines saying that she wasn't very well. Her wing was dropped. There didn't seem to be any sign of the cob," she tells me, explaining in case the term was new to me (which it was) that male swans are referred to as cobs (and females as pens). "And she's got five babies." The ambulance crew was dispatched over to Staines and they fetched the pen and the cygnets. Medics treated the wound, surmising it was caused by a dog bite.

But plenty of the ambulance calls are in response to human abuse of the graceful, gorgeous birds. Beeson looks strained as she recounts her swans' enemies: anglers fishing in the Thames and other English rivers and lakes. Her strawberry blonde hair hangs below her shoulders. She's wearing jeans and a short-sleeved pink and purple striped T-shirt, and when she's not recounting swan abuse, she displays a cheerful smile. "Pairs are shot," she laments, "and babies get so tackled up that they get their throats ripped out. It's just horrible." Shortwood Common Lake in Staines, she says, is a particularly problematic locale. More than thirty years before we talked, Beeson rescued the first cygnets she reared from the lake. Every year since she's rescued swans victimized, she says, by fishermen at Shortwood Common Lake. "One of the horrific cases I dealt with involved two kids who bought a can of lighter fuel, poured it over a swan, and set fire to him. What is going on in their heads?" she sighs, sad and confused. She is convinced that young animal abusers often grow into adults who perpetrate mayhem against fellow humans. She describes a swan pair that she "homed" to a private lake that were victims of a dog attack, saying the dogs' owner encouraged the attack. "Ripped the male swan's wing off, and ate some of the babies in front of the mum. They left here with one baby and the mate's got one wing now." "Outrageous" and "sickening" is how she refers to the swan abuse she's witnessed over the years.

"It attracts a low life element," she says in a soft and slow voice about the nearby lake. "They've got a few cans of beer and they set their lines up. It's just a hole of a place, although it's beautiful to look at. They're just pig ignorant," she says about the fishermen, a strange metaphor to choose since pigs are often respected for their intelligence. Sometimes it's the swan's fault for ingesting a bait-laden hook, but many fishermen respond to the loss of hook and bait by reeling in the bird. "The fisherman will draw the swan in with a hook down the esophagus. That hook tears like a razor blade so that the bird needs to be opened up and the hook removed and the esophagus repaired." The World Cup was being played just before my visit, so the swans at Shortwood Common Lake were safer than usual while the "yobs" drank their beer in front of the telly instead of lakeside. "The minute England lost," Beeson reports, "it was just like the Gates of Hell opened." Her staff went from answering one or two calls a week during the soccer matches to a couple of dozen.

I ask Dorothy Beeson what led her to become the swan queen of Staines. Her laugh sounds like a machine gun as she leans back to tell her tale. "I was at a low point in my life, and I used to go out bird watching." She observed a swan pair go through the mating ritual. "The day their cygnets were out on the water for the first time they were so used to me that they brought them over to see me." The babies were cute, but the cob was suffering from a tangle of fishing line dangling from his beak. She finally found a vet who agreed to operate on the distressed bird. The vet asked Beeson to look after the recovering swan for a few days. "Which I did," she says, and looks back at me as if there is no need to explain further.

"And that resulted in this?" I ask, pointing out the pens of recuperating swans in her barn, the well-equipped clinic, the land available for recovering birds to live on until they feel fit enough to return to the wild—if they wish.

"I decided that I would create the Swan Sanctuary for my queen and country," Beeson tells me with a smile. The queen is known as the Seigneur of the Swans in quaint English tradition, a role that can be traced to the twelfth century when the bird became a popular dinnertime treat and any swan on public waters was considered royal property.[51]

"Swans were being wiped out. They were all dying from lead poisoning." Ingesting lead weights used by fishermen was killing them. "These pieces of lead were going into the gizzard. The gizzard is a digestive organ and it was grinding them up. Then the lead was going into the kidneys and causing the deaths of so many," she says. In 1989 lead fishing weights were banned in England and the swan populations began to recover. "I do think that any serious angler shouldn't fish where there's a flock of swans."

"Over thirty years you've gone from someone who cared about one pair of swans to quite the expert on swans and swan phenomena," I suggest.

Beeson's response is a droll, "Some people say I'm an expert. I suppose if you were darning socks for thirty years you'd be an expert at that." She laughs.

"But you probably know more about swans than most people."

"I'd say that. I certainly know quite a lot about swans and their behavior and their illnesses and their treatments."

She considers them God's creatures and that no matter the animal "if it's sick it deserves some assistance," especially since about 90 percent of the swans she sees at the Swan Sanctuary are injured or sick "and those are problems inflicted by humans."

In addition to the royal connection in England, people every-where—apart from the miscreant anglers—consider swans special. They take a role in most cultures that differentiates them from their duck and goose cousins; they seem aristocratic. Leda and the swan—the Greek myth of Zeus and Sparta's queen. Tchai-kovsky's "Swan Lake." Maybe it is the long and graceful curved neck. Or the languid manner with which they drift on the water. Or the soft white plumage most of them sport.

Beeson agrees, and then some. "You're going to think I'm some kind of nutter," she says. "There is a very spiritual side to a swan. I've seen things that probably people wouldn't believe. If you've got a pair and one dies, the other has this silent grief." They know she wants to help them when she rescues them, she tells me. "They give out these little sounds."

"What is the sound like?"

"It's just a bit like this." She makes a series of soft grunts. "They know that you're not going to harm them."

Plenty of people stay far from swans because of their aggressive reputation. Beeson doesn't consider swan aggression a concern even though she was knocked out cold by one once.

"It was sent to me in a packing crate and when I unpacked it, it flapped its wings and struck me right in the head."

But she doesn't see aggression against people as a swan trait. Cobs will protect their territory against other intrusive swans during mating season. The invader risks being killed by drowning. I imagine swans with gaffs and swords strapped to their legs, attacking each other in a ring, a crowd betting and cheering them on. Not a chance, says Beeson, swans only fight to protect their territory.

We're interrupted by the arrival of an expected goose at the office. The Swan Sanctuary does harbor other birds in need.

"Oh my God," Beeson sings out. "Well done, RSPCA." That's the Royal Society for the Prevention of Cruelty to Animals, "looking out for animals," as it identifies its mission, since 1824. She says the goose was confiscated from a Romanian family's garden. "Foreign visitors to our country are stealing our waterfowl and eating them, so it's said," Beeson complains.

"But if it's wild waterfowl," I ask, "can't it be hunted for food?"

Her response suggests the removed attitude so many Brits I've encountered in the Mother Country hold about us in the Colonies. "No, no," she says. "It's not like in your country where you can go out and blast at anything. Good God, no!" There are some waterfowl hunting seasons, "but not just willy-nilly down the Thames, popping one off!"

"I think we have some restrictions, too," I counter defensively. We're laughing, and we leave her office to tour the hospital wards full of sick and injured birds in various states of repair.

Fluffy cygnets brought in with their sick mother look darling as they scurry for food. Swans primp and swim wherever I look, in hospital enclosures, floating stately on ponds, coming up to fences to greet their caretaker.

"Hello, Charlie!" she calls out to one. "This is Charlie," she introduces us.

"Hello, Charlie," I say. It's the first time I've been formally introduced to a swan.

"And that's his mate, and his babies."

"Nice looking babies!" When I come closer to them Charlie makes it clear with a shrill trumpeting that I've crossed his comfort zone.

"Hello, Charlie," she says again as he rattles against the fencing. "He's trying to show what a big strong gent he is." The sanctuary's fences are high enough to keep the injured birds from flying off.

Dorothy Beeson lives on the bucolic Swan Sanctuary site. "I can run out in my nightie, in the middle of the night. I couldn't do that if I lived in Staines."

"And what do they call you in town?" I ask. There must be a nickname for this woman who has dedicated her life to saving sick and injured swans. I suggest the Swan Lady.

"Oh, I don't know." She acts as if the question never occurred to her. "Probably barmy." Perhaps a bit barmy—who wouldn't be after a lifetime caring for victimized swans? "I find it quite depressing, actually," she concludes about her work as we say good-bye.

CHAPTER TWELVE
The Self-Taught Lion Tamer

TRADITIONS CHANGE. FOX HUNTING WITH HOUNDS WAS BANNED IN Britain in 2004. You can still see bullfights in Spain, but not in Barcelona. In 2010 the Catalonia parliament outlawed what Hemingway lusted after but called "a decadent art."[52] Hundreds of so-called dancing bears attempted to entertain passersby on Indian subcontinent streets until just a few years ago. International animal welfare agencies teamed with the Indian government to outlaw the practice and find sanctuaries for the mutilated bears: Their snouts were punctured and laced with a rope, they were castrated and their teeth pulled—then, unable to escape their handlers, they were forced upright onto their hind legs to prance for rupees.

～～

Is it animal use or animal abuse for a circus performer to stick his head in the mouth of a huge adult male lion? Sounds more like the potential for performer abuse to me.

Budapest, a sunny summer day in 2010. I'm in a taxi heading from a friend's house in the Buda hills to the Hungarian State Circus, a venerable Middle European institution still entertaining and thrilling audiences in its intimate quarters next to the city zoo. But not all Budapesters are amused. When I tell my taxi driver where I'm going, his response is immediate.

"I hate circuses," Peter Csabai announces. His voice is calm, but firm. We've been chatting since I got in the car—about the weather (it's hot and the cab's air conditioner feels good), about travel (Csabai tells me about his jaunts throughout the world), and about Hungary's precarious economy (he's driving a taxi again because a business he founded is faltering).

"I was eight or ten," he says. "I was taken to the circus like all children." But he was disturbed watching the animals in the show. "They were forcing them to sit down, stand up, do something stupid. If it's for fun, it's okay," he says about such antics. "But it's not okay if it's forced."

I start to take notes. Interviewing a taxi driver is a cliché for foreign correspondents, and I tend to shy from using them as easy sources. But Csabai is worldly and articulate, and it's rare to find a man troubled by circus acts since boyhood. He watches me as I scribble in my notebook, and after he ascertains that I'm a writer, he asks another question.

"Are you happy?"

As he maneuvers the Mercedes through traffic, I acknowledge that I'm pretty content.

He tells me a man needs three things in life to be happy. "You need your soul friend, your wife. You must enjoy your job, not just for the money. You must make something for fun." Painting or gardening, he offers as examples, stressing that what you make must be productive. Playing video games he dismisses, saying that doesn't count. The trick, he explains the obvious, is to combine your job and what you do for fun. "At this point," he says about the ideal combination, "I am not happy. But I am happy about my wife."

I arrive early for my appointment with Vladislav Goncharov—the man who famously sticks his head in his lion's mouth—and duck out of the heat into a bar next door to the circus. It feels almost air conditioned, and I order a bottle of water. On the wall I spot a poster that calls out in English, I WOULD RATHER DIE OF THIRST THAN DRINK FROM THE CUP OF MEDIOCRITY. I take a swig of the chilled water. Another sign advertises Zack brand Unicum, the bitter digestif ubiquitous in Hungarian bars.

Lion tamer Goncharov shows up and we sit at a shaded table on the sidewalk in front of the bar. He's wearing Adidas shorts, a shirt reminiscent of a Hawaiian print, and he needs a shave. His piercing blue eyes size me up as I explain my mission. Before we talk about use and abuse, I want to learn how one chooses to become a lion tamer. The story is fantastic. Vladislav Goncharov is not only a lion tamer; he is a *self-taught* lion tamer. The circus was not in his family's blood. He mustered himself out of the army in 1997 wondering what he was going to do with the rest of his life. Security guard seemed an option, or police work, or another tour with the army. While he was mulling over the possibilities, a friend suggested he take a job selling tickets to the circus. The idea appealed to him and off he went to Siberia. Literally. He barked the shows and sold tickets to the circus in Chita and Novosobirsk, and in Siberia he met his future wife, a circus acrobat. "It was she who brought animals close to my heart," he tells me, and she did it to get him out of the box office. "She told me that if we as a family want to be together then I should myself become a circus artist, and that I should get involved in working with some kind of animals: dogs, chimpanzees, or maybe bears."

Goncharov considered the circus menagerie and decided to adopt a baby lion. But he was untrained and did not know what to do with the seventeen-day-old captive-bred lion he chose for his first circus partner. "It loved me because I was feeding it." He nursed the cub with a bottle. "I wanted the small lion to feel that I am his mother actually. So I wanted it to come to me as early as possible." He knows now that taking a lion from its mother at such an early age is wrong. "I was feeding it and it was growing bigger, bigger and bigger." But Goncharov did not know how to train it or what to do with it. He gave it to a zoo, but he refused to quit. He took in another lion and studied his behavior, experimenting with how he needed to act in order to convince the lion to do what he wanted him to do. But that lion also proved difficult.

"He even became bigger than my first lion and didn't want to get in contact with me," he says, and then he marks what caused the behavior change. "When he became a big boy. When he became sexually mature."

"What did he do?" I ask. "How was it clear he no longer wanted to relate to you?"

"I could see it in his behavior. He was a real man, not a little puppy that was running to me and licking me."

He seemed threatening, and Goncharov gave lion number two to a zoo. But he felt confident he was learning how to change his own behavior toward the lions as they matured.

"I was also growing in all this process, developing, so I became mature enough to know how to circumvent problems. How to deceive the animals."

"You're completely self-taught?" I ask, amazed.

He looks back at me with his compelling coolness and answers simply, "Yes."

"No mentor?"

"Nobody was prepared to tell me anything because I was viewed as competition. Nobody wanted to tell me their secrets."

That I could understand. Harder to understand—but easy to appreciate—was Goncharov's decision to soldier on with his attempts to create a circus career performing with big cats.

"Many people told me that it will come to a sad end. That either the animals will tear me up during the show or behind the scenes. I had to prove that I not only like animals, but I'm capable of working with them."

Work with them he does. For his show he's in the ring with seven huge male lions.

"But while you were teaching yourself how to work with these lions"—he knows where I'm going with my question—"were you . . ."

He interrupts me. "Was I afraid?"

"Yeah, afraid. Or intimidated?"

"Yes," he acknowledges without hesitation.

"So what motivated you to continue?"

"My love for the animals, my desire to work with these animals, and my wish to work with animals in a circus. It's very prestigious in our country to work with predators. You immediately become highly respected."

"And your wife is encouraging you," I suggest. "She's saying, 'Vlad, go out there and tame those lions.'"

"She was always behind me, supporting me. She was always saying, 'Everything will be all right.' Thanks to my wife and thanks to the animals that I work with, they have made me into a real fighter."

"Fighter?" I ask. "Meaning what?"

"I have the character of a manly, strong, highly motivated person."

"Do you figure that working with lions made you stronger than had you stayed in the army and chosen a military career?"

His answer comes back without a second thought. "Absolutely. Going into a cage with seven male lions who are ready to sort out who is the strongest—not only with you, but also with one another—that is something that teaches you a kind of mentality."

"Because mentality is the key word, right? Since you are not the strongest, they are the strongest."

"Yes," he agrees, and says his character sends the lions a message. "I show them that I am strong."

"How?"

"With my energy. When I come into the cage I behave very decisively. I will be sure that if there is a lion behind me and it's looking at my back that it will not attack me because there is an energy coming out of me." Sitting at the bar table he demonstrates what not to do. He looks behind himself and acts startled. Being unsure of yourself in the ring, he tells me, could be a disaster.

"Right," I agree. "But even if you are completely self-confident, any one of those seven lions could tear you to pieces in minutes."

"They can. But thanks to the training that I've given them from a very tender age they do not do that."

Goncharov selects year-old, captive-bred lions for training. Training, he tells me, is all done via positive reinforcement techniques and rewards—no beatings, no whips. He says his dozen years of experience have taught him how a lion is going to behave under various circumstances and what he needs to do to prevent problems for himself or amongst the lions. But he respects the fact they are wild animals even if they are captive bred, wild animals he's convinced to allow him to control them. I ask if he believes he knows what the lions are thinking or does he just know what they will do under certain circumstances. His answer is that he understands them about 50 percent of the time. Sounds like pretty poor odds to me, but Vladislav Goncharov exudes confidence.

"Do they want to do the tricks you teach them?" I ask.

"Everything depends on the character of the animal. Those that do not want to do these things I turn over to the zoo."

"Do you think your performing lions are happy?"

"Yes," he says. "I think that they are."

"Do they like you?"

He rejects "like" and instead answers with "respect."

"Are you friends, you and the cats?"

"Partners."

"And what do they get out of the partnership?"

"Thanks to me they receive a lengthy period of working in the circus. And all the human care that they cannot receive in the zoo or in the wild." He lists the benefits for the lions, from his point of view. They receive vaccinations against disease and other medical care, vitamins, and an excellent diet including live rabbits and chickens. He is the provider, Goncharov tells me, and for that the lions should be grateful. Natural selection doesn't necessarily kill them when they get sick; here they are treated. If they're too old and tired to chase down a zebra to eat, they're not forced to feast on whatever dead meat they can scavenge. "The circus is better than a zoo or nature because here on Earth there is a creature, man, that is higher than these animals."

"You believe that we are superior to the animals?"

"Definitely. We are in charge of what happens on the planet."

"You are a famous star now." I point out the obvious; posters of him with his head deep in a lion's mouth are plastered all over Budapest.

"Thank you very much." He's gracious as he tells me about winning gold medals for circus performance in both Moscow and Budapest a couple of years ago.

"Those lion tamers who rejected your requests for help as you were learning the business, do they embrace you now that you're an accomplished professional?"

His answer is music to the ears of anyone who's been snubbed by colleagues. "Some have started turning to me for advice. They would like to know how I do it."

"That must make you feel great."

"Yes, I feel good." And then he adds, "I try to help them because when I was a beginner, when I was twenty, nobody would tell me. I'm trying to help those people who need this advice. There is a God that's watching who will probably help me be successful as a result of that."

The climax of Vladislav Goncharov's self-taught act—the head-in-the-lion's-mouth trick—is an extraordinary pose to consider.

"And this lion will hold my head in his mouth as long as *I* want him to hold my head in his mouth and not as long as he wants," Goncharov declares, self-satisfied.

What must that be like to do not just once but two times a day? "What does it feel like to stick your head in the mouth of a critter who can bite it off your neck if he so desires?" I ask.

"Emotions and adrenaline," is his response, explaining that he feels good because putting his head in a lion's mouth is his work, and it feels good to do his job well.

"What are you thinking about when your head is inside that guy's mouth?"

"When this moment will end," he says in a calm voice.

For some reason I never expected such an answer. I expected something philosophical like, "I feel one with the entire animal kingdom," or something personal like, "I feel at peace with the fates." But I never expected that something he does twice a day and has brought him fame would be something he wants over as fast as possible.

"I want it to end well and quickly."

"So it's safe to say that as brave as you are and as big as the smile is on your face now, it's scary."

"Yes," he says patiently. "It's a predator. It's an animal."

"Any day he could bite your head off!"

"Yes," he agrees, repeating, "predator."

Earlier, animal rights advocate Elliot Katz said that the inherent thrill for the audience is "when is he going to get his head smashed." Katz said he didn't think blood lust was what motivates most ticket sales. "People are not necessarily going to see him get hurt, but to watch his courage. Even though for him there's probably not that much courage because he's raised that cat. It's like a kitten to him."

Not like a kitten, Goncharov reminds me, but a one-year-old, and a year-old male lion can weigh in at as much as two hundred pounds.

"Do you think every day could be your last, because of your friend the lion?" I ask.

"Every day is a birthday for me."

"Of course every day is a birthday for all of us," I counter, and he laughs. I point to the busy street next to the sidewalk table where we're sitting. "A car could crash into us."

He agrees, and says that means then that he has *two* birthdays each day. "I have a birthday because I'm not killed by the lions and also because I'm not hit by a car."

We talk about Siegfried and Roy, and the day their act exploded into chaos when a tiger Roy raised attacked him with wild vigor. Goncharov nods. "An animal's thinking is much lower than a man's," he says. "It thinks, 'I want to eat something' and that's it. It won't get as wild as in nature because it has had human contact all its life." But it might have gotten up on the wrong side of its cage that morning, he theorizes. "Maybe the tiger had a bad night or had too little to eat or had problems with its making excrement or maybe something's itching there and that's why it bit him. You mustn't come to the conclusion that this animal is going to bite you the next day," he says about an errant beast, because that's not how its mind works. "It can be friendly with you tomorrow," and he feigns lion kisses. Goncharov's never been bitten by one of his cats, but one "made gestures that it wants to grab me. It happened twice and then it stopped. It's a predator," he shrugs.

I tell him about Peter Csabai, my taxi driver that morning who said, "I hate the circus," and complained that the animals are forced to act. "If he were here with us, what would you say to him?"

"I would tell him that if he doesn't like the circus, nobody forces him to go. And he shouldn't force his opinion upon everybody who likes the circus. If I don't want to travel in a taxi because it's expensive, I will take trolley bus. I won't be telling everybody, 'Don't travel by taxi because it's too expensive.'"

What about animal rights activists like Dr. Elliot Katz, I ask, who believe lions cannot lead a reasonable life if they are kept captive? "What is your message to them?"

"I would recommend that they start dealing with other issues. The homeless. Or they should protest about miners going under the earth because there are methane explosions there. Or that oil doesn't get into the seas. I could give you a list for the rest of the day. Shall I go on?"

Nope, I say. I get the point. And I ask him the litany of questions Dr. Katz suggested.

"Where do your lions live when they're not performing?"

"The lions live in a cage," he informs me. Of course, where else could they live?

"What happens to your lions once they become too old to perform?"

"I give them to the zoo," he says, another predictable answer, and so their further care is the zoo's responsibility.

"Do your lions ever become dangerous to the point where they can no longer perform in your act?"

"Yes, sure." As always, his candor is refreshing. "But it happens very rarely."

And Katz's final query: "What would you do if one of your lions hurt you or someone else?"

"Nothing could be done," he tells me. "It is my problem. I am to blame."

I ask Vladislav Goncharov if he eats meat.

"Yes, I eat meat, because I want to have muscles."

"But you love animals?"

"Very much. If I didn't like animals I would have a different job."

"Do you have pets?"

"I have three dogs."

"But the lions are not pets?"

"They are partners."

CHAPTER THIRTEEN

Yes, He Really Does Stick His Head
in the Mouth of a Lion

THAT AFTERNOON I GO TO THE CIRCUS TO WATCH VLADISLAV GON-charov and his "partners" perform. The Hungarian State Circus is well over a hundred years old; performances are one-ring affairs, with the audience placed intimately close to the acrobats, clowns, horsemen, and dancers. As I wait for the show to start, I wonder about crowd safety. Goncharov is going to bring his lions this close to me? Are they declawed? Would claws matter if they got loose? Hundreds of pounds of lion wouldn't need the advantage of claws if it wanted to swat me.

The clown is funny, the acrobats daring, the horsemen gracious, and the dancers graceful. The crew erects high netting between us in the audience and the ring. Goncharov finally appears, his hair slicked back and his face clean-shaven. He's changed into a stark white shirt and black pants held up with black suspenders. One after another his lions enter until all seven crowd into the ring with him. The band is playing swing-sounding dance music and Goncharov keeps his feet—in shiny patent leather shoes—moving in time with it as he cues his lions to pose on their perches. One after another he assigns them routines: lions jumping over one another, lions roaring, synchronized lions rolling over like the family dog, and lions sitting on their haunches clapping their front paws in time to the music as they rock side to side like feline Rockettes. (I can't even get my housecat Schrödinger to stop scratching the sofa.) The crowd gasps. The crowd laughs.

The music changes to a slow and gentle tune as Goncharov isolates one of the lions from the pride. He pets it and moves his hands to its jaws, and then—amazing to behold!—he sticks his head deep inside the beast's mouth and parks himself in that bizarre position for several breathless moments. I think about what he told me that afternoon, "I want it to end well and quickly." It does. He pulls his head out and triumphantly straddles the lion horseback style.

Despite the climax, his show is not over. He lies on top of all the lions. The lions roar on command; they clamber up on the netting separating them from the audience and grab in our direction with a vivid display of their long dagger-like claws. As the cast takes their bows, I join the standing ovation, clapping madly. I point to Goncharov and wave. He waves back. As I leave the old circus building and head out into the streets of Buda, I realize I'm a convert. I loved the show, even as I wonder about Dr. Katz's concerns about the life the lions live. Use or abuse? I'm not so sure.

Later, Vladislav Goncharov and I exchange e-mail messages. I congratulate him on his performance and he says he's glad I took the opportunity to see that his act is an appropriate use of animals. That's his conclusion. I'm still ruminating. But no question it was a rousing performance and it delighted the child in me.

～～

Not so lucky was Oleksie Pinko. The Ukrainian lion "tamer" was mauled by two of his cats in the middle of his circus act in Lviv in September 2010, a few months after I saw his colleague Goncharov. While the crowd screamed, an American tourist, Doug Shepard, captured the attack with a video recorder. His wife and children scattered along with the rest of the audience—terrified—and not just because of what was happening to Pinko. They were worried about the flimsy-looking net separating the chaos from their ringside seats, and they fled as the circus crew first jabbed at the two marauding lions with long steel rods, and eventually subdued the cats with jets of water from fire hoses. "I do not want to go to the circus ever again," Shepard reported the response from his son, and added his own opinion, "I don't blame him."[53]

⸺

In the highlands of Michoacán, Mexico, many years ago, I was researching a book about the guitars and guitar makers of Paracho. Across the street from the first hotel I secured (bare lightbulb, bugs, and $20 a night), just outside of the village on the highway to Uruapan, a tawdry roadside circus set up its tent. The multicolored big top was impossible to ignore. My son Talmage and I wandered over to what he would later call The Circus of Despair and we bought tickets.

Folding chairs were set up on flimsy plywood stages; we sat on ours and waited for the show to start, expecting, as Tal said later, "wild magnificent animals right in front of us doing amazing things." Instead a parade of sad and dejected creatures greeted us: malnourished looking, their coats ragged, appearing much too old for show business. Neither Tal nor I can forget, these years later, how they were whipped, prodded, and poked as they entered and exited the stage and performed their acts.

"The circus turned from a wonderful fantasy to a show of cruelty and despair in a matter of minutes," Tal remembers, "with us feeling guilty for paying the admission fee—as if we were co-conspirators in the obvious torture of these animals, as the carnies made a quick buck off the country locals." As we watched, Tal fantasized out loud about sneaking back that night, setting the animals free, and locking the trainers in their cages. Instead, after about fifteen minutes, we stood up in the middle of the performance and left the tent—looking for enchiladas and tequila. Tal says he still can visualize the look in the animals' eyes: "trapped, lost, hurt, and helpless."

⸺

Bullfights in Mexico (along with Spain and other countries where the bull rings attract matadors and spectators) are under continuing pressure from animal rights activists. The sport (or abuse, take your pick) suffers from declining fan interest; attendance at fights is down. It didn't help the status of Mexican bullfighting when, in mid-June 2010, bullfighter Christian Hernández entered the Plaza de Toros in Mexico City dressed in the finest skin-tight pink and gold matador regalia, faced his bull, experienced immediate second thoughts about his chosen profession, and fled.

The crowd booed as Hernández flashed his bright red cape, looked at the huge charging *toro*, and ran as fast he could for the fence around the bull ring. A surge of self-survival adrenaline fueled the twenty-two-year-old ex-bullfighter over the fence and into an early retirement. The victorious bull just stood in the ring, perhaps confused by the matador's disappearance. Once his nemesis was corralled, Hernández reentered the ring for a moment to wave at the hooting crowd. He spoke to waiting reporters with refreshing candor. "There are some things you must be aware of about yourself," he said. "I didn't have the ability, I didn't have the *cojones*. This is not my thing."[54] Understandable, especially since Hernández was gored in the leg by another bull about a month before his final bout.

A short time later, Hernández found himself arrested, booked for violating his contract because he ran from the bull. He paid a fine at the police station and was released. Seizing the public relations opportunity, People for the Ethical Treatment of Animals (PETA) offered to reimburse the former bullfighter for the cost of his fine. The animal rights organization sent him their "Real Men Are Kind to Animals" certificate, which they suggested he "wave in his detractors' faces."

In their news release, PETA wrote, "Townspeople may paint Hernández as a coward or imply that he is somehow less of a man for refusing to torment and kill bulls who are physically harmed, driven into an arena with a roaring crowd, run around in dizzying circles, jabbed with knives, and finally stabbed to death at the point of complete exhaustion—but, as we know, bullies are the cowards. So let's hope Hernández sees that he can have fans when he doesn't hurt animals for a living—and to all the 'real men' out there who save animals rather than stab them," PETA suggested giving their hero Hernández a big "Olé!"[55]

In Portugal I saw a sordid bullfight several years ago. It was a warm sunny day; I was ensconced in a sweet little bed-and-breakfast somewhere between Oporto and Coimbra. Midday I needed a break from work and I took the car for a cruise around the countryside. In a nearby village I happened on a field where preparations were being made for some sort of event. I stopped to watch. The scene reminded me of the rural Little League team I used to coach when I lived in Nevada. Whatever was about to happen was designed for the local populace; this was no show put on for out-of-towners. The audience was sparse, scattered around a rustic pole fence that enclosed a field about the size we needed for our baseball games.

As soon as I saw the stars of the show, it was obvious that I was watching preparations for a bullfight. A trailer was backed up to an opening in the fence, and when its tailgate was raised, I saw three tethered forlorn bulls that looked as adolescent as their adversary. Sitting high on horseback, his back straight and wavy black hair greased into place, the matador seemed to feign confidence. He waved to the sparse group of onlookers, with a look on his face that I took to be a severe attempt to hide his qualms about the pending encounter. Or perhaps that look was just youthful arrogance from a player who knew that the odds were stacked against the bull. His white ruffled shirt contrasted with a black suit coat and vest, and black and white striped pants. When the coat draped open, the lining flashed fire engine red in the bright sunlight.

Opening ceremonies consisted of a couple of drummers and a bagpiper serenading the scene in casual slacks and sports shirts. They were standing in the field adjacent to a woman peddling ice cream sheltered from the sun under an umbrella. The bull was released and proceeded to chase after its adversary until the matador turned his steed and began the process that would lead to the bull's demise.

If Hemingway was correct and there is potential art in a bull-fight—decadent or otherwise—it certainly was not on display that afternoon in Portugal. The matador ran his horse first from and then after the bull, engaged in what looked much more like chaos than choreography, although he managed to land a few of his *bandeiras*, stabbing the bull with the colorful small spears. The *forcados*—on foot and outfitted in blue jeans, white shirts, and wide red sashes to match the matador's coat lining—then teased and antagonized the bull, a process that, of course, enraged him and again he was chasing the horse and rider. An ambulance was parked near the ice cream vendor in case the bull prevailed. But he didn't.

Killing the bull during the final act was illegal in Portugal when I stumbled on the fight. The bull I watched died from wounds he suffered during the "battle," not as the climax of the show. Bullfighting has been controversial in Portugal for a couple of hundred years. In 1828 Queen Maria II outlawed it: It is not a "sport" for a civilized people, she told her subjects. But in 1921 the practice was again legalized with the stipulation against killing the bull added in 1928. That ruling was reversed in 2004 by Jose Manuel Barroso, when he was the country's prime minister,[56] a decision cheered by the likes of Jose Fernando, president of the National Association of Forcados in Portugal. "Fans don't come to see the bulls suffer," he claims, "but to watch the courage they show."[57]

The stabbing continued, now from the matador's lance—also festive-looking, covered in a rainbow of ribbons. The bull slowed, stumbled, eventually came to a rest in the dust, and collapsed. Dead. Not from a coup de grace, but from the bloody results of his various wounds and sheer exhaustion. The matador tried to look victorious; the crowd acted mightily unimpressed. The bull was dragged across the dirt and loaded onto a waiting flatbed trailer.

Chapter Fourteen
Dead Chickens without a Fight

NESTLED BETWEEN THE URBAN SPRAWL OF THE SONOMA COUNTY seat Santa Rosa and the almost-too-cute wine tourist destination Healdsburg is sleepy rural Fulton, along the Russian River and unknown to most commuters and wine country visitors hurtling past on the nearby 101 freeway. Victorian houses share the main street with Mexican day laborers hoping for work. BRODERICK FOR JUDGE suggests a billboard tacked to the side of a weathered barn. Lush rows of grape leaves line vineyards that butt up against the town's few streets. A fruit stand on River Road offers local bargains: "red ripe" tomatoes for 89 cents a pound, "large" California artichokes for 49 cents each. With a few extra minutes to spare, I stop. Artichokes they are, large they are not. But the tomatoes are red and ripe, and I choose some tomatoes along with a variety of fruits and vegetables too tempting not to buy. I josh with the clerk about the weather as he packs the produce in a box. Rustic Fulton looks lost in the early last century.

This rainy spring morning I'm in Fulton to watch chickens being processed from live birds into foodstuffs. Interesting, I think, that we call cows beef when we eat them. And juvenile cows veal. Pigs become pork. But there is no euphemism for poultry. When we eat chicken, we call it chicken. I've been listening to cockfighters compare the lives of their birds to the chickens raised for food. Cockers crow about what a grand life their roosters live before their fighting days start, and about how well the winners continue to live. Chickens raised for food, most fighters are quick to point out, live a short regimented life before their throats are slit.

Fulton Valley Farms operates a slaughterhouse just across River Road from the fruit stand. I visit about a month before the

93

place is scheduled to close—operations are moving to the Central Valley, where most of the company's chickens hatch and grow. I chose Fulton Valley Farms because if any commercial chicken is going to be a happy chicken, it seems like it will be one of theirs: The company shies away from antibiotics, likes to feed its chickens a vegetarian diet, and doesn't jam them into overcrowded coops.

John Cochran is the jolly general manager. He looks up from a desk piled with paperwork when I arrive as scheduled. There's a sign on his office door that reads, SI NECESITA COMPRAR ALGO O TIENE ALGUNA PREGUNTA, POR FAVOR VAYA A LA VENTANILLA—If you need to buy something or have some question, please go to the little window. The "little window" is a box office–like window adjacent to the door. The sign is not translated into English; Spanish is the work language of America's slaughterhouses. A banner on the office wall states PURE POULTRY and shows the image of a chicken with a halo over its head. NO HORMONES, NO ANTIBIOTICS OR ANIMAL BYPRODUCTS, it proudly announces. With his bushy white moustache and wire-rimmed eyeglasses, Cochran looks the part of an all-American butcher. He welcomes me with some examples of just how varied his customer base is. He sells fresh-killed birds to a local cheetah aficionado as a treat for his cats; chicken heads to a falconer whose birds fancy them as a delicacy; and chicken livers to a local entrepreneur who bakes gourmet dog biscuits with them. We talk and the phone keeps interrupting us as Cochran organizes orders for his customers. Getting fresh chickens to the market fast is a critical aspect of his stock in trade. "Fresh chicken is a completely different experience," a local butcher said, lamenting the news that Fulton Valley Farms was moving. His shop would no longer get roasters and fryers, breasts and thighs just a few hours after they were processed. The move would add about twelve hours travel time to the finished food product.[58]

Slaughtering chickens is not animal abuse, Cochran explains with patience. "When you have happy chickens, you have healthy chickens. When you have healthy chickens, you have great-tasting chickens."

I stop his speech. "Of course it's possible for you to ascertain that your chickens are healthy, but how would any of us be able to know if a chicken is happy?"

"The chicken is comfortable. It's not sick. It's not requiring medication because it's a healthy, happy chicken." He makes the points as if they should be obvious. "They're not crowded in cages. They're calm when they're brought here. They're not stressed. They're happy."

I tell Cochran I trust him on the healthy and look forward to seeing the calm. But I say that I just cannot understand how he can attribute "happy" to a chicken.

"They're some of the funniest creatures in the world," he laughs about his chickens. He recounts chasing around ranches after chickens that try to hide from him ostrich-like, by sticking their heads under bushes. "I love it. It's one of my favorite things to watch. They're hysterical."

"But is there enough going on in those little heads and hearts for them to experience happiness?"

"That's my interpretation," he insists, but admits, "I don't know."

Scott Rumbeck, another plant supervisor, gives me rubber boots, a hairnet (to meet U.S. Agriculture Department hygiene standards), and a long white smock to borrow that's labeled JAVIER in cursive stitching. We head out to what is a *disassemble* line.

"We'll start in the live hang area," Rumbeck says. But first we stop by a sink and wash our hands. "It's all about food safety," he explains, "to protect the consumer." We look at a truck loaded with cages filled with chickens. They appear, as John Cochran promised, remarkably calm. They sit in the cages clustered together, but there's plenty of extra room if they wished to get up, walk around, stretch their wings. A worker hangs each chicken by the feet onto hooks that slip around their ankles, and as the line hauls the birds toward an electric stunner, they hang silent and passive. There's no cackling or squawking, no flailing about or other indications of either distress or attempted escape.

"The moment you hold 'em upside down, they're cool with it, and things are okay," Rumbeck says. "The loading process onto the (dis)assembly line is cool and calm. There're no broken wings. There're no dislocations. Everything's intact."

Rumbeck grabs a bird from the line and points out that it's undamaged and not struggling.

"They look pretty calm, don't they?" he asks me.

"They look calm, yeah," I must agree, watching chicken after chicken swing past me, all hanging upside down by their feet, all looking remarkably unperturbed. Calm is the correct word.

"They have no idea what's going to happen to them," he notes, and we both laugh the laugh of a couple of guys who are not—as far as we know—going to be killed in less than a minute: relieved, ironic, and perhaps—at least in my case—feeling somewhat guilty.

The birds are about to be stunned; a quick electric shock knocks them unconscious, the effect of the jolt designed to last for about twenty or thirty seconds. But the birds never regain consciousness. After the shock the chickens' heads, erect before the jolt, flop and go limp. The line keeps moving, sending the chickens toward what is known in the trade by a straightforward description: the neck slicer.

"While they're still unconscious, they'll get their jugular slit, and then they'll bleed out."

The chicken heads are guided into a slot and a spinning blade does the trick. Usually. Sometimes the guidance system fails to align a head properly and a chicken gets a momentary reprieve. But it is just for a moment. Standing just downstream from the mechanical neck slicer, in a yellow rain slicker splattered with chicken blood, is the backup man. Armed with a knife, he slits the throats of those chickens that miss the automated hatchet man. Under both man and machine is a collecting vat, flowing red with blood. Rumbeck looks at it with approval and advises me to ask general manager John Cochran later what the plant does with all that chicken blood.

I already know what happens to some of it. After their throats are slit and they're dead, the electric shock wears off and the bodies twitch and jump, the production line equivalent of the proverbial chicken running around with its head cut off. The result is some more blood splatter; a red splash lands on my notebook. And the heart is still pumping the blood, now pumping it right out the neck. In fact, the electric shock increases the heart rate and hence speeds the bleeding process, most of which occurs in an adjacent collection room.

About seventy chickens a minute lose their necks as we watch.

We look in the pungent blood room where, in a couple of minutes, the chickens bleed out—to use the industry's term of art. At that point they are immersed in scalding hot water to loosen their feathers. From the bath they move on to the feather removal machinery. Once the body is blown free of its feathers, it finally and literally becomes a chicken with its head (and feet) cut off. Those body parts not processed for human food are discarded—heads, feet, some of the guts, and feathers. "We keep the gizzards, the liver, and the heart," Rumbeck tells me as we step over a pile of intestines and other guts destined for a rendering plant, being careful not to lose our footing on the slippery remains. "That'll all get washed down," he assures me. The byproducts that go to the rendering plants are used for a variety of purposes—including plastics and makeup. Given the carnage, the plant is remarkably clean, and even the wastewater is reused. It's pumped across River Road to a pasture where it irrigates acreage planted for sheep pasture.

The birds are almost ready for the butcher counter. First each one is checked by a USDA inspector, then—if it's "whole body worthy," a trade term for Grade A—it's chilled and packaged for distribution.

Scott Rumbeck is an enthusiastic tour guide. He's proud of the Fulton Valley Farms process and he likes his chickens. He speaks fluently in Spanish to his workers. "I think that's why I got the job!" he jokes. He smiles easily; his blue eyes smile with his mouth. A three-day growth of beard contrasts with his hairnet. He accepts the fact that the chickens we just watched being processed may have been a little confused the last few hours of their lives, lives that last about seven and a half months on average.

"If there's a quicker way," he says about his slaughterhouse's routine, "let us know."

"We could stop eating meat?" I offer.

"I respect what people might want to do," is his response, "but this is the United States, and you're not going to tell me what to do and I'm not going to tell you what to do. California agriculture feeds a third of the world and this," he gestures to his chickens, "is what we have to do to keep up with the demand."

"Do you eat chicken?" I ask.

"All the time," he answers without hesitation. He attributes his meat eating to his upbringing and the norms of his culture. Rumbeck learned Spanish while living in Mexico, and he watched a cockfight while south of the border. It wasn't much to his liking. He references the Shirley Jackson short story "The Lottery" as an example. "It's all about tradition, the way you're raised, your political surroundings." Talk about strange! Here we stand, in blood-soiled smocks, surrounded by chickens in various states of disarray, suddenly talking literature. "People get stoned at the end of 'The Lottery,'" he recollects. "It's all about tradition. How does one culture say to another culture, 'That's not right'?" We have no business, he believes, telling Mexico that cockfights are not humane. But it seems a strange story to cite as evidence of cultural empathy and understanding. The tradition in "The Lottery" is an annual stoning of a citizen chosen by chance. In the story Bill Hutchinson's wife "wins" the lottery. As the story comes to an end, "she held her hands out desperately as the villagers moved in on her. 'It isn't fair, it isn't fair,' Mrs. Hutchinson screamed, and then they were upon her."[59] Jackson's story is all about the dangers of not questioning tradition, especially when we know the tradition is morally wrong.

The cockfight Rumbeck attended was at a fair in León, Guanajuato. "I don't like cockfights. I don't like fighting. It's not necessary. You're gambling an animal's life for money." That fowl death he sees in a completely different light from those in his slaughterhouse. "It saddens me. That animal does have feelings. It can feel. It's got to be scared," Rumbeck says about the gamecocks forced into the cockpit. "It doesn't know what's going on."

Back in the office I ask manager Cochran about the blood. All that blood, he tells me, is hauled across the San Francisco Bay to the East Bay Municipal Utility District. There it is fed into enzyme digesters, a combination that produces methane; the methane is used to produce electricity, electricity that is sold to the California electric grid. "This is seriously cool stuff," he says with great pride and with happiness about using the entire chicken. "East Bay MUD is thrilled, they just love it."

I take off Javier's blood-splattered white smock, doff my hairnet, and pull off the boots I'd borrowed, big thigh-high rubber boots now wet with the water used to keep the slaughterhouse clean and sprinkled with a few chicken parts I picked up along my tour. I say my good-byes to John Cochran and Scott Rumbeck, look up at the huge chicken illustration on a sign outside the slaughterhouse, and head home. I'd prepared myself to be psychologically walloped by the tour—maybe even nauseated by the sights, sounds, and smells. Perhaps disgusted by the wanton death I witnessed (I did a quick calculation: I'd been in the slaughterhouse for an hour and ten minutes—at seventy chickens a minute, 4,900 chickens lost their heads during my tour).

At least I figured I would feel some holier-than-thou superiority since I eat no poultry.

But no. The experience left me oddly at peace—possibly because the chickens I watched traverse the disassemble line also looked oddly at peace. Or maybe it was because I didn't get to know them out at their ranch; by the time I saw them they were anonymous, motionless, and upside down. But they were raised for food and food they were. I still don't want to eat them, but if I ever choose to resume eating meat, I'd like mine to come from a place like Fulton Valley Farms.

South down the highway a few miles is Angel Motors, where my Volvo is maintained. I stop to pick up my car and talk with proprietor Angel Ochoa about animal happiness and animal suffering, and he's not convinced a chicken knows the difference. But he is sure about our responsibilities. "The chicken doesn't know he's suffering, but we do," Ochoa tells me. Whenever my car needs servicing, a dose of the mechanic's philosophy is included—at no extra charge. "It's our obligation not to allow it."

CHAPTER FIFTEEN

The Nemesis of Cajun Cockfighters

THAT SENSE OF OBLIGATION IS SHARED BY FORMER LOUISIANA STATE senator Art Lentini. Lentini drafted the bill that became Louisiana's first law against cockfighting—it outlawed gambling at the fights. Now a lawyer in private practice, I find Lentini in his office in Metaire, a suburb on the west side of New Orleans, on the road to Cajun country.

"With all the problems facing Louisiana, why bother with cockfights?" I ask him.

"I do like animals," he says, almost as if it's an afterthought, "although I was a hunter at one time." His initial concern was the gambling at fights, not the roosters' welfare. But there was another factor: Lentini was told by his predecessors and colleagues in Baton Rouge that Louisiana legislators would never vote to ban cockfights. He took on the task as a challenge as much as a cause. But as soon as he rolled up his sleeves and started work on the anti-cockfighting bill, stereotypes began collapsing for him.

"I was taken aback." Lentini's language is formal; his voice is soft and slow—fitting for a warm Louisiana morning. The French cuffs on his stark white starched shirt are embossed: A. J. L. The proponents of cockfighting "were not the type of people I thought they were going to be. They were nice people."

"What did you expect to find?"

"To be honest with you, I thought they were going to be the type of people who were engaged in dogfighting, that they would be rough and in my face, aggressive, that they would think I was a wimp or a pansy because I was worried about animals. They're not, and it really threw me at first." Crowds of cockers and their supporters packed the debates on the bill. "They all seemed to be very nice people and they really, sincerely believed that they were not doing anything wrong." The supporters kept insisting what I'd been hearing: that it was a sport, and part of Cajun culture. "One time a guy told me, 'If you ban this, what are our kids going to do? How are we going to keep them from committing crimes? It's like football.' And they really meant it, most of them." We're talking a few years later and he still remembers his surprise. "I really didn't have anyone to dislike. I thought, because it involved animal cruelty, that I'd be offended by these people. But they were very nice people."

In fact, the state law on animal cruelty needed to be changed before cockfighting could be outlawed in Louisiana. That law—which already forbade animal torture, torment, "cruel" beating (is some beating not cruel?), and abandonment and mandated that animals be provided proper food, drink, and shelter if they are confined—included an exception written especially for cockfighters. "For the purpose of this Section," reads the now-obsolete Newspeak statute, "fowl shall not be defined as animals."

Nice people they may have been, but Senator Lentini was not moved by their arguments to be left alone along the bayous with their fighting cocks. He watched a film depicting a cockfight and became convinced that the roosters were suffering. He looked at the gaffs and the knives. He listened to testimony from Humane Society lobbyists about what occurs at cockfights. He heard about cockers sucking the blood out of the necks of badly injured birds in order to allow oxygen to keep flowing into their air sacs. He knew children witnessed the spectacle and figured it desensitized them to unnecessary violence. He concluded that cockfighting *is* cruel regardless of the waiver written into Louisiana law at the time.

"The activity was abhorrent to me," he realized, "but the people weren't. That was what was difficult to grasp."

But Senator Lentini didn't blink. His bill banning gambling at cockfights became law, followed by another law forbidding the fights, making Louisiana the final state to outlaw the animal cruelty or traditional sport—take your pick on the terminology. He led the opposition, but he's never been to a cockfight and, good politician that he is, he's equipped with a glib answer to charges that he can't know what he's opposing if he doesn't experience it. When he was asked how he could vote on something he'd never seen, he answered his challengers in his easygoing manner with a question of his own, "Have you ever been to an abortion?" But Lentini thinks he understands why some people dismiss the feelings of chickens. He attributes it to where their eyes are situated on their heads. Fish, lizards, birds, and other animals that have their eyes on the side of their heads, he tells me even while suggesting that his theory may sound crazy, don't elicit the same kind of sympathy as those that can look at you with both eyes at the same time.

He dismisses the insistence of cockers such as Paul Huln who claim emotional bonds with their chickens. "I can't believe that they care for them in the sense that we care for a domestic pet." If they did, he says, they couldn't strap gaffs and knives to their legs and watch them tear each other apart. "They care for them in the sense that they want them to be strong and well nourished so that they can fight and win the fight."

Bottom line, says Lentini, is that "cockfighting involves extreme cruelty to animals for no other reason than human entertainment. We're not eating them. There's no purpose other than to watch two animals and see which one will destroy the other." And he rejects any comparison with some other animal activities considered cruel by some animal rights advocates—such as dog racing and horse racing. In a race, the goal is to cross the finish line first. In a cockfight, the goal is to kill the opponent. But he's not arrogant and didactic.

"I heard all the arguments," he assures me, "and I've got to tell you, I don't have all the answers. People would say, 'What about hunting?' Well, people hunt, but they eat what they hunt."

"Not always," I point out. "Some people hunt for trophies."
"They do," he nods, and adds, "what about furs?"

Point taken, and I add, "That's a form of entertainment, to wear a fur coat."

"And I don't have the answer to that," he says. "It's murky. It's not something that's well defined to me. But a cockfight is extremely brutal and it is dehumanizing to sit there with a bunch of people yelling and screaming, betting on which one is going to kill the other, and reviving the bird so that it can go back. It's a lot of suffering."

Suffering is a point of contention. Cockfighters don't necessarily believe the birds suffer, at least in the sense that a human suffers. Anglers don't necessarily think a hooked fish suffers. Or don't care.

Senator Lentini rejects any comparison to chickens raised for food—even if a fighting cock enjoys a couple of years of a coddled lifestyle before he is thrown in the ring (compared with just several months getting fattened up for a slaughterhouse). "We're not sitting there at the chicken plants gleefully watching the chickens being killed for food." That's an appropriate word to sum up the differences, I think: gleeful. No question that none of the workers at the Fulton Valley Farms operation looked gleeful to me as seventy chickens a minute lost their heads, and I saw no money changing hands on bets about which chicken might miss the automated neck slicer and be spared a few seconds until the knife-wielding backup man found the jugular by hand.

"I'm proud of this," says Art Lentini about his role ushering Louisiana into the post-cockfight era. On a table in his office is a pair of pewter fighting cocks, a gift from a friend.

———

It's been a few weeks since I watched the bloodbath portrayed in *The Cove* and announced to my wife that I could no longer include fish in my diet, that I felt forced to eat no animal products: no red meat, no poultry, no eggs, and no dairy products. Sheila's irritation was not just with the complications this caused her in the kitchen; she worried about my health.

"Where are you going to get your calcium?" she complained. She looked out toward the Bodega Bay and across Doran Beach to the Pacific, filled with salmon and rockfish, halibut and sole. "I cannot believe that you won't eat fish anymore."

Together we've enjoyed the bounty of our waters, available fresh and filleted at the docks just blocks from our home. But now it seems wrong to me to buy packaged animals that were killed for me to eat since I can exist well without them. I don't want to be a bore and a problem mate, so I offer her a deal.

"If you," I say to Sheila, "go out and catch the fish and if you personally kill it, if you gut it and dress it for the kitchen, I'll cook it and I'll eat it." I make a fine halibut smothered in mayonnaise (actually in a product called Vegannaise) and baked with dill and lemon. I get rave reviews for my simple salmon steaks coated with olive oil and baked with that same dill and lemon accent. I've replicated a soup from Sheila's favorite Berkeley restaurant. It's a dashi stock, shiitake mushrooms, chopped spinach, and soba noodles surrounding hunks of smoked trout. It seemed a fair compromise to make, a slight gender change from the nursery rhyme, "Fishy, fish in the brook/Daddy catch it with a hook/ Mommy fry it in a pan/Baby eat it fast as he can."

"Okay," Sheila accepted the challenge. "Okay." Party boats leave daily from the Bodega Bay dock near my office. Arranging a trip to haul dinner out of the Pacific fishery would be no problem. In fact, Sheila would not even need to leave the shore. A few miles inland from us the Hagemann Trout Farm is in business. We've passed it for over a dozen years on Highway 1 and never stopped to try our luck angling on the ranch pond, said to be stocked with fat and juicy rainbow trout. "You catch 'em, we'll clean 'em," the farm advertises. Sheila will need to pass on the cleaning to keep her half of our bargain.

In terms of animal use versus animal abuse, I think I can rationalize fish back in my diet if my wife catches, kills, and eviscerates them—especially if the Hagemann Ranch is raising them expressly for the purpose of dinner tables.

"In fact," I told her, "I'll eat any animal you catch, kill, and clean." After all, how can I make a differentiation between a fish and any other animal, although I must admit, I felt safe with this offer. She just isn't the deer hunting type.

CHAPTER SIXTEEN

From Central Park Horse Carriages to Ants on the Kitchen Counter

JUST A FEW BLOCKS WEST FROM THE NOW-DISNEYLAND-LIKE TIMES Square, at 538 38th Street, Manhattan's hectic pace slows at an old four-story redbrick building that seems detached from the twenty-first century car repair shop on one side and the modern hotel on the other. The smell on a hot summer morning might offer a hint about the operation: Inside are stables for the horses that pull lovers and tourists in frilly carriages through Central Park. How romantic! How New York! What fun!

"Animal abuse!" cry the naysayers, insisting that such dray-age on the hot city streets is not a fair life for the old gray mares and other horses. Animal rights activists want the surreys in New York, and elsewhere, shut down. "Help put horse-drawn carriages out to pasture," pleads *Glee* television star Lea Michele in a PETA-sponsored advertising campaign. "Don't get taken for a ride," advises Kristen Johnston in another PETA ad, the Emmy-winning actress Lady Godiva–like atop a prop that looks like a horse. The Coalition to Ban Horse-Drawn Carriages circulates gruesome photographs of carriage accidents, featuring horses lying prone in the streets. The group insists that even a routine day on city streets—a day with no wrecks, exhaustion, or hoof injuries—constitutes unnecessary cruelty for the horses: heat and cold, traffic and noise, no opportunity to graze and frolic. Advocates calling for an end to the New York tradition point to the stables on 38th Street as abusive because of the steep ramps horses are forced to negotiate after a long day of work just to get to the upper floor stalls, where they're housed overnight in what the protesters call stalls much too small for adequate comfort.

Traditions can change. Paris, London, Toronto, and Beijing are examples of cities that have outlawed the carriages. Despite what most of us might think, the horse-drawn buggies of Central Park do not pre-date the automobile age. The nostalgic sound of horse hooves on Central Park South, across from the Plaza Hotel where the carriages line up for fares, dates only from the mid-1930s.[60] While PETA is using media and celebrities to put an end to these urban buggy rides, there are other public figures and celebs trying to preserve this New York fixture.

On a late spring morning I stop by the 38th Street stables and talk with one of the carriage drivers, John Gokeeniz, a Turkish student who is paying for his schooling with Central Park buggy tours.

"It must be quite a chore for you and the horse to navigate the streets of New York," I suggest to him. "Even walking can be a chore here."

"Sometimes it's busy," is his understated response. "You never know when the horse might get scared."

"What types of things scare them?" I ask, and his answer comes without hesitation.

"Garbage trucks. They come very fast and make too much noise." Not all the horses spook when they're on the streets with a garbage truck, however. "The oldest horses don't scare much, they're experienced. But younger horses get scared."

"Does it bother them to be on the street all day?"

"They're not on the street all day, only when we are going to the park." He makes the distinction between the business districts and Central Park. "Otherwise we are in the park. It's very quiet."

Gokeeniz has been driving the carriages for two years when we talk, and he likes the work, considers it fun. "I love horses." His time outside with his customers and his horse offers a nice counterpoint to his studies in statistics at Brooklyn College. He looks like he's happy checking out his horse and wagon before heading off to troll for customers. "It's a good job."

The horseman shows off his carriage to me. It looks like the original surrey with the fringe on top. The cushions are plush and bright red velvet, a nice counterpoint to the body's rich off-white color scheme. The convertible top is poised to close if it rains. The carriage is festooned with bright bouquets of flowers that look real enough, along with an American flag.

A quick ride around in the park starts at $34, a twenty-minute excursion is $50, and each ten minutes more is another twenty bucks. Gokeeniz says he makes a good living, and he advertises his contentment with a souvenir from Amish country, a MY HOBBY IS DRIVING ME BUGGY placard affixed to the back of the carriage alongside the license plate.

———

Horses race for our entertainment and they pull buggies. Dogs race, too. I met my first greyhound that wasn't a bus at the Greyhound Hall of Fame in Abilene, Kansas (boyhood home of Dwight D. Eisenhower). Her name was Dutchess, and she occupied a privileged spot on a cushion near the entrance to the museum. She seemed happy in her retirement, a luxury not shared by other ex-racers.

Russ Cohen is a sportswriter and a member of the American Humane Association's Red Star Rescue team, a group that rescues pets that are victims of disasters. At home he takes care of a couple of rescued greyhounds. One of them is Rey, who "ran maybe like twelve, thirteen races. She wasn't very good, she fell around the turn a few times." The owners quit racing her when she was a year and a half old, ten years before Cohen and I talk when we meet at a New York trade show and discover our mutual interest in animal use and abuse. "She's still doing great," he tells me about Rey. "She runs around the yard." And he takes her for lure coursing exercises. "The lure, instead of a rabbit or a squirrel, is a white plastic bag. Any greyhound that sees a white plastic bag on the horizon, they'll go right for it." They think it might be a white rabbit.

"Why is running the dog on a lure course different than racing the dog?" I ask Cohen, who acknowledges he is entertained watching Rey run.

"It's for their exercise," he says. "They really love it."

Jordan is his other greyhound. She's just over three years old when we talk. "She came from Oklahoma. She never raced. They rejected her. She came with a broken tail and is afraid of doors. She probably got a door slammed on her." He was told there was more abuse. "They basically left her in a cage for six months and she never had any socialization."

The Cohen family adopted her and he considers her a great dog. He cannot understand why she failed as a racer because she runs well on the lure courses. "She loves to run." Even so, Russ Cohen opposes the greyhound racing industry. "I hate greyhound racing because the owners don't care. They're in it for the money." Although he checks himself here. "Not all owners are bad. I've met a few guys that take care of their dogs. They might even keep them as pets. But most of them don't take care of their dogs. They don't feed them as well as you would think." He says at the track most are fed what he calls "4D meat"—poor quality.

He's convinced that the dogs are looked at as expendable commodities by the racing business and its patrons. "Most of these guys are addicted gamblers, even the owners. Once they're done with that dog in the sense that it's not winning for them, that's it. If someone is there to adopt it, great. And if they're not, then what happens? They're getting euthanized."

Russ Cohen stumbled on choosing greyhounds for pets. "We were looking for a dog to adopt and we had heard about the cause," he says about the efforts greyhound rescue groups make to find homes for dogs no longer valuable to the racing world. "The dogs are terrific. They're unbelievable pets. They're intelligent and they love you. They're not a kissy kind of dogs, but they love people."

Last night falafels were on the menu for dinner. No animals were harmed for our family meal, right? "Let's do the dishes in the morning," Sheila and I agreed as we headed for bed.

As is often the case when you leave food out, I'm greeted in the morning by an army of ants marching from a hole in the corner of the kitchen wall directly to the sink where remnants of last night's dinner still litter our plates.

It's both a beautiful and a disgusting sight: ants and ants and more ants. I grab the sponge and start mopping them up by the hundreds, rinsing the sponge and washing them down the drain. I rinse off the plates and stick them in the dishwasher and then grab the sponge for a second assault on the ants. I've no compunction about reclaiming my kitchen.

Message received. The ants are no longer sending soldiers toward the sink. I've won this battle, but know better than to think I've won the war.

So why don't I care about these creatures, miracles that they are? Is it that ants are too low on the food chain, and they don't come when you call them? Of what use are these endless ants? Is it abuse when I annihilated them by the scores—perhaps by the hundreds—with each swipe of the sponge? They were all coming out of the wall like circus clowns out of a midget car. They all looked exactly the same. So it's hard for me to consider that wiping them off the face of my Earth is abuse.

But are they faceless and nameless? Just days before, Sheila— who also has been dispatching ants by the hundreds into the garbage this year (it's been a particularly invasive season)—spared an ant that was in the path of her assaulting wet paper towel. She noticed that it was struggling with an extraordinary load: a hunk of crumb that was much too bulky for it to carry with ease and grace. What possessed that ant to assume the unwieldy chore? Why were other ants hauling loads that looked easy by comparison?

"I just couldn't kill it, it was doing such a good job," she told me later, explaining that although she did spare the hard worker, she sent ants scurrying in front of it and behind it to their maker with abandon. But not with pleasure. On the contrary. After each of her paper towel counterattacks to their continuing invasion, she expressed remorse.

CHAPTER SEVENTEEN

Who Is Abusing Whom?

CALIFORNIA BEARS WERE ONCE IN JEOPARDY. THE MIGHTY GRIZZLY (pictured on our state flag) was eliminated by farmers and ranchers back in the Wild West days when it was open season on just about anything that moved. But our black bears now are thriving. The population is estimated at forty thousand by the state Fish and Game Commission—four times the number that roamed the mountains a generation ago—a number that allows for a few thousand a year to be hunted without jeopardizing the species, according to the officials who sell the permits.[61] Odd concept: government permits to kill animals living in the wilderness, their homes.

Late one night when I was hosting a radio talk show at KCBS in San Francisco, I happened on the news that bear hunting season was about to open in the Sierra Nevada foothills. It had never occurred to me that we hunt bears in California, and since the station's signal reached into the Sierra, I solicited calls from listeners who hunted bear. I asked them to explain to me, and the rest of the urban dwellers in the audience unfamiliar with the hunt, what lured them out of their homes to stalk and kill their bear neighbors.

The answers were fascinating, although they certainly did not compel me to want to pick up a gun and go after bear. But most of the callers spoke from the heart, explaining the respect they felt for their prey. They talked about feeling psychically connected with the wily and dangerous animals they stalked. They expressed a strange-to-me emotion of completeness when the bear in their sights fell dead. What exactly this emotion was, I have never understood. But then, I'm no animal hunter. However, it was intriguing to hear their passion for the hunt and the kill.

Every summer, tourists pack national parks like Yosemite, and every summer, the photographs are shocking: automobile doors and roofs peeled back like sardine can lids, the result of bears foraging for easy pickings left inside the cars. It's a scenario well known to Stewart Breck, a research wildlife biologist for the U.S. Department of Agriculture national wildlife research center in Fort Collins, Colorado. His task is to study the conflicts that develop when human beings and other wildlife clash, and to conjure solutions that may mediate such conflicts. These conflicts include invasive species inundating landscapes, such as the Burmese pythons that saturate Florida's Everglades, and birds that collide with airplanes, like the geese sucked into the engines that famously brought a U.S. Airways jet taking off from La Guardia down into the Hudson River. Dr. Breck's specialty is the encounters between humans and large carnivores.

The urban-wildlife intersection continues to expand as some Americans leave our densely populated cities and opt for a homestead in neighborhoods populated by the kind of large carnivores Breck likes to observe. That's not necessarily bad news for the animals. The types of people who tend to make their homes or their second homes at places like Lake Tahoe or Aspen tend to choose such locales exactly because they want to commune with wildlife. There is greater acceptance of bears and wolves as neighbors among the current crop of urban refugees, Breck tells me, than was shown by the original settlers of the North America wild lands. Wolves and grizzly bears were almost wiped out in the Lower Forty-Eight by the early pioneers. "In the past few decades," he says, "there's growing tolerance for these animals. The result is that black bear populations are expanding their geographical reach." Breck specializes in developing non-lethal tools designed to encourage the bears to stay away from human enclaves.

Research by Dr. Breck and his colleagues ascertained that minivans—the soccer-mom's trademark car—are more likely to be torn open by Yosemite bears than any other car model. The scientific language of his study mixes with down-home reality as his report offers several hypotheses regarding why bears now seek minivans to target for fast food. "Minivans are designed for families with children and small children in particular are notorious for spilling food and drink while riding in vehicles." That's not all. "Passengers of minivans were more prone to leave large caches of food in vehicles parked overnight." In addition to these user-caused temptations, the researchers theorize that "it is possible that minivans were structurally easier to break into than other vehicles." But my favorite hypothesis is their last one. "Selection of minivans could reflect the foraging of a few individuals that developed a learned behavior for breaking into minivans."[62] That theory makes me think of Yogi Bear telling his pal Boo-Boo, "Hey there, Boo-Boo. Check out this minivan and all these peanut butter sandwiches in the back seat."

Bears' foraging for human food is not only a problem facing park visitors and campers. "One of the real growing issues is bears in towns," Breck says, and not just in the Wild West. Bears are rampaging in rural New York and New Jersey, West Virginia, and other unexpected places. "It's ubiquitous, wherever we have bears coexisting with people," cars are attacked as if they are refrigerators. And it's not just minivans. "Bears are breaking into houses. People leave their doors unlocked and bears are very adept at getting inside. In some cases bears attack and kill people, which is," he says from the human perspective, "the worst-case scenario." Of course, the reverse occurs too: bears killed by people who believe they are acting in self-defense. "Wildlife managers are struggling with what to do." As the number of encounters grows, one sobering result usually is that "more bears die." Breck's studies in Aspen determined that bears in search of food surprise homeowners and give themselves a death sentence.

"I don't think in any case there was a bear trying to hurt some-body. But somebody comes in the house, there's a bear in the house, the bear gets scared and ends up in a couple of cases swat-ting somebody." The sad result is the bear becomes victimized. "There's just zero tolerance for that kind of behavior, so those bears end up getting euthanized."

The concern of Aspenites and others is understandable. These aren't teddy bears; these black bears can grow to three or four hundred pounds of hungry muscle. Land-use decisions become a form of animal abuse. "That's the take-home message for a lot of this conflict," says Dr. Breck. "There are simple things people can do to minimize their conflicts with wildlife so we don't have to get into this cycle of killing." His voice sounds sad as he relates the tales of foraging bears killed as they seek food left in tempting places. "Bears play an important role in the ecosystem. They're a species we love having around. They're a part of American history and culture."

Indeed. That's why in California the bear is memorialized on our state flag with its proud profile.

Once bears taste human food and learn how easy it can be to obtain, they can become dependent on it, exacerbating the conflicts with the humans whose food they're stealing. "In Tahoe there are cases where bears just become garbage bears. No one wants to see that." Under normal conditions bears come out of hibernation eating grasses and forbs. As the season progresses they enjoy berries and acorns. Ants, other insects, and small rodents are part of a bear's natural diet. They are omnivorous, and if there is a failure—natural or otherwise—in their usual food supply, they'll go looking for alternatives. That's what often insti-gates the house break-ins, and the result is a bear that learns to love to eat what we love to eat. They're very intelligent, Dr. Breck knows, "so they'll adapt very quickly."

I ask the researcher if he's encountered bears in the course of his fieldwork, and his answer catches me by surprise.

"I climb into bear dens every winter."

"You climb into bear dens every winter?" I try to imagine the scientist tiptoeing into a cave, hoping he doesn't wake the slumbering hundreds of pounds of bear whose home he's invading.

"That's our preferred method for changing their collars," he explains about the need to update the radio tracking devices he and his colleagues attach to bears so that they can track their movements.

I'm still awestruck. "You're going into the dens where the bears are hibernating?"

"Yes," he sloughs off my surprise. "Black bears are quite docile. We go in. We'll tranquilize them. Come back and wait until they're asleep and then we'll go back in and change out a collar, take our measurements, and then let 'em be." But he's also chased bears out of Yosemite campgrounds and enjoyed a chance encounter with a Montana bear, an animal he watched in close proximity while it was unaware of being watched. "That was certainly one of the highlights of my experiences with bears." It wasn't doing much that would entertain a circus audience anxious to see a trained bear ride a tricycle or dance. "It was scratching and rubbing against a tree, just doing what a bear does, which is not a whole lot during the summertime."

CHAPTER EIGHTEEN

Saving Chickens

KIM STURLA IS THE FOUNDER OF ANIMAL PLACE, A SANCTUARY IN California for farm animals rescued from slaughter. For a generation she and her colleagues have been saving so-called domesticated animals—chickens and pigs, cows and sheep—and then placing the animals for adoption with caretakers who have no desire to eat them or keeping them on the organization's ranchlands to live out their lives free from a supper table destiny. I ask her about the argument she's heard often, that these animals are on Earth exactly for the purpose of providing sustenance for us.

"Some people believe that," she readily acknowledges. "We support a reverence for all life. Our mission is compassion for all animals, whether that's your companion dog or cat, wildlife, or animals raised for food." Sturla is an absolutist. "We rescue animals that have come from horrendous conditions—factory farms, auction yards, slaughterhouses—and we do an awful lot of education." She's a vegan; so are the rest of the workers at Animal Place. But she understands that not all people will want to give up eating meat. She wants those who do choose to eat meat to gain intimate knowledge of how those animals destined to be human food live and die. "In our ideal world, everyone would agree that no animal would die just for human consumption."

"Why should no animal die for human consumption?" I ask her. What's the philosophical basis for such a world?

She takes a historical perspective and points out how most farm animals were raised prior to World War II. "You really did have primarily small backyard farms that would have a few chickens and perhaps cattle grazing until they were slaughtered. It's all mechanized now. They're all on huge factory farms." She offers an example of what she considers wrong and what she's doing about it. Some two thousand chickens were spared by Animal Place a couple of years before Kim Sturla and I spoke; they were removed from a factory farm in Gilroy, a reprieve that saved them from the soup pot. The Gilroy outfit, she tells me, is an egg-laying factory, a facility horrible to witness. "I think if anybody went inside one of those they would never want to have an omelet again." She cites the small size of coops jammed full of hens.

Most of us have heard the horror stories of factory farms; some of us have toured the facilities or at least seen photographs documenting what appears to be inhumane, or at least insensitive, treatment of animals about to be food. What intrigues me about Sturla's story, what's intriguing about Animal Place, is the mission of rescuing mundane animals in relatively huge quantities. After factory chickens lay eggs for about eighteen months, their egg output decreases, making them no longer cost effective for their owners. Off they're usually sent to slaughter. In the case of the Gilroy operation, Sturla convinced the farmer to turn the spent hens over to Animal Place. It's hard enough for a country animal shelter to unload unwanted kittens to good homes. What the heck do you do with a couple of thousand spent laying hens? She managed to place about eighteen hundred of them in loving homes.

"We placed them with folks that have little backyard flocks and want some fresh eggs for themselves. These chickens were saved from a horrendous death and are now living out their lives in peace with freedom." Before Kim Sturla took the chickens from the factory, they'd never been off their cage floor. "They never roosted. They never had sun on their backs. They spent their entire lives in cages where they could not even stretch their wings out. It's a rehabilitation process," she tells me, "to get them to just be a bird."

"Two thousand saved chickens sounds like a lot of hens," I tell her. "But two thousand of them must just be a peck of corn in the mass of spent hens populating factory farms."

"It's just a drop in the bucket," she agrees. That's why she organizes what she calls "nose to snout" tours of Animal Place, hoping hands-on education about the lives of farm animals will help wean consumers from a meat diet. "Come see that they have personalities," she says about cows and pigs. "They're individuals. They can suffer just like your dog or cat can. They know their names. They come up to you, they're engaging." Sturla says her goal is to "sensitize people to all life forms, not just those that they're familiar with."

Kim Sturla's life has been dedicated to animals and animal protection. She was the director of the Peninsula Humane Society south of San Francisco for many years before founding Animal Place. I ask her if she remembers the last piece of meat that she ate.

She thinks for a moment and then answers slowly, as if she's considering the question. "I don't remember the last piece," she giggles, "but it was decades and decades ago." She's a vegan now.

"It's pretty darn easy, actually," she says about the restricted diet, since restaurants and grocery stores cater well to vegans these days, especially in California. "It was perhaps a little more challenging about thirty years ago," she remembers, but no longer. "The soy ice cream is to die for. The faux meats!"

"You go for the fake meat?" I ask. I tend to shy from vegan fare that attempts to replicate meat products. I do not miss the taste of ham hocks and lamb chops, chicken breasts and goose liver. "You like to eat textured soy protein that looks like a T-bone steak?"

"It doesn't look like that," she mocks me with a smile in her voice. "I'm fine with the faux meats. I don't have an objection to that. Some folks do," she acknowledges my prejudices. "As long as an individual did not suffer, that's my bottom line."

No soybeans were harmed in the production of faux chorizo. In fact, I confess to encountering some fake meat products that I've become enamored of eating. For example, Field Roast brand Italian sausages ("seasoned with fresh eggplant, zesty red wine, pungent fresh garlic, and plenty of fennel") make a terrific breakfast, sliced and fried with potatoes. And each sausage packs twenty-five grams of protein.

Before I say good-bye to Kim Sturla, I ask her if she's witnessed the slaughter of farm animals for food.

"I've not been to a slaughterhouse," she tells me. "I've been to auction yards and I've been to a number of factory farms." She's seen pictures of slaughterhouse realities, but she's not been inside.

"Because it hasn't come up as an opportunity or because you don't want to expose yourself to that kind of trauma?" I ask.

"I wouldn't want to," she says about a slaughterhouse visit, "but I would do it because I think it's helpful when any of us see anything firsthand. We can speak more from direct experience." Her voice is soft with reflection. "But I have not yet had the opportunity."

CHAPTER NINETEEN
Dominion over Every Creeping
Thing That Creepeth

THE PIERCE COLLEGE SPORTS TEAMS ARE THE BRAHMAS, NAMED AFTER
the rather exotic bulls that roam the pastoral campus, which is
surrounded by the San Fernando Valley sprawl. At this working
agricultural college in the middle of greater Los Angeles, Brahma
bulls feel right at home.

Campus signs point to the "sheep unit" and others warn of
tractors and bulls crossing the campus road. From this bucolic
farm scene the high-rise office buildings of Woodland Hills can
be seen in the near distance, adding glass and steel to the urban/
agrarian contrasts. Pierce feels like an oasis as I wait for Leland
Shapiro to show up. A former dairy farmer, Dr. Shapiro has been
teaching animal ethics at Pierce since the early 1970s; he's written the textbook *Applied Animal Ethics*. I've decided to check in
with him as I continue to search for where animal use becomes
animal abuse. It's mid-morning and the Southern California sun
is already warming the farm—I eavesdrop as a couple of Shapiro's
colleagues talk about setting up shade shelters for the cattle. I
enjoy the pungent grasses instead of the Ventura Freeway, where
the lingering morning rush hour a couple of miles distant smells
of exhaust, not hay. A red frame chicken coop is next to the Agriculture Science building, and the chickens are clucking with what
sounds to me like a happy cackle. On the door of the coop is a
sign offering FARM FRESH EGGS FOR SALE, illustrated by three eggs
holding rolled diplomas and wearing mortar boards. $3.00 PER
DOZEN/PLEASE SEE VICKY.

It seems I should trade my suit and tie for Oshkosh overalls
and my rented Hertz Mustang (car not horse) convertible (so
perfect for those L.A. freeways) for an old Chevy pickup.

Shapiro's office is in the low-slung Mission-style Agriculture Science building. With its red-tile roof and its stucco walls, it matches the dry Southern California hills, brown now in June. A morning owl hoots, one of the bovines bellows low, and Dr. Shapiro ushers me into his office, jammed literally floor to ceiling with over forty years of science and memorabilia. Bumper stickers: DRINK MILK. SAVE A COW and BEEF. GOOD TASTE. GOOD HEALTH. IT'S WHAT'S FOR DINNER. There's an Old Glory with a likeness of a cow superimposed on the flag and a poster headlined, ALL I NEED TO KNOW ABOUT LIFE I LEARNED FROM A COW. The ethics professor is dressed in blue jeans and a black T-shirt; on the back of the T-shirt is the image of the Pierce College mascot, the American Brahma Bull.

Leland Shapiro teaches Ag 120, "Ethical Issues in Using Animals," a course designed to teach students the difference between animal use and animal abuse. Dr. Shapiro loves animals and is a harsh critic of loud, radical animal rights organizations and activists.

"PETA will tell you that Jesus was a vegetarian." Shapiro launches right into his disagreements with People for the Ethical Treatment of Animals. He speaks rapidly, confident about his research. "But if you really read the New Testament, Jesus ate meat himself. He fed meat to his disciples. He fed fish to them."

"Since there is disagreement in our society about what's ethical and what isn't," I ask the professor, "how do you guide your students?"

"I point to the flag," he gestures to Old Glory on display in his office, "and I say, 'In America, what's the right way? You have a right in America to disagree with me.'"

"Does that mean," I ask him, "that you think each of us should decide for ourselves what is right and what is wrong regarding the treatment of animals?"

Not really, is his answer, and he returns to his classroom example. "I say, 'I hope all of us in the room would agree that beating an animal just because you want to see it suffer would be wrong, cruel, and a person who does that should be thrown in jail. In my personal opinion, the only time you can hit an animal would be if your life is in danger.' The example I give them is if a horse kicks you out the barn and you get up and go back and hit the horse to teach it a lesson, that's abuse." But if the horse is kicking you and you're trapped against a wall, he says, it would be okay to try to hit the horse to stop it from hurting you. "Just like your child. You see your child doing something wrong, you might have to spank him lightly for shock. But if you find out your child did something two days ago, and you hit him, all that teaches your child is physical violence."

A vegetarian may say it's wrong to kill an animal for food since meat is not necessary for human survival, while a meat eater may argue that as long as the animal is killed humanely there's nothing to be concerned about. How does Shapiro teach ethics when there are so many opinions about what is right and wrong regarding human interaction with other animals?

For starters he teaches pragmatism. "My students ask me when they find out I'm Jewish what I would do if I were starving. I say I would eat pork with cheese on it, if that's what I needed to survive. I know how to hunt and I know how to kill. I would survive. I would eat rat and squirrel and snakes and lizards. I don't want to eat those things, but I want to live." However, Shapiro condemns bullfighting, cockfighting, and dogfighting as unnecessary and vicious.

"What about cricket fighting?" I ask. Is the morality of what we do with an animal different depending on what we consider the animal's status to be in a hierarchy we devise—Aristotle's *scala naturae*?

Shapiro says yes. He sees the human being at the top of the heap, and if sacrificing a "lower" animal will save a human, he considers it an ethical act. "I delivered my own two children. I cut the cord. I've delivered thousands of animals over the years. To me, life is beautiful every single time." He acknowledges his own hypocrisy or ambiguity. "I eat meat," he says with enthusiasm. "I just don't want to kill 'em."

I leave Leland Shapiro and race the Mustang across L.A. to a rendezvous in Gardena with animal cops, thinking about his conflict: So many of us like to eat meat, but only meat removed in our minds from the animal it once was.

CHAPTER TWENTY
Sea Turtle Cowboy Boots

THE SCENE IS THE McDONALD'S ON REDONDO BEACH BOULEVARD IN Gardena, in the heart of the Los Angeles basin. Fish and Wildlife Service wildlife inspector Juan Ramirez is stripped down to his undershirt, and FWS special agent Ed Newcomer is strapping a transmitter to his chest. Special Agent Newcomer and I had a lunch date, and he asked me if I wanted to join him earlier to witness Ramirez's second encounter with a shopkeeper who sells *ropa vaquera*—cowboy clothes—out of a shop on New Hampshire Street.

Inspector Ramirez stumbled on the cowboy clothing store one day after lunch. He saw the goods on display and decided to check out what was on offer to test his skill at identifying sources of leather—just to practice. His job is to check goods coming into American ports as part of the continuing attempts to keep things made from endangered and threatened species from crossing international borders. While Ramirez was checking out the boots, the shopkeeper made a suggestion: How would he like a pair of "special boots"? The conversation was in Spanish. Inspector Ramirez was offered cowboy boots made of *caguama*—sea turtle. All marine turtles worldwide are in jeopardy. They suffer as fishing bycatch. They're hunted for their eggs, meat, shell, and skin. Turtle habitat is degraded. Trade in marine turtles is prohibited by international treaty.

Sea turtles are called *tortuga del mar* in textbook Spanish; *caguama* is slang for the prized animal and its leather. As soon as Inspector Juan Ramirez saw the pair of boots, he was convinced they were, in fact, *caguama*. He made the positive identification from the scales. "There's no real pattern to them," he tells me in the McDonald's parking lot, "and it's creased from the movement of the flipper."

"Aside from the fact that they're endangered and it's illegal to buy and sell them, are they spectacular to look at?" I ask him. He doesn't seem the cowboy type. He looks in his early twenties; he's wearing jeans and a colorful sports shirt is now over his undershirt (the transmitter is well hidden by the sports shirt). His footwear is decidedly not *ropa vaquera*—he's wearing blue running shoes.

He dismisses my question. "I'm not really into cowboy boots. They don't look that good to me." Newcomer joins Ramirez in rejecting the turtle boots as a fashion statement. "I don't particularly care for the reptile look in cowboy boots. To me they look a little gaudy—so animal-like, over the top."

The boots cost $750, and the shopkeeper also offered Ramirez a matching turtle skin belt for another $150. He bartered with the retailer and took the boots and belt for a total of $800. While FWS lab technicians were evaluating the purchases to ascertain that they were indeed sea turtle, Newcomer and Ramirez decided to return to the store and try to learn more about the boots and belt, and the role of the shopkeeper in the sea turtle leather trade. The shopkeeper had told Ramirez he procures his *caguama* products in Mexico. Where in Mexico was he getting the goods, and from whom? Did he act as a distributor to other stores? What other stores were selling the illegal footwear? Developing such information has the potential of shutting down a distribution network, and it also can help prosecutors add charges like conspiracy to the list of grievances against smugglers and retailers.

"He's just going in today to howdy-and-shake," Newcomer says. "We're not going to make a buy. He's just building on that relationship he started last week, and reporting back that the boots and belt are a hit." Traffic on Redondo Beach Boulevard is competing with our conversation, as are birds singing in the trees. Los Angeles is a clash of the hyper-urban and the resistant wildlife.

Newcomer is finishing up with the covert equipment. "This is the transmitter." He points out a unit about the size of a mobile phone. Whatever transpires in the store will be broadcast to

Newcomer's car, a half block from the store, where he'll be listening and recording. The wire is not just to gather evidence. "If something were to happen he would say something in English that would cue us that it's time for us to come rescue him."

"Does that make you uncomfortable?" I ask Juan Ramirez. "Are you nervous about going back in there knowing you're the good guy and they're the bad guys?"

"No," he brushes off the idea. "I flow with the conversation. I'm a customer. That's all I think about. I'm just in there to buy something."

"If something were to happen," Newcomer explains, "Juan would say something to the effect of, 'Hey, you don't need a gun,' or 'Don't point a knife,' or 'I'm no threat to you.' If we hear those words, he knows we're going to be about twenty to thirty seconds away." Ed is working with a backup special agent, Sam Jojola. "The minute we come in the door, he's going to hit the ground. And we'll be there," Newcomer says with complete confidence, "to deal with whatever's going on."

The transmitter is in place, held with white adhesive tape. Cars are coming and going past us, in search of Big Macs and fries. "Wiring him up in the parking lot of McDonald's on Redondo Beach Boulevard isn't a worry?" I ask. But I answer my own question. "This is L.A., it doesn't make any difference. This is just his new iPod you're helping him install. No one cares what you're doing."

"We're far enough away that it is unlikely we'd run into those people," Newcomer says about the mom and pop shopkeepers. We're about a dozen blocks from the store, a world away in the packed megapolis. "Nobody thinks twice about these things," he says about passersby.

"We could be making a TV show," I suggest. "This is L.A."

Inspector Ramirez dons his sports shirt and Newcomer looks at his handiwork with approval. "Yeah, it's not going to show through that shirt. You can't see it in your armpit. That'll be good." Next he arms Ramirez with the pièce de résistance, a new gadget they want to test that records both audio and video of the coming encounter. (For security reasons, the agents requested that I not reveal the specific details of how they make covert recordings, but let's just say that the world of technological miniaturization provides platforms nearly impossible for suspects to uncover. Think *Get Smart* Agent 86's shoe phone meets today's Bluetooth apparatus.)

"Don't be nervous now. Remember, big breaths before you go in so you're not shaking. A couple, three or four deep breaths," Newcomer counsels. Ramirez looks as cool as if we *were* shooting a TV cop show.

We jump in our vehicles, and I follow the agents in my Mustang as we whiz down to the store in question. Newcomer parks his SUV a discreet distance from the suspect shop. Ramirez parks his run-of-the-mill pickup truck closer, and—looking like he belongs in the neighborhood—eases out of the cab and ambles over to the store. We listen to his footfalls on the sidewalk, and suddenly the radio comes alive with his tinny voice.

"Hey, the place is closed!" It's midday on a Friday.

"You're kidding me," responds Newcomer.

"The place has the white fence across it and it's locked."

"Go up and take a look at it and see if there's a sign," Newcomer orders. "Maybe they're at lunch or something."

"Alright," the radio squawks. And then, "No sign."

Closed it is. The team shrugs—the liability of undercover work. They'll be back. We motorcade back over to Redondo Beach Boulevard and find a restaurant. Over plates of Chinese food, we trade stories. Making cowboy boots out of endangered sea turtles, we all agree over a lunch filled with red meat and fish (on their plates, not mine), constitutes animal abuse. Sam Jojola explains why he doesn't hunt animals. "It's more fun," he says, with a nod to the proprietors we missed that morning, "to hunt the people who are hunting the animals."

CHAPTER TWENTY-ONE

Cockfight First Responders

THE MASSIVE SONOMA COUNTY SHERIFF'S HEADQUARTERS BUILDING sits like a stalwart statement to law and order in a civic center just north of our downtown county seat, Santa Rosa. There I meet with Lieutenant Scott Dunn, the de facto cockfighting specialist of a county much better known for its gourmet Pinot Noir, towering redwood trees, and pristine beaches than for illicit cockfights and the equally forbidden gambling that inevitably accompanies the matches. While I was bantering with Cajun cockfighters in Louisiana, I realized what chauvinistic arrogance I was displaying: traveling to the rural South and acting like a city slicker observing the quaint antics of the "coon-asses" as if I came from a sophisticated landscape free of controversy about animal abuse. Cockfights, I learned quickly, are as much a part of Sonoma County life as wine tasting and sunbathing.

A March 2009 news release from Dunn's office disabused me of my urbane self-righteousness. Deputies, it reported, responded to a call west of Rohnert Park and "found over fifty suspects fleeing the scene," a barn on farmland where they arrested fifty-three "males on charges associated with cockfighting." They added burglary charges to the rap sheets of two suspects because they ran into an occupied house trying to escape cops who were after them on foot, with squad cars, and from a helicopter. They seized a flock of birds and a stash of cash.

⌒‿⌒

About a quarter of our population in Sonoma County is Hispanic, and police records suggest the majority of cockfights organized in our midst are for the diversion of immigrants from south of the border. "Every case I've been involved in, all the parties are Latino," Dunn tells me as we sit down to talk on a quiet weekend morning. "I can understand cultural issues." He's heard the arguments that cockfighting is routine in Mexico. "However, you're residing in a country where this is illegal. It may be culturally okay down there, but it's not here." The lieutenant is nearing retirement. His steel-gray hair suggests the many years he's been on the force, but his face looks remarkably relaxed for a man who has spent the majority of his career in law enforcement. His voice is soft and his answers to my questions are measured with a slow cadence that allows plenty of time for him to think before he speaks.

Of course the topic of use versus abuse comes up; that's why I'm here. Lieutenant Dunn reflects on arrests he made in the early 80s when there was an influx of male students from the Middle East into Sonoma County colleges. "How they treat women in the Middle East is different than how we treat women here. Culturally, a level of abuse," he chooses his words with care, "is acceptable in their communities. We don't tolerate it here." He remembers arresting shocked wife beaters who would complain to him, "Why am I under arrest? All I did was slap her."

"If I go out and poke around in rural Sonoma County," I ask him, "am I going to find a cockfight?"

"Yesterday I met up with one of the animal control guys." Dunn's answers usually start with a story. He's talking about Bob Garcia, the county's supervising animal control officer. Animal control estimates that their department averages about three busts a year of cockfights in progress. But they get over a dozen complaint calls annually that result in no arrests and no confiscated chickens. "By the time we get there it's gone or we can't find evidence of it or it's secreted so well it's difficult for us to locate." But he knows the fights are endemic in our neighborhood because of one telltale sign. "People are raising the birds and there's nothing illegal about raising birds. There are a number of places that you can just drive down the road and see banks of birds, and your suspicions are up." But suspicions don't necessarily equal crimes. "If you were to contact them," Dunn knows, they would explain their bird raising as completely without any connection to fights. "They're raising them for show," he says in a tone of voice that includes the underlying message, "Yeah, sure." Sonoma County cockfights include illegal gambling, and result in maimed and abused animals. Those two crimes are serious enough to warrant attention from the sheriff's department.

The typical Sonoma County cockfight is well hidden from passersby, camouflaged to prevent sheriff's aircraft from spotting them. The cockpits often are set up in farm or ranch outbuildings. "You walk into this barn and typically you'll see sections of plywood nailed together circling this makeshift ring. It all takes place right there. There's somebody who is taking money as people are coming in; they'll even have a little refreshment area." Such attention to the wants of the audience elicits an ironic quick laugh from the lawman. "It's not a huge facility, but they will pack people in."

Lieutenant Dunn and the officers assigned to cockfighting cases rarely plan raids; their intelligence networks do not extend into the subculture that organizes the fights. Instead they get calls from neighbors who see activity that makes them suspect something is amiss next door: a noisy party, an unusual number of cars parked on rural roads adjacent to a ranch. "We get there and the next thing we know we've got a hundred people running in different directions." He makes it sound like a scene out of a movie. The slick operators stage spotters on the roads leading to the fight, and in those cases, before the police are in a position to encircle the action, the participants start running—inevitably the outnumbered cops cannot catch all the chicken fight aficionados. Officers watching the events of the 2009 Rohnert Park raid from a sheriff's chopper said that as the audience scattered it reminded them of ants fleeing a nest that's been waterlogged.

The arrestees were processed, as the cops tend to say, without incident—except for the severe injuries suffered by one of the animal control officers. As she was grabbing a rooster, he slashed her with the knives lashed to his flailing legs, cutting her arm open. The arterial bleed resulted in consequential blood loss and required several stitches.

Some 150 fighting cocks were seized during the raid and destroyed. "They're trained to fight," says a matter-of-fact Lieutenant Dunn about their fate. "They can't become pets."

"How about chicken soup," I suggest, "or coq au vin?"

"From what I'm told," says the pragmatic cop, "they're not very good food quality because the lean muscle mass is not as desirable as just a barnyard chicken."

"But isn't it a paradox that the law considers it abuse to allow them to fight, so you kill them in order to prevent them from fighting?"

"It is unfortunate," he agrees, "but look at where that rooster is destined. He's going to be slashed to death versus humanely euthanized." It's the same rationalization used by the Humane Society's Julia Breaux in Louisiana.

"But he might not be slashed to death," I protest. "He might be the victor!"

Lieutenant Dunn is not swayed. "Even as the victor they frequently are injured." He allows as how some of the owners do cater to their birds' needs like a Fifth Avenue matron does her well-coiffed poodles. They treat their prize birds' wounds with antibiotics and whatever other compounds and techniques they can think of, especially if they believe the animal is of genetic value as a stud.

"Most of these guys get hit with relatively small fines," Dunn tells me, and a misdemeanor conviction. The worry for those running from the deputies may well not be limited to charges related to the cockfight. A substantial number of the Sonoma County Latino population is north of the border without proper immigration documentation. A Sunday afternoon cockfight could turn into deportation. In order to prove that what they bust is a fight and not a bird show, investigators pounce on any fighting devices they can seize, especially the knives and the gaffs. Just as is the case with equipment designed specifically for the use of illegal drugs, it's illegal in California to make or own paraphernalia like the knives and gaffs because they are fabricated for one purpose and one purpose only: cockfighting.

The Rohnert Park raid did result in deportations; charges were dropped against several suspects found far from the barn because of insufficient evidence against them. Other suspects paid fines but then failed to appear for scheduled court dates; warrants were issued for their arrests. The police seized $45,000 in cash; prosecutors identified the money as gambling loot (or it was abandoned by gamblers who feared prosecution were they to claim it as their own). The courts gave the cash to the cops to use "to support law enforcement operations."

Lieutenant Dunn again emphasizes with his droll delivery that it's the exception for his department to bust cockfights because of prior knowledge that they've been planned and scheduled. "Usually it's an in-progress type thing. It's very rare that we get fights that we can anticipate: okay, something's going on this weekend, let's get our ducks lined up and try to get it. So when everybody's scattering to the wind . . ."

I interrupt him; I can't help it. "With all due respect, Lieutenant," I say, "I don't think you want to take ducks to a cockfight. You must work on that metaphor, okay?"

He looks at me with resigned anticipation. "I can see that one in the book."

"No question, Lieutenant. You're a dead duck, so to speak."

A jolly Bob Garcia is the point man for Sonoma County animal control—he's witnessed humans dealing with other animals for over thirty-five years—and he doesn't hesitate to profile them, telling me, "Most of the cockfighters in California are from Mexico." And most of the rest of the California cockfighters, he says, are Filipinos. The weapons used, he informs me shortly after we sit down to talk at his office in the pound, differ depending on the ethnic group involved. "If you see a slasher, it's indicative of what a fighter from Mexico uses, as opposed to Louisiana where they use a lot of gaffs." Dogs in the kennels provide a background accompaniment to our conversation, and as Garcia attacks cockfights, I glance over to a corner of his office where there is an altar-like display of cockfighting paraphernalia seized by him and his officers on their raids around my home county.

No question in Garcia's mind, cockfighting is cruel, but the subculture and its trappings obviously intrigue him. He understands that gamecocks bred for the pit instinctively want to fight. But that does not mitigate the cruelty issue for him. "The animal goes through a lot of pain." He speaks from experience. "We've broken up cockfights."

Supervising Animal Control Officer Garcia considers dogfights even worse atrocities than cockfights. "You see two dogs fight, and then you hear one squealing, see blood spurting out of its eye, the other dog has its canine in its eye, grueling stuff like that. Yet people are watching it and enjoying it. That's a dark side of humanity, in my opinion." Bad as the antics of Michael Vick were, Garcia credits the publicity around the Vick dogfighting case as an opportunity to educate. Vick's crime raised awareness amongst the public about animal cruelty in our midst. Not just dogs profited, but chickens and maybe even crickets.

I tell Garcia that I'm a soft touch when it comes to just about all animals. I try to escort flies out of the house. I see their magic and their miracle even as they annoy me (although I will swat them if they're stubborn about being herded to the great outdoors where they belong), and tell him I've become a vegan thanks to researching this book (although my shoes are leather and my late

Aunt Lillian's fine fur coats still hang in my bedroom closet—I'd wear them if they fit me). But I find it odd that I stratify animals. I do find dogfighting more abhorrent than cockfighting. Rover and Spot seem to mean more to me than Paul Huln's fine tough-fighting cock that I held in my arms down in Louisiana. And I simply cannot get exercised about the morality of cricket fight-ing—they look like elegant cockroaches to me. I ask Bob Garcia for some moral guidance through my moral relativism.

It's cultural conditioning, he reckons. "We're exposed to tak-ing a fly and swatting and killing it. Most of us don't have any feelings about doing that." He hesitates; this man's life's work is steeped in the relationship between humans and other animals. "I don't know if I can really answer," he says about my request for advice, and it gives me some comfort that this professional animal control officer is stumped when it comes to animal use versus abuse. But he continues to attempt an answer. "You experience a closer relationship with a dog than a chicken," he says.

"Because?"

"Because it responds to you more, and has more feelings and reciprocates with compassion towards you."

"The chicken doesn't fetch the newspaper," I offer as an example.

"Probably not," he agrees with a smile.

Despite the hierarchy, Garcia is an enthusiastic supporter of California's laws forbidding cockfighting.

"I think that cockfighting is cruel." That's not all he dislikes about the fights. He's convinced that the injured and dying birds suffer, and he knows the fights are facilitators of illegal gambling.

"There are lines that we need to have in society." Lax enforce-ment of what some of us may consider victimless crimes erodes society, he tells me with his easygoing soft and slow voice, a voice I can imagine has calmed kennels full of anxious animals over the years. He's pleased to report that throughout his long career he's watched as Sonoma County has grown more compassionate about animals, more caring and responsible. As an example, he cites the fact that fewer and fewer dogs and cats are being euthanized/put down/killed—pick the terminology that suits—in part because owners are spaying and neutering their pets. "In 1995," he says, pulling up the feline figures, "forty-five hundred cats were euthanized here in Sonoma County. That's a lot of cats."

"That's a lot of cats," I agree, "and most of them came from the house of the lady who lives across the street from my house!"

"Could be," he laughs, and then proudly informs me that at the time of our 2010 chat, the number of surplus cats killed by Sonoma County was down to about twelve hundred a year even as the human population in the county substantially increased. Guidelines help teach people to treat animals with respect, he says, and "cockfighting is not acceptable."

Yet it continues in the shadows of the county's tourist attractions and economic powerhouses: lush grapevines, luxury B&Bs, gourmet restaurants, and spectacular scenery. No question that cockfighting intrigues even those, like Bob Garcia, who work to suppress it. He draws my attention to his collection.

"I use it for my staff, for training purposes," he explains. But it is on display with almost museum-like attention to its intrigue. He gets up from behind his desk and walks over to the mementos. "These," he says, picking up steely gaffs, "are probably what you saw in Louisiana." They look vicious, and several months after my visit, far south from Sonoma County in Tulare County, a spectator at an illegal cockfight was stabbed by a blade attached to a fighting rooster; two hours later Jose Luis Ochoa bled to death. But the gaffs Paul Huln was making were much longer than these Sonoma County models. "Yeah, they have different styles," says Garcia. "I've never confiscated any gaffs in Sonoma County. Those came from someone who gave them to me for my collection." He laughs at the absurdity of the anti-cockfighting animal control officer collecting what he is charged to keep off the streets. Or at least that's what I think he's laughing at. Perhaps he's laughing because he is uncomfortable being intrigued by what he's convinced himself should be banned. There's no question the gaffs are fascinating to study. They are works of fine craftsmanship designed for only one function: to aid chickens trying to kill each other.

Garcia picks up a knife. "What we normally find are these slashers." He shows me what looks like an elongated miniature sickle. "A rooster has natural spurs." He explains how the blade is attached to the leg, just as I learned from the experts in Louisiana. "They trim the bird out," he says, using cockfighting jargon. "They cut the comb. They cut the waddles." Removing the comb and waddles minimizes body parts susceptible to cuts and the resulting life-threatening blood loss, and no comb makes it easier for the lighter bird to jump at its opponent. "They vent the bird. In the anal area you'll see feathers plucked out so the bird won't overheat." This customizing of the chickens is important for law enforcement officers to recognize because such anatomical changes can be used as evidence against suspected cockfighters who own chopped and channeled fowl. "They cut the natural spur to a stump." Now he demonstrates how the slashers are lashed to the cocks. "They attach the implements to that stump." The knife harness is equipped with a cup that fits over the stump. "They tie that with this wax string that I have, and they attach the slasher," he's demonstrating, "like so." Ritual is infectious; I'm intrigued as I watch.

We're interrupted by a worker with a routine message from the outer office. "There's somebody picking up their dog," she tells her boss, "and the 'designated as vicious' paperwork . . ."

"Let me deal with it," Garcia waves her off. "I'll be up there in a minute."

Just another day at the office: show-and-tell about fighting cocks and vicious dog forms.

He shows me what looks like little boxing gloves. Called muffs, these are used for practice fights in place of the slashers. The cocks spar and the handlers get an idea of how they fight. Are they high fliers? Are they aggressive? Do they strike out with precision?

Breeding the fighters and training them to fight is legal in California, as is selling the birds to buyers in places like Puerto Rico where cockfighting is legal. Arrested cockers often use the breed and train defense, claiming they're not engaged in fighting and gambling. But it's illegal to possess slashers in California, and a suspect caught with birds *and* fighting paraphernalia is in an awkward position to claim innocence; the muffs and the special vitamins and the handmade carrying cases decorated with inlaid wood images of fighting cocks all add up to circumstantial evidence often embraced favorably by the courts against the defendants. Bob Garcia's collection includes a bottle of Jose's King of the Ring Terminator Formula.

"Some of this stuff is testosterone," he says about the various bottles of rooster snake oil in his collection. "I don't know what this is," he says about Jose's formula. "It's probably just vitamins, with a nice name."

Animal control officers work in conjunction with the sheriff's department on periodic cockfight raids because of all the chickens that need to be tended when their owners are arrested. "We're dealing with this creature that has to be cared for." Not just one. Scores of them. "When there are hundreds of birds, we'll impound them on the property." Bob Garcia sounds somewhat weary as he recalls past raids. A representative number of birds will be taken as evidence. There's no county facility to keep hundreds of the seized fowl. The next step is disturbing. The birds are, to use Garcia's euphemism, destroyed.

"The birds are destroyed," I repeat and tell him I'm still somewhat flummoxed by the logic employed here, "so that they won't fight and kill each other. It seems a bit of a paradox." Or more than a bit.

"I guess you could say that." But he is quick with an explanation, from his point of view. "It's how they die. The fighting is not

139

clean and quick." Nor, he says, is the response of the handlers. "A lot of these birds, after they're spent, they throw them in a garbage can still alive, all cut up, bleeding. They will eventually die. But it could be hours. To allow an animal to suffer needlessly like that is something in my opinion—and I think our society's opinion—unacceptable." Handlers take very good care of the birds, he agrees, until they've served their purpose. "They're not put out of their misery. They're allowed to sit there and suffer." He and Julia Breaux agree again.

Yet, I point out, some of the fighters—the winners—would live because they prevailed in the cockpit, and when the raiders swoop down on a fight, all the birds die.

Bob Garcia sees no alternative. "You can't put them in a barnyard with other birds. They'll kill them." There are some sanctuaries that will take over the care and feeding of some confiscated fighting cocks. But no effort is made by law enforcement to match bird and do-gooder, at least in part because there are more fighting cocks than protected perches. He says there's no use for fighting cocks other than fighting because of the selective breeding and training that results in the doomed animals. They're too tough to bother eating, worse than spent laying hens, for which there's hardly a market. Those opposed to cockfighting want to see an end to the genetic lines that fuel fighting cocks. Hence animal lovers like Garcia promote euthanizing the captured chickens.

"You're consciously trying to get rid of the genetic strains that the cockers spend generations developing?"

"We're ending it," he nods. "That's important."

When does use become abuse for an animal control officer, I ask Garcia. "I'm certainly not opposed to euthanizing an animal," he answers carefully (and with obvious candor), "or using it for human consumption, when it's done humanely. Quickly and so that the animal does not suffer." Abuse, he says, is when an animal is allowed to suffer. Fighting cocks is an example, from his perspective, but so is neglect: failing to adequately feed and water an animal.

I leave his office, and its barking dogs, and head back home to Bodega Bay with a new appreciation for the farmlands between San Rosa and the Pacific, wondering behind which barns I might find a neighborhood cockfight.

CHAPTER TWENTY-TWO
Cricket Fighting for Science

CRICKET FIGHTING IS A CENTURIES-OLD PASTIME IN CHINA, AND IT'S experiencing a resurgence on the mainland after being labeled "old culture" by the 1950s Communist party and outlawed as a distracting amusement until after the Cultural Revolution. To condemn cricket fighting as a blood sport akin to bull-, dog-, or cockfighting may be a stretch since the crickets often just push each other around. Neither is it a given that either fighter suffers life-threatening injuries during a bout (except to whatever may pass for cricket pride). Some scholars, though, worry that so many fighting crickets are bought and sold during the fighting season (estimates range up to 100,000 bugs a day traded just in Shanghai) that some Chinese cricket populations may be in jeopardy.[63] The fighting bugs are bred for strength and aggressive behavior, and some handlers dope their crickets and outfit them with sharp metal apparatus to augment their little mandibles.

The *Wall Street Journal*, in a dispatch from Shanghai on the cricket fighting business, confirmed that despite the possibility of combatants leaving each other with damaged or missing limbs, "the fights are vicious but rarely deadly. One cricket usually gives up and runs away—or vaults out of the arena. The loser often gets flung into the street by his displeased owner."[64] Or not. New School for Social Research anthropology professor Hugh Raffles ventured to Shanghai to mingle with cricket handlers and gamblers in the city's industrial suburbs. He watched as losing crickets were retired, their careers, he learned, finished. "The referee collects him in a net and drops him into a large plastic bucket behind the table," he reported, "for release 'into nature,' everyone told me." His translator informed him that he should not worry about the bucket of losers, that they would be treated well, because "the curse on anyone who harms a defeated cricket guaranteed it."[65]

———

University of Texas neurobiologist Hans Hofmann takes time off from his family weekend to sit down in an Austin cafe with me and talk about his cricket research.

The streets around Pease Park are jammed. It's Eeyore's Birthday Party, an annual Austin fundraiser named for A. A. Milne's depressed donkey. It's a perfect Texas spring day—blue skies and no humidity—except for the hay fever that keeps attacking Hofmann and me, as costumed Austinites parade past celebrating Eeyore, striving to obey the city's "Keep Austin Weird" motto. This subdued scientist studies male aggression among insects, and his academic research inspired an uncommon hobby: Dr. Hofmann is an expert cricket handler. He and his cohorts fight their research subjects for fun as well as scholarship. Weird as that work and hobby may seem, Hofmann draws no attention to himself with his plain black T-shirt, wire-rimmed glasses, and mild-mannered professorial demeanor.

I learned of Hofmann because of an article in the journal *Nature* about the work he and his coauthor conducted in their cricket-fighting lab at Germany's University of Leipzig. "The contestants initially fence with their antennae," the two wrote, "and then display spread mandibles which later interlock before the animals finally wrestle." The match ends when one of the crickets retreats—again, unlike cockfighting and dogfighting, cricket fighting is not an exercise that usually ends with the death of the losing combatant. But the losers, learned the scientists, tend to (figuratively, of course) lick their wounds for about twenty-four hours before they can be coaxed into another fighting match. They won't fight earlier unless, as veteran Chinese cricket fighters know from folklore and experience, a cricket's handler shakes the losing cricket for several seconds. Expert cricket handlers take loser crickets in their cupped palms and shake them, and then they throw the poor fighters into the air a couple of dozen times, tossing and catching them. That exercise eliminates what is known as the loser effect; a losing shaken cricket will climb (figuratively, of course) right back into the ring and start swinging. Hans Hofmann wanted to know why shaking crickets (and it's the males that fight) restored their aggressive instincts.

"I didn't believe a word of this," the skeptical scientist tells me with a smile about his initial reaction to the cricket-shaking yarns. But Hofmann went back to his lab. "I took a bunch of crickets and I set up ten fights. I took the loser every time and I did this," he's grinning as he pantomimes his basic cricket shake and catch-and-throw act, "and I put it back." Without such manipulation, he says, about one in ten crickets will fight again right after losing. But after Hofmann shook and threw his losers, six out of ten were itching for another match, filled with cricket aggressive energy and ready to do battle. The scientist (and cricket fancier) was thrilled. "I thought, 'There is something real going on.'" It wasn't just that the six were cured of the loser effect. Hofmann perceived a consequential behavior change: they fought harder than they did during their first bouts. "They fought like crazy. I think that I'm actually giving them a winner effect. But that has not been rigorously studied, so I don't want to call it that." Always the scientist, he's careful about his labels. The initial experiment was followed by further work until Hofmann's technique was refined to the point where he could, as he puts it, "reset" up to 90 percent of his crickets to fight hard immediately after losing.

Convinced that what he was observing was no fluke, Dr. Hofmann wanted to know why.

"I tried everything. I thought it was the stress." He inserted crickets into centrifuges to subject them to more stress. He taped them to fan blades and spun them.

"You're a sadist," I tell him.

"No," he corrects me, giggling. "I'm a scientist. I did everything I could to stress these animals out."

A colleague offered him use of a wind tunnel. They suspended crickets in front of a fan from a string connected with wax to the backs of the insects, and as a result the bugs would fly without moving, what the investigators call "stationary flight." Because the crickets stay in one place while engaged in stationary flight, they can be connected to all sorts of test equipment. Hofmann put his losers into the wind tunnel, they "flew," and he forced them back into the arena where "they would fight like crazy."

He decided he was wrong; it wasn't stress that reset their fight drive, it was flying. He made video recordings of the crickets he subjected to his catch-and-throw routine and, sure enough, momentarily during the up and down in the air, they flew. And the amount of time they spent engaged in flight movements, he learned, made no difference. Just seconds of attempted flight reset their fight instinct. Further experimentation convinced Hofmann that his crickets also reset their fight instincts quickly when—immediately after losing a fight—they were faced with protecting their shelters or were offered the opportunity to court a female, and he observed that the biochemical octopamine plays a critical role in these behavior patterns. "Octopamine is the signal that implements the reset," he tells me. "Flying stimulates the release of the chemical and if octopamine is introduced into a loser cricket, it will reset without flying."

Further experiments in the basement of the old Leipzig lab showed that forcing the octopamine into the mix could result in the equivalent of the ninety-eight-pound weakling at the beach beating up the muscleman who kicked sand in his face.

"I would take the smallest cricket in there," Hofmann is describing the collections he was using for his basement experiments, "and make him fly for a minute and put him back in the arena. He would just beat them up like crazy."

"Beat up the big boys?"

"Everybody. They would just run. This guy was just out of control. He was so aggressive. He became the top dog." (Love these animal metaphors!) But not for long, "only for an hour or so. It didn't last because he was the smallest cricket."

Confirming the validity of cricket tossing may influence matches in China (and elsewhere around the world), but Hans Hofmann sees greater potential value for what he's learned. "We're exploiting the crickets as a model to give us some fundamental and general insight about how animal communication signals evolved, including our own." He thinks we humans might learn about ourselves from fighting crickets, about our nervous systems and about how we respond to each other. "We signal all the time. We just don't think about it." But shaking and tossing crickets isn't just for research. Hofmann and his colleagues capture the fancy of university freshman science students with the insects' antics, showing them a good time while they learn.

Science is his profession. However, Dr. Hofmann doesn't hesitate to acknowledge that he isn't just taking notes when his crickets spar; he enjoys a good match and he shakes his head with an emphatic "No!" when I ask him if he sees anything wrong with cricket fights staged purely for amusement.

Crickets, chickens, dogs, bulls. Does the difference most humans distinguish between these animals translate to assigning the cricket a value less than that of the family dog? (Don't try to convince Pinocchio of that; he relied on Jiminy Cricket for sage advice.)

"Where do you draw the line?" Hofmann rephrases my question. "Are animals sentient beings?" He answers without waiting for me to offer an opinion. "They clearly are, no question about it," he says, and quickly adds the caveat, "most of them," and then modifies his response further, "to different degrees, there's always variation."

"What about dogfighting and cockfighting?" I ask this cricket fighter.

"I find them pretty disgusting," he says without hesitation, but then cautions, "one has to be very careful with ethical and moral judgments." Without my prompting he adds, "With insects, I don't have a problem with people letting them fight." And people do fight other insects, too: Atlas beetles and praying mantises, for example.

"Why do you think that is?" I ask. I find the distinction intriguing.

"I think it probably has to do with a deep-seated aversion to how Western society treats animals," and Dr. Hofmann takes off on a theme he clearly has given careful consideration. "We are very schizophrenic about it. On the one hand, we eat them. But, of course, we have no idea what is being done to those animals that we eat before they get killed. The agricultural industry is atrocious. On the other hand, we mistreat animals with our love. We call them pets." He proceeds to tell me stories about growing up on a Bavarian farm, surrounded by animals, none of which he considered a pet. Even the family dog was there for a purpose that did not include acting pet-like. "Nobody would ever cuddle up with that dog. We had cats. I never petted a cat. The cat had a job to do; it had to catch mice." He says his family had a contract with the cat; they fed it and provided it shelter in return for mousing service. He bred rabbits when he was growing up to make pocket money. He skinned them and dressed them, selling both the meat and the fur. "I was not attached to them. They were livestock."

Perversion is what he calls the relationships he observes between his urban Austin neighbors and their pooches, because they leave their dogs confined while they're at work all day. "I say about them, 'You are so selfish and you don't even see it. It's completely unacceptable what you are doing to this animal, and you are telling me that fighting crickets is immoral?'" He's incensed at the suggestion of such a judgment.

Back in his graduate student days, Hofmann didn't just fight his crickets, he was the bookmaker for campus cricket gambling. "On a Friday afternoon we would set up some matches. We just fooled around. Scientists can't be serious about this kind of stuff." Science with the crickets during the day, then beer and bets on the cricket fights through the night. "As a modern scientist," he says with satisfaction, "I learned something from this folk science. It's not earth shattering. I'm not going to get the Nobel Prize for it, but it's better than nothing."

❧

Zack Lemann, the staff entomologist at the Audubon Insectarium in New Orleans, probably will not earn a Nobel Prize either for his work cooking up insects for museum goers to sample. Crickets are on his menu: He bakes cricket chocolate chip cookies—which he calls chocolate chirp cookies—the chocolate chips, he says, hide the cricket texture and the familiar flavor helps the squeamish transcend the trauma of eating bugs. He garnishes the cookies with a cricket topping specifically to show them off as identifiable insects. If the crickets aren't obvious to cookie eaters, he says, "invariably you have people who feel cheated."[66]

I asked Lemann for his recipe and he was happy to oblige. "When I make chocolate chirp cookies, I simply use a regular chocolate chip recipe that I like and add the crickets." But there is a trick. "Before baking the cookie dough, I cook five-week-old house crickets on a baking sheet at 350° for about thirty minutes. Crickets this age do not have wings yet, and it makes the eating easier." He uses four or five crickets per cookie, not mixing them in the batter, but placing them on top of the cookies. "If one mixes crickets into the batter, they are usually not visible once the cookie is made. Where's the buggy fun in that? Really, you don't want your entomophages to feel short-changed, and you also don't want to give mischievous folks a chance to offer an apparently normal cookie to someone else in an attempt to snicker at and trick them."

The Insectarium is closed the day when Lemann escorts me to its cricket-fighting exhibit. He loves his bugs and he loves sharing his experiences with them. His enthusiasm bubbles into his rapid speech. "Look at this!" he says pointing out another something that amazes him as we walk through the old converted Customs House on Canal Street. He wants to show off everything in the place, but eventually we're looking at his crickets and his cricket paraphernalia.

"This is the fighting arena," Lemann explains. We're studying a wooden rink about three inches across contained by walls. "It's the cricket equivalent of a boxing ring. The point is that they can't hop out and they can't scale it."

"There's something intrinsically attractive, for better or for worse, about some level of violence," Lemann says as we look at an *Acheta demestica*, a house cricket, and read a line of Japanese poetry inspired by *Homoeogrylus japonicus*, the Japanese bell cricket—so named because of its sweet song. "If a jewel of dew could sing, it would tinkle with such a voice."

Adjacent to the cricket exhibit is another fighting insect, the Atlas beetle. A traditional Southeast Asian beetle fight requires two male fighters and a female beetle. She's secured close enough to the combatants to stir their aggression against each other. Despite their fierce appearance—the Atlas beetles sport nasty-looking horns—Lemann tells me their fights can hardly be called a blood sport. They tend to end before any damage is done: The loser knows he is overpowered and simply retreats.

Before we say good-bye and I head back to my hotel in the French Quarter, I ask Zack Lemann about a story I was regaled with as a youngster by my father. He was a violinist in the merchant marine, leading a dance band, and when his ship was off the coast of South America some of the crew amused themselves by pouring lighter fluid around a tarantula and encircling it in flame. Before I could finish, Lemann interrupted me. He'd heard a variation of this scenario.

"They say it bites itself to death." Lemann is an insect specialist, but he also knows his arachnids—spiders, he tells me, are his favorite animals. "This is something you hear about scorpions as well, that you put them in a ring of fire and they stung themselves to death." He debunks the suicide theory. "I think what happens is that the heat becomes intense enough that the heat is killing the animal—it is effectively cooking it alive. When that happens, the animal is going to flail and struggle. In the case of the tarantula, the fangs go up and down. I'm not sure the spider can manipulate its body so that it is even capable of biting itself, other than its own legs."

"I hasten to add," I tell my guide, "that my father didn't subject the tarantula to this fate, but he watched as others did it."

"Good for him," says Lemann.

But of course if we're in the cockfight audience or paying admission to a bullfight or betting on the Kentucky Derby or mimicking the monkeys at the zoo, aren't we aiding and abetting the uses or abuses of these animals?

"Use or abuse?" I ask him about the tarantula act.

"Oh, that's abuse," he declares without hesitation. "That's abuse," he repeats but then tells me, "I'll confess something to you. It's not something I'm proud of but it's part of my life. When I was a young boy, I would put fishing spiders in a jar together to watch them fight." He blames "whatever pre-teen testosterone might have been coursing through my body or notions of violence that seem to be attractive to males of our species."

"So your work here at the Insectarium is to absolve yourself of pre-teen guilt?"

He laughs, but then points out that he's feeding countless crickets daily to his other bug charges. "In nature they would be killing another animal anyway," is his rationale.

"But is the Insectarium just a cleansed sideshow, making money off of the thrill-seeking public? Is it just another version of pouring lighter fluid around a tarantula?"

"In some people's minds it is," Zack Lemann acknowledges, but their criticism doesn't worry him. He's convinced feeding those farm-raised crickets to his other insects and spiders does no harm, and that the education the crowds who come to his museum receive is well worth the price the crickets pay.

CHAPTER TWENTY-THREE

A Jordanian Princess Changes Arabian Horses Mid-Life

"I THINK IT'S WHAT THEY CALL A JUNGLE CAT," THE PRINCESS TELLS me, "something between a lynx and a lion." She's pointing to what looks to me like the mountain lions that prowl the Coast Range near my California home. The cat is in a cage on the grounds of what was a dairy on the outskirts of Amman, Jordan. This is now home to the Princess Alia Foundation's animal refuge; Princess Alia is the daughter of the late King Hussein— her privileged experiences riding Arabian horses led her to a new career caring for abused animals. "There's such a lot of abuse that goes on in the equestrian disciplines," and she offers an example. "They electric shock them." Experiencing show-training techniques from the inside made her question the right of human beings to subjugate horses. "Do you really have a right to do that because you want to win a ribbon? It's insane." She cites extreme mental stress that damages horses coaxed to jump and prance for dressage. "These poor horses are under such pressure all the time. Misuse is becoming abuse."

That phraseology—misuse becomes abuse—I recognize as an extension of my probe into seeking the point where animal use becomes animal abuse. It is appropriate to place this other factor on the continuum: first use, then misuse, and finally abuse.

In order to avoid misusing animals, don't discipline animals, Princess Alia advises. Work with them and create positive relationships that are based on communication rather than the whip.

"You're convinced it still will do what you want it to do if you spare the rod?" I ask.

Not only is she sure, she believes leaving the horse the opportunity to express itself can be a lifesaver for both horse and rider.

"When you're riding there are times when the horse doesn't want to do something because it doesn't make sense to it or because it knows better than you. You don't want it to be obeying you blindly; you want it to be aware of danger. You don't want to forbid it to take natural reactions, because it would need those skills to survive in the wild. Accept that sometimes it knows better, and it will trust you in return."

I nod, but point out, "You can interact with animals in this type of idealized relationship because you come to them from a privileged position." I describe a scene I saw en route to her refuge, a scene by the side of the highway from downtown Amman. "We were passing Bedouin tents with goats and donkeys tethered nearby. That lifestyle may not be one where the happiness of the animals is a factor. The goats and donkeys are food suppliers and cargo carriers."

She disagrees with my premise. No matter the circumstances of the humans, "you can give the animals as good a life as you can. They needn't be stressed. When you're going to kill them it should be as quick as possible. It should be without them realizing anything bad is going to happen."

She's no radical animal liberationist. The princess eats meat (although she is careful about choosing the slaughterhouse where her meal makes the initial transition from living creature to the dinner plate). "If that happened to you," she says as if she were speaking to an animal slaughtered in an inhumane manner, "I don't feel right about eating you."

"Do you believe that we humans are the super-animals, more important than the others?"

"In ways," she acknowledges. But her full answer is diplomatic. "I think everything has its place," she adds, and then gives the others their credit. "I believe they're here to help us. And I believe they try to help us, but sometimes we close ourselves off."

I'm meeting with Princess Alia because my friend George Papagiannis—who's working for UNESCO in Iraq—forwarded a bizarre e-mail to me: an alert from his office manager about expected gunfire in the streets of Baghdad. "With immediate implementation Iraqi Authorities gave an order to shoot all stray dogs in Baghdad," it read. "Including the IZ." The IZ is the International Zone where many foreign humanitarian organizations, such as UNESCO, were based and where their employees, such as Papagiannis, lived. "This has been approved by Ministry of Health and they will be picking up the carcasses. There might be some shots sounds in the IZ." It seemed such an odd memo: the mundane, matter-of-fact wording combined with the extraordinary image of streets littered with writhing and bloody dying dogs. After a quick check I learned that shooting street dogs is not unique to the chaos of post–Saddam Hussein Iraq. Amman's city government also decided to deal with its stray and wild dogs with a bullet to the head—and when the princess learned of their fate, she chose to intervene.

Shooting stray dogs is just a temporary remedy, she tells me. New packs—their progeny—roam the streets within a few months. The answer, she's convinced, is dog birth control—spaying the canines. And she's managed to talk Jordan municipalities into testing a catch, spay, and release program—the critical element being the catch. "They bring them in, spay them, and put them back where they were found," she says, telling me her crew does manage to grab large numbers of the rampaging dogs. The dogs don't increase in number; they keep interloper dogs out of their territories, and eventually die a natural death instead of a death by gunshot or poison. "You can't catch them all, but they'll be reproducing in much smaller numbers."

But the princess's portfolio is not restricted to stray dogs. Three jungle cats were rescued by the foundation in addition to the one I'm looking at, all from a private, for profit zoo. Those three were released into the wilds of the Jordan Valley, but the one the princess and I are looking at was damaged. "It looks as if it's had a blow to the head. He's always had his head down. It's just not right." He looks like a large house cat—a *very* large house cat, and he looks unhappy. "He just stays there," she says about his spot at the rear of the enclosure. The other three ran when offered their freedom. "They were always pacing, wanting to be free." They were set free after about a week at the refuge, where their health was checked.

Rescuing animals from abusive conditions at private zoos and lobbying to close zoos that exist to profiteer at the expense of animals are two roles that the princess added to her to-do list after she created her foundation. The original goal of her work was to improve the last moments of animals facing a messy death at Jordan's slaughterhouses. A film portraying the prolonged death of a Uruguayan bull motivated her; it was hit over the head, tied up, and stabbed repeatedly. It was an incompetent job, she tells me, and unnecessarily so. "The poor thing was lying there, screaming." Within a year she and her colleagues realized that their portfolio was expanding rapidly as they tried to fill a void advocating for animals abused in the pet trade, animals struggling to survive in private zoos, and animals abducted as stock for illicit trafficking. Jordan, she tells me, is a crossroads for the smuggling of wildlife.

Her Royal Highness, as her compatriots refer to her, is dressed down when we meet at the refuge. She is no dilettante dabbling in do-gooder work from a distance. Rather she is a hands-on worker with the rescued animals, and one who is convinced that misinterpretations of Islam—the dominant religion in Jordan—add to the woes of her country's animals. She sees Islam as a valuable weapon in her fight for improved animal welfare. "It's quite specific," she says about Koranic instructions regarding animal rights and the responsibilities of humans vis-à-vis the rest of the animal kingdom. But interpretations of any religious literature differ from believer to believer, of course. The morning when we meet during breakfast I read in the *Jordan Times* about an imam in Iran who proclaimed that the faithful should not keep dogs as pets.

"The only actual confirmed saying of the Prophet that is agreed upon by all," she tells me about dogs as pets, "is that if you're going to eat of a dish which you fed a dog out of, scour it." Which, she points out, "is normal basic hygiene. But it's also implying that you're likely to eat out of a dish that a dog's eaten out of." The implication, she says, is that dogs are our house-mates. She speaks as fast as a New Yorker on too much caffeine; she's wild with enthusiasm about her project and its cultural complexities. With little prodding she offers more animal-friendly hadiths, or sayings of the Prophet. "There are so many of them, including the famous one of the murderer who saw a dog panting, so he went down into a well and gave him water from his shoe and he went to heaven because of it."

We tour the refuge and I meet two baboons and two lions, striped hyenas and spotted hyenas, and a pack of wolves. The lions—Saba and Seeta—are en route to a permanent home in a large cat sanctuary in South Africa. The director of the Lions Rock sanctuary joins us and explains why the two captive-bred cats cannot fend for themselves in Africa. "They have an instinct to kill," says Amir Khalil, "but they don't know how to hunt. That is a huge difference." Dr. Khalil tells me the hyenas—they look calm and relaxed in their quarters at the refuge—were fighting and biting when they were rescued from the zoos.

We're looking at a particular striped hyena, which is a local native wild species. When the zoo where this particular hyena was on display was inspected, the report was that he and other hyenas there seemed neurotic and terrified. Their aggressive behavior was blamed on their keepers, who were intent on exhibiting their own toughness by intimidating the animals—animals notorious for their own machismo.

"This one had an injured leg," says the princess, and unlike some of the others taken from the zoo, he will not be released soon and may live out his life being cared for in the old dairy. "He had mange; you can see it on his face."

The hyena, keeping his distance as far from me in his cage as possible, does look scared.

"Hey, Dobby!" she calls to him ("Dobby" refers to a badly abused elf in the Harry Potter books).

"When you call him, he relates to you like a dog?"

"Sometimes," she says, and then with a sense of regret in her voice, "not to me so much. This one in particular is quite special."

Others of her crew call to Dobby and bang on the cage. "Dobby, come! Come on out!" And finally a cooing, "Handsome boy!"

That does it; he ambles toward us. Flattery apparently will get you where you want to go with a hyena.

"What an outfit he has on," I say, looking at the jaunty stripes.

In another cage spotted African hyenas sit, watching.

"Pretty animals," I say, as the crew calls him to come closer to us.

"Yes, beautiful," she agrees. "Amazing creatures."

"Seeta, Seeta," the princess's cousin Sarra Ghazi calls to the cat, and it comes up close to the cage wire. Ghazi is the foundation's managing director. She and the princess are partners in the project—and both exude passion about their work. Princess Alia Foundation workers and volunteers take advantage of new Jordanian regulations to force the removal of animals like Seeta and Saba from abusive or dangerous zoos and other poor living conditions.

"I suppose there's no black and white," she says about different interpretations of when use becomes abuse (although she does dismiss cockfighting as certain abuse), but she offers wise counsel about interacting with animals. "Do the best you can by them." She reminds me of the seven wolves she keeps fenced—albeit in the natural settings of a relatively large enclosure—and explains why they should never be let loose. "We can't release them into the wild because I don't think they could cope. Plus they're quite friendly. They'd probably come into someone's house and get shot."

But the story was different for three hyenas she and her crew released into the wild days before we met. They were trucked to the desert near Petra. Handlers opened the doors of their cages, and the surprised animals returned to the wild. "Seeing them go free, it's wonderful!" Her face brightens with a satisfied smile. "I hope they'll do okay, but it's a chance." The rehabilitated animals are on their own—equipped with no tags, no radio signal devices—to fend for themselves in the wild. "They got out of the cages and they looked," she revels in telling the story of what was the opposite of a hunt. "They looked at us as if to say, 'Really?'" She laughs. "They were staring at the scenery." Rangers spotted each of the hyenas three days later, and all of them appeared to be doing well. The princess is convinced that the wild will provide a better life for the hyenas than the confines of a cement enclosure.

We left the other hyenas, the cats, the baboons, and the wolves at the refuge and retired to a family house up on a nearby hill to drink fresh lemonade and philosophize about the relationships between humans and other animals. But Sarra Ghazi corrected me when I suggested their work was about animal welfare. "It's not just animals. It's promoting respect and compassion towards all creation. It's the animal, the human, and the environment."

"That's a hefty challenge," I offer, taking a sip of lemonade. But the two of them do not seem daunted.

"There are plastic bags all over the place," says the princess. She's referring to pollution and the damage the bags cause animals.

"We are intrinsically all part of one creation," says Ghazi. "What we do to the Earth affects us. What we do to the animals affects us." I could have been back home in California listening to a New Age guru. Despite the clichéd language, the message rings true.

"These are living, breathing entities," the princess is talking about the baboons now and makes a leap, "with equal rights."

"Rights equal to our own?" I ask.

She nods an affirmative reply, and then qualifies it.

"Unfortunately humans are dependent on animals, be it for work animals for income and production, or consumption. Can we live equally?" The princess answers her own question with a quick "no we can't, because of our greed." Human beings need to maintain a balance, she says. Our surroundings at her palatial home are sumptuous, and I muse to the two of them again about the contrast between their lifestyles and that of the Bedouin tent dwellers alongside the highway.

The princess again rejects the argument that animal welfare depends on the economic status of humans. "I don't think being humane is a matter of privilege," she says. "Quite often the poorer people are the ones who are the most decent with their animals, the most sensitive." Ignorance, she says, often explains why animals suffer abuse, ignorance combined with greed. She worries that society is becoming desensitized to violence in part because of our treatment of animals. Most meat eaters don't hunt for their own food, so they're unaware of the conditions that lead to their hamburger—slaughterhouses like the one that tortured the Uruguayan bull. "The more we desensitize ourselves and allow ourselves to do this to animals, the more we're doing it to each other. That's frightening." She hopes the few animals her foundation helps, along with the publicity generated by her work, influences society's relationships with animals by word of mouth.

Sarra Ghazi agrees. "The minute a child stands and has got that rock in his hand and he questions, 'Should I?'—you're halfway there, because he's not just throwing it immediately. You're implanting that question in him." She worries that we've lost our empathy.

"We've become coarse with each other in part from the anonymity foisted on us by technological wonders," I suggest. "We deal with each other anonymously. ATMs and supermarkets with automatic check-out, e-mail and text messages, toll roads without tolltakers."

"We're not interfacing," laughs the princess.

We finish our lemonades and Princess Alia walks me to the door where a car is waiting to take me back to my Amman hotel. In the foyer we walk past the display of a huge and gorgeous elephant tusk. "I don't think that's politically correct," she says quickly and with a laugh, "but for the record my husband bought them [a pair] at an antique auction." The date on the tusk establishes it as taken long before the ban on elephant ivory trading. "But I still feel awkward about it."

"That's an example of how we're always compromising when it comes to our complex relationships with animals," I offer in response.

Her husband comes down the foyer stairs to greet me.

"I was just blaming the elephant tusks on you," she says as she introduces us.

We shake hands and he wastes no time to clarify. "This is legal ivory." We laugh, but he wants to make his rationalization clear. "These are eighteenth century." We look at the massive remnant of a long-dead beast. "They came from Germany." The trade in animal parts is worldwide. There is a global secondary market in long-dead beasts.

"I always have to explain these," the princess is giggling, "because I think it is a bit hypocritical."

As long as we covet animals and their parts, endangered species will be threatened by illicit traffickers and their customers.

CHAPTER TWENTY-FOUR
A Jailhouse Meeting with a Militant Vegan

I ARRIVED IN DENVER AND MOVED INTO THE ELEGANT BURNSLEY Hotel on Capitol Hill. The neighborhood is a mix of stately mansions from its glory days, mid-century high rises like the Burnsley, and some down-at-the-heel stretches. My room, if I go out on the balcony and search for it, offers a sliver of a view of the Rockies in the distance. It also looks out on the restaurant across the street, Charlie Brown's Bar and Grill ("Something for Everyone"). I glance down at its outdoor patio and can't help but notice an entire pig pierced nose to tail on a spit over a fire—roasting for the dinner hour. Its tongue is hanging out, its eyes are glazed, and its hide is starting to sweat and drip fat.

A half an hour in a taxi toward those mountains gets me far enough away from the restaurant to forget the pig and out to Jefferson County and its impressive administration building, the site of the county jail where I hope to interview an inmate awaiting trial on arson charges. The civic center rises out of the foothills five stories high, topped with a glittering glass dome. "It looks like a warlord's castle," I tell my Ethiopian cab driver. We've been discussing the ongoing unfortunate political crises in his country. He's glad to be far from the turmoil in his homeland. It's a glorious Colorado summer day, still too early for the heat to feel uncomfortable when I get out in the direct sunshine. I learn later that the local nickname for the building is the Taj Mahal.

In the lobby while I wait for my escort to the jail, I spot a poster on display. Of course I'm always seeing animal stuff since I'm immersed in the research for this book. But this particular signboard is eye-catching. It's patterned after the iconic UNCLE SAM WANTS YOU recruiting poster, but Uncle Sam is portrayed here with a dog's face and the caption says, I WANT YOU TO VOTE

EARLY, VOTE OFTEN, GET PAW-LITICAL FOR THE ANIMALS—part of a campaign to raise money for a new Foothills Animal Shelter facility for Jefferson County. The human–other animals interface permeates society, so of course it makes sense to use a dog to sell the dog pound.

Jefferson County stretches into the Rockies, a mix of urban sprawl, affluent exurbs (Columbine High School is located here), and isolated rural enclaves, all nestled together in some of the most spectacular landscape in America. When Wellesley English professor and poet Katharine Lee Bates wrote the lines "O beautiful for spacious skies, for amber waves of grain, for purple mountain majesties above the fruited plain," her inspiration easily could have been Jefferson County. In fact, she wrote the lines that have become America's de facto national anthem during an 1893 trip to nearby Pikes Peak.[67]

Walter Bond was arrested two weeks before I arrived here, and Jefferson County—its jail—had been home since then for the self-described "militant animal rights activist," housed by federal authorities who charged him with arson.

Early in the morning of April 30, 2010, the Sheepskin Factory was set on fire. A Denver institution since its founding by Greek immigrant Louis Livaditis in 1980, the Sheepskin Factory—as its name suggests—sells goods made out of sheepskin and other animal hides: car seat covers, boots, rugs, coats, mattress pads, slippers, hats, earmuffs, mittens. Soft and cuddly products, like the sheep and lambs that originally owned the wool and skin. The human appeal of the animals' coats is stressed in the company's sales pitches: "For peaceful nights and happy days," is the suggestion of the advertising for wraps designed for babies and made from baby lambs, a line the Sheepskin Factory calls BabyCare. "BabyCare lambskin comforters keep babies cozy, warm and secure in the natural softness of a uniquely processed lambskin. These genuine sheepskin baby lambskins provide security and comfort wherever baby goes. Wool fibres [*sic*] keep baby warm and cozy in cold and chilly weather while keeping babies cool and dry in warm weather. Lambskins are not only sanitized to ensure protection but are also machine washable."[68]

The damage from the fire was estimated by investigators at half a million dollars. Livaditis reopened in an adjacent building, and the arson investigation seemed stalled until authorities were contacted by a concerned citizen who told them Bond—an acquaintance who had been out of touch for a dozen years—called from a public telephone in Salt Lake City to claim responsibility for the fire. According to federal investigators, Bond agreed to meet with what they term a "confidential informant," not knowing that he or she was wired and that agents were listening as Bond both took credit for destroying the Sheepskin Factory and announced that he had targeted the relocated business for a future arson attack. Later that day, about three months after the fire, Bond was arrested in the Denver suburb of Northglenn. Police released his mug shot, and when I saw it I started working to secure a jailhouse interview with him. I'm seeking as wide a variety of responses on the animal use/abuse question as I can while I try to answer it for myself. The entire front of Walter Bond's neck is adorned (or defaced) with a huge uppercase announcement: VEGAN. But that's not all that attracted me to his case.

"When he got his face tattooed, I just really thought he was a weirdo," Billie Jo Riley of Northglenn told the *Denver Post*. Riley claimed to the paper that Bond dropped by her house two days before he was arrested, that he was a friend of her husband's. The couple, she told the reporter, were grilling burgers, and Bond ate two "beef patties."[69]

Federal authorities say they culled more from wiring the informant than Bond's claim that he torched the Denver store. He directed the contact to the Animal Liberation Front website and anonymous postings (signed by A.L.F. Lone Wolf) claiming credit for a fire that wrecked the Tandy Leather Factory in Salt Lake City because it sold leather goods, and the Tiburon

Restaurant in Sandy, Utah, because it served foie gras. All three were his jobs, he indicates on the recorded conversations, according to affidavits filed in federal court by investigators.

Fire is nothing new to Walter Bond, say prosecutors. When he went by the name Walter Zuehlke, he was convicted in 1997 of setting a Mason City, Iowa, house ablaze and served over three years of a ten-year sentence before he was released on parole. That fire, according to the Animal Liberation Front website, targeted a meth lab,[70] and prompted the band Earth Crisis to write a song about Bond they call "To Ashes," which they included on their 2009 album, *To the Death*. Earth Crisis guitarist Scott Crouse says it makes sense that the group is interested in Bond. "We, as a band, support a vegan/vegetarian, drug-free and environmentally friendly lifestyle. We write songs about things we find interesting and inspiring and that is how we choose to further that message." Crouse and his bandmates were moved to write "To Ashes" after hearing Bond's stories about his brother's methamphetamine use. "We met Walter in Denver in 2008," he told reporter Amy Sciarretto. "He told us his story of burning down the meth lab. He explained how he attempted to confront the dealer face-to-face, go to the police, and that both were ineffective. He decided to take things into his own hands because he saw the only way to save his brother was to stop the problem at the source. It's an amazing story whether you agree with his actions or not, enough so that we thought we'd write a song around it. A lot of Earth Crisis lyrics have always come from 'real life' inspirations."[71] Their lyrics recommend that every meth lab be burned to ashes.

I'm escorted to a cinder block room in the Jefferson County jail. It's called a "paper pass through" room by the deputy who escorts me; lawyers use it to pass papers to incarcerated clients. I sit at a table with prison bars down the middle of it and wait. The door I enter is held ajar by the foot of the deputy, who sits just outside the visiting room listening and announces he'll intervene if Walter Bond causes trouble. I cannot imagine the accused arsonist would try to bother me. I'm told not to give anything to him or touch him. There is a one-way mirror on a wall on the other side of the bars and a door.

A buzzer sounds, long and loud.

Bond enters his side of the room, his Buddy Holly/Elvis Costello–like glasses clashing with his heavily tattooed face: swirls of black patterns extending well up onto his balding pate. He's wearing a bright orange prison jumpsuit, which leaves his forearms exposed, showing off more tattoos. He thrusts a friendly hand through the bars for me to shake.

"Thank you for the offer," I say, "but I've been told we're not to touch."

"Okay." He looks surprised and says a Channel 9 reporter stopped by the day before and shook his hand.

"I'm glad to meet you and I appreciate your time," I say. "I'm fascinated by the case. I'm curious about your background, and what leads you to be . . ." I'm staring at the tattooed VEGAN across his neck and he interrupts me.

"A militant animal rights activist?"

"Is that how you define yourself?"

"Yeah, yeah," he says with a congenial smile.

"What does militant animal rights activist mean?"

"Primarily it means that I'm an abolitionist, which means that I believe in total freedom of animals from human use." He's calm, self-assured, and gesticulates to make his points. He says he long ago gave up just trying to better the living conditions of animals used and abused by humans. Now, he says, "I fight for the total liberation of animals."

I need another definition. "What constitutes the total liberation of animals?"

Bond responds with a litany. "Instead of promoting vegetarianism, I promote veganism, which is the nonuse of animals whatsoever in your diet. It means that I support antivivisection

[vivisection is scientific testing on a live animal]. I don't believe that there's any reason to ever use an animal to be tested as a model for humans. It means that in any venture I undertake I'm going to speak out for those who can't speak for themselves."

He's thoughtful and well spoken. I can relate to his point of view. "And the adjective 'militant'? What does militant mean in the context of your work to save animals?"

"It means that I support animal liberation by any means necessary and whatever it takes, so long as it's not violent to any human or animal. I'm not going to talk about my case but I do support groups like the Animal Liberation Front, which has been doing illegal activities since 1976, to bring about the liberation of animals and the retaliation against those who profit from blood trades. I guess that would be my militant deal."

He and I agreed before the interview that we would not talk about the specifics of his case. I had arranged our meeting during a telephone call he made to me at my request. Inmates can only be contacted by phone if they place a collect call, a call that is monitored by the jailers.

"And the Animal Liberation Front," I acknowledge, "is a . . . shadowy organization or whatever is the right term."

"It is a clandestine group, for sure," he agrees.

"Would you consider yourself a member?"

"I wouldn't consider myself a member. I can't speak on that at this time. What I can say is that the ALF is not a traditional membership organization. A lot of people have this idea of the ALF as a paramilitary animal rights group you join. It's not. It's a set of guidelines. Anybody who follows those guidelines has the right to think of themselves as an Animal Liberation Front activist. So it's leaderless resistance, you know? If two people were at a rally and both of them were ALF neither of them would ever know. This model was set up a long time ago in England so that the movement itself can never be destroyed. They," he says about authorities such as the federal agents who arrested him, "might get one person, or they might get a group of people, but they can never stop the Animal Liberation Front."

We look across the desk at each other, through the bars. I tell him it sounds to me from his description of himself and the ALF that he's a member. He appears content.

"That's how they work," is his only response.

"You're articulate," I compliment him, but it's true. "What's your background? Where were you schooled?" We're both talking fast, taking advantage of the limited visiting time.

"I don't have much formal education, but when it comes to animal rights, I've been around for quite a while." He's thirty-four years old when we talk and pegs his initiation into animal rights back to when he was a teenager.

"When I was nineteen years old, I built slaughterhouses, one in Perry, Iowa, and one in Logansport, Indiana. I got to see what goes on behind the scenes in the production of animals for food, and it was terrible." He was engaged as a construction worker, he says, not as a worker on the killing floor. But he observed the details of the meat business firsthand. "I saw the entire production day in and day out, what was happening. I finally got disgusted with it, sick of it—I could tell you hours of stories of the terrible things I saw over the course of the months in that slaughterhouse. It was then that I went vegetarian, quit that job, and then quickly after went vegan."

"Of course it's impossible not to look at your neck."

"Yeah."

"I was mentioning to a colleague of mine that I was going to talk with you today and I sent your picture to him. He said, 'Maybe he's a vegetarian and the tattoo artist couldn't fit the whole word on his neck.'"

No laughs.

"No, no, I'm definitely vegan." And he tells me that reading bioethicist and philosopher Peter Singer's seminal book *Animal Liberation* reinforced his convictions.

I tell him I've met Singer at his Princeton University office and know his work.

"I started working with animal sanctuaries and did a lot of vegan outreach. I educated people about the plight of farm animals."

"What was the catalyst that moved you from this sort of traditional work to what you define as militant?"

"It comes down to tactics. We in the animal rights community, we're all very idealistic people, and we would like to believe that if we're really nice and we talk to people a lot and they think that we're really nice people that eventually we're just going to change the entire world. I, after talking with hundreds of people and having some successes at that, was just starting to see that it wasn't having the effectiveness that I wanted."

"Was there a specific event that moved you to what you define as a militant?" I ask.

"No," he says; he was tired of feeling ineffective, "like I was just wasting air and not getting enough of results in return. I started to drift more and more towards a militant mindset on it, you know what I mean?"

Not really.

"It's coupled with a sense of urgency," he tells me. "This is the thing that a lot of people I don't think understand. They look at people like me—a militant, you know, militant activist—as if we're doing this out of some sort of pathology and it's really not; it's out of a sense of urgency. When you take what's happening to animals and if you imagined if that was happening to you, would you want somebody to just wait around generation after generation, year after year, while you're tortured and killed and those that are your kin are tortured and killed forever?" His voice is intense and he's using his hands for emphasis. "You know what I mean?" he asks again. But without waiting for an answer he tells me. "I'm placing myself in the shoes, if you will, of a suffering animal." That mentality, he says, is what made him a militant activist.

"Is there a hierarchy in the animal kingdom," I ask for his opinion, "in which humans are at the top and animals are here for us to use?"

"You're in the minority if you think otherwise," Bond replies. "The general populace thinks animals are definitely lower in the hierarchy. I don't take that stance whatsoever."

"Is there a hierarchy within animals? Do you think that a chimpanzee has more value than a guinea pig?"

"No. I respect all animal lives. I don't pretend to be an animal lover across the board. There are plenty of animals that creep and crawl that I don't want anywhere near me." He expresses no problem with defending himself if an animal were to assault him. "If an animal was attacking me, then I would kill it. Or if vermin are infesting my home, it comes down to a natural order type of thing where you have to protect your home. You know what I mean?"

I sure do: Ants infesting my kitchen died by the hundreds in one swipe of the sponge.

"Nature definitely does pit creature against creature," Bond says through the bars. "But I personally don't think that human beings—especially in a technologically advanced society—have the right or the pretext to use animals for the most trivial of reasons."

"Trivial such as?"

"Like the taste of their dead bodies. Or to shove shampoo into their eyeballs."

"You mean animal testing?"

"Right, right," his voice is rapid and intense. "These things are, in my mind, as outdated as cavemen raping women, you know?"

"But it sounds like there is a hierarchy for you," I say. "You define it. If there's vermin in your house, you'll kill the vermin. If an animal's attacking you, you'll kill the animal. So you're top dog in the world of animals, yeah?"

Bond rejects my premise. "I wouldn't see that as a hierarchy. I see that as an instance where nature pits one animal against the next. You know what I mean? My view of hierarchy is an attitude that you're inherently better than another animal. And I don't agree with that."

"That vegan thing is a real trademark." I point again to the tattoo.

"Uh-huh," he agrees.

"How long have you had that tattoo?"

"Oh, I've had this tattoo about three or four years now."

"Any regrets?" I simply cannot imagine defacing my neck with any message, especially a polemic. Maybe LOVE, but VEGAN?

"No, none at all," his lips smile above the VEGAN billboard. "Actually it was great. When I first got it, so many more people in the public sphere would ask me about veganism and I felt good; I'm getting my message across easier this way. Instead of doing an outbound I'm doing an inbound, now they're coming to me."

"And the rest of the tattoos? You're tattooed all over obviously."

"Oh, yeah, I have tattoos all over. I have a lot of the animal rights tattoos. I have Straight Edge tattoos. Straight Edge is a lifestyle that's no drugs, no alcohol, no smoking. It's a stance against those things for the rest of one's life. Straight Edge and veganism have kind of gone together for quite a long time. You'll find that some of the most militant wings of veganism come from the Straight Edge quarters."

"Here's something that could be surprising to you," I say through the bars. "I'm vegan."

"Oh," the accused arsonist does look surprised, and he offers a wide smile.

"But I would never call myself a militant vegan." I tell him more about myself. "As you can tell by my gray beard, I date from the Vietnam War era and I was a Vietnam War resister."

"Uh-huh," he's listening.

"There were, you could simplistically say, two camps: those who were militant, to use your term, Vietnam War resisters and those who were nonviolent. I'm having a very difficult time wrapping myself around the idea of a militant animal rights activist. If I were engaged in an activity to express my opposition to the Vietnam War and someone threw a brick through a bank window, I would separate myself from that person. Help me understand why violence is an appropriate tactic to use to save animals."

"Let's look at other movements throughout history that have had to use force," he says. We're talking as if we're speculating in a university seminar, not locked in a jail dealing with the reality that Walter Bond is charged with arson and facing a long prison sentence if he's convicted. "We have the Suffragettes," he offers as an example. "They threw bricks through windows, they destroyed property, they civilly disrupted the organization of society. Now, looking back at them, I don't think anybody would say, the Suffragettes had no leg to stand on and it was wrong of them to go to that level. We could see the same thing with black liberation movements. Yes, you had your Dr. Martin Luther King, who was an amazing man. But you also had your Malcolm X's and Huey P. Newton, the Black Panther party. And let's not forget that people like Martin Luther King never used passivism as an excuse to not put themselves in harm's way."

"Not putting yourself in harm's way is very different than causing harm," I interrupt.

Walter Bond sighs. "How does militant direct action cause harm? It causes harm to property. Nobody has been harmed."

He's talking about his case, if indirectly. "But if property is damaged," I say, "then human and animal life could be damaged without intent."

Bond is nodding. "Uh-huh," he says. "That's true. There's always that risk of error. But thus far it hasn't happened."

"To your knowledge."

"Yeah, to my knowledge it hasn't happened."

"But why would one want to take that kind of a risk? Even if you didn't care about the people, were they injured or killed the bad publicity would be counterproductive for your cause."

Bond doesn't take the bait. "It's one of many tactics," he says about militant direct action, the euphemism we're using for arson in order to avoid talking directly about his case. "There're a lot of people in animal rights that are fighting by welfarist means, that are fighting by educational means, that are fighting by absolutely legal means. What we don't have are enough people pushing the envelope further: fighting for animal liberation and retaliating against those who profit off of blood trades—by any means necessary. I don't use these tactics or the philosophy of these tactics to negate any others. I am absolutely not against legal activism. I'm not against educating people. And I'm not against good PR. You know what I mean?"

Time to change tack. "What's your utopia? If you could change Colorado and get what you wanted for animals, what would it be?"

"Ideally I would want," he lets out a slight laugh at the idea of winning one for the cause, "I would want a state, or Western civilization, free from animal cruelty. Do I think that these militant tactics that are happening today, allegedly by me and by animal activists around the world, are going to change this moment? No. But politicking isn't changing it this moment either."

I interrupt his stump speech. "No animal cruelty. You're a vegan. But can you be content with others eating meat? Or with someone like me? I eat a diet like yours, but I'm wearing a leather belt and leather shoes. If there were no bars here, would you strangle me?"

"No, I'm not a violent person. I don't attack people."

"Would you rip the belt off of me?" I realize that I am annoyed with the prisoner for rationalizing the crime he's charged with committing as if it were exemplary moral behavior.

"No, I wouldn't rip the belt off you," he answers. "I realize that there're differences in people. I'm not so single-minded to not tolerate other individuals. I don't live in a vegan world. I know people who are not vegan and don't share my ethics. But if you ask me ideally what I think about that, I don't think there's a reason to. You can easily go to a secondhand store and get non-leather items. You can get non-leather items at a department store. We are living in a civilization where veganism is easier than it's ever been."

"Oh, much easier," I agree. "Especially for me, I'm from California."

"I find it harder and harder to justify not supporting veganism. It's really as easy as grabbing that product instead of this one."

"Are you surprised to find yourself sitting here in jail, with these bars between us?"

"No, not really."

"Because?"

"Whenever you effectively resist the system there's going to be ramifications and consequences."

"Are you now feeling yourself a cause célèbre?" I ask. Bond's case is in the local newspapers, on the TV newscasts in Denver, and all over websites that deal with animal rights issues. "Do you think your arrest will benefit your cause because some attention is on you and the crime you're charged with committing?"

"I'm not sitting here and feeling like I'm some great celebrity. Any attention that I'm given right now, it's kind of like being all dressed up with nowhere to go." Bond has no Internet access in jail, and he says he's not seen the TV reports on his case. "But from what I can gather from letters that I receive, it seems at this point in time that people either really love me or they hate me."

"You may be a reverse cause célèbre," I suggest. "You may disgust people to the extent that those who are teetering in your philosophical direction will say they don't want anything to do with this crowd."

"That's true," he accepts the possibility, "I may. But you can never tell what's going to happen down the road in a person's mind. I talk a lot about veganism with people. There're one or two occasions I can remember where years later people came back to me and said, 'A lot of stuff you said made sense.' I'm not your typical bunny hugger–type of stereotype."

I look at him, and agree.

"All the tattoos and everything," he says. "A lot of the times I plant seeds."

"You may be locked up for a good long time if you're convicted. You might not see daylight for a while."

"That's true. With the case I'm now facing and the allegations that are pending it sounds like in Salt Lake City, there's a good chance that if convicted that I won't see the light of day for quite some time and maybe never."

"You sound sanguine about that."

"The fight goes on. Whether I get out and work in an aboveground capacity or I am locked up for the rest of my days, I will use the time to write books and refine my philosophy and try to get my points across as best as I can."

I remind Bond that this book I'm writing deals with the point where animal use becomes animal abuse. "Where's that point for you?"

"That point for me is when we use animals. I believe it is abuse."

"No riding horses?"

"No, no riding horses," he says.

"No taking the dog for a walk?"

"In my world," says Bond, "after we had taken care of the last generation of domesticated animals, there wouldn't be pets. I believe in the exclusion of animals from human society, not the inclusion."

"What if the animal wishes to include itself in our society? What if an animal comes to your door as my cat did? An abused cat. My wife let it in and rehabilitated it. Was she doing the wrong thing in your mind?"

"No, not at all," he says, because the cat came from a domesticated population. "We have a responsibility since domestication is literally just genetic slavery. Look at world history and what humans do to humans. Even when we speak clearly in our own language not to use and exploit each other, we have a profound history of not even honoring that. Given the course of human history and how we've interacted with each other, I think it's just too difficult to know when we're cohabitating with an animal or when we're using it for our benefit."

"So you say keep us separate but equal?"

"My motto is hands off the animals. Leave them alone. They don't need our love, compassion, or use. At this point in time and with the record of animal abuse in society, I think they simply would be best left alone by human beings."

I ask Bond about his family. What do his parents think about his life's path?

"I guess they're both proud. They don't eat vegan and neither of them are vegetarian. But they both raised me to be an animal lover through and through. They both understand that my feelings come from compassion."

He hasn't been in touch with them since he was locked up.

"Knowing my folks they probably support me 100 percent."

"Do you eat dairy?" I quiz him. "Or honey?"

He shakes his head.

"Eggs?"

"No."

"And you don't wear clothing made from animal skins?"

"Oh, obviously."

"What are you eating in here?" I ask him about the jailhouse food.

"They have me on a vegetarian diet. I told them that I am lactose intolerant. I eat everything that's obviously vegan on my plate. We have a commissary here so I'm able to get soups that are vegan and snacks that are vegan."

"Some of the reports about your arrest suggest that you were overnight at a friend's house. There was a barbecue and the girlfriend of that friend says you ate two hamburgers."

Walter Bond laughs.

"True or false?" I ask.

"False," he says, speculating that the Alcohol, Tobacco, and Firearms agents who arrested him told her to spread the hamburger story in an effort to taint Bond's character. Whatever the genesis of the hamburger story, no question it left a lasting public impression.

Consider the sensational approach taken by local Denver television station KUSA and its "9 Want to Know" investigative news reporter Jace Larson. Channel 9 sent Larson and a camera crew to the jail where he asked Bond if he was the Lone Wolf who took credit for the arson attack on the Sheepskin Factory. Predictably, Bond ended the interview, removing the Channel 9 microphone from his prison jumpsuit and calling for the guard to take him back to his cell. On that evening's newscast Jace Larson and his anchorwoman, Adele Arakawa, referred to the hamburger story.

"He has told you he is passionate about animal rights," says Arakawa to Larson and the Channel 9 audience. "But there has been some question about exactly how passionate he really is."

"Yeah, that's right," agrees Larson. "The day after his arrest, an acquaintance of his told '9 Wants to Know' that they watched him eat two hamburgers at a barbecue earlier in the week. We wanted to ask Bond about that," Larson looks with concern at the camera, "but he ended the interview before he had any time to explain."

"Not veggie burgers," smirks anchorwoman Arakawa.

"They were not veggie burgers," ascertains Larson, sharing the attempted joke. "They were hamburgers." [72]

Within a matter of seconds, the voices of television news "authorities" had changed a neighbor's allegation into a statement of fact.

Months later Jace Larson, speaking to my interviewing class at the University of Oregon, acknowledged the error and said, given the opportunity for a redo of his live broadcast give-and-take with Adele Arakawa, he would make it clear that the hamburger was hearsay.

Not everyone following his case is disgusted with him, Bond tells me. "I've gotten plenty of letters from people who write, 'Walter you're amazing. I'd pin a medal on you.' I'm not pretending to be a perfect human being. I make mistakes. I just try to do the best I can. And I get letters from people who've told me that there's a special place in hell for arsonists and to enjoy my cage."

"My parents' house was burned down," I tell him, "by an arsonist. There was accelerant spread in front of the house. I, vegan like you, abhor arson. I think it's one of the most heinous crimes imaginable, no matter the motive. That's why I'm really curious how someone could possibly rationalize arson for political purposes."

He doesn't seem moved by my personal story and instead just explains that arson is a tool for "stopping what you're seeing directly happening in front of you."

"With no knowledge of what happens to the fire? Fires all the time go out of control. Even controlled burns set by professionals right here in Colorado . . ."

"Right," he agrees.

". . . get out of control . . ."

"Right."

". . . and run amok."

"That is true."

"That's why as a tactic it seems so wrongheaded to me," I say.

"It's a tactic that one should not take lightly and should take every precaution one possibly can and be willing to deal with the outcome."

"You're dealing with an outcome."

"I'm definitely dealing with an outcome."

"I spoke with the owner of the store in Denver," I tell the prisoner. "Here's a guy who's an immigrant from Greece. He has worked hard for a couple dozen years and created a business. I'll be meeting with him tomorrow. You and I may not agree with what he's doing, but he is operating a legal business."

"Correct."

"He's an upstanding citizen of Denver. Does he deserve to be treated in this manner?"

"Whoever did this," Bond says, "I'm sure they weren't attacking the status of this person as an immigrant and a pillar of the community."

"But it's one and the same," I argue. "It's holistic. You can't separate these things."

"It's just a matter of perspective," Bond tells me. "Are you looking at it from the business owner's perspective and his rights, or are you looking at it from the fact that this is a blood trade, and he's literally selling the animals' dead body parts? I mean, I don't think anyone would call somebody who torched an SS officer's office full of lampshades made out of Jews a filthy and despicable character."

"Are you equating the business of making sheepskin rugs and seat covers and boots with the Holocaust?"

"Absolutely. Unequivocally I would say it's worse than the Holocaust."

"How can it possibly be worse than the Holocaust?" I am aghast.

"Because animals since basically the dawn of human civilization have been used and murdered. If we believe, as I do, that a life is a life, then what humans are doing to animals far exceeds anything in any holocaust that's ever happened."

We're interrupted by a rap on the door signaling that my time with the prisoner is up. Months later Walter Bond pleaded guilty, and before he was sentenced to five years in federal prison told the judge, "In a society that honors money over life, I am honored to be a prisoner of war."

CHAPTER TWENTY-FIVE

Stoic Arson Victims Reopen Their
Sheepskin Business

WHILE CONDUCTING MY RESEARCH, I SHARED WALTER BOND'S MUG shot with some of my e-mail correspondents. I figured Bond's image would amuse some friends and colleagues, and perhaps evoke some intriguing commentary. I was correct.

"Arson is where, in my view, he crosses the line from harmless kookdom to being a seriously dangerous influence on the too-easily influenced," journalist Gil Haar wrote back to me. "I think where all these vegans fall down is in anthropomorphism run amok. Notwithstanding their pure intentions (I assume), Felix Salten and Walt Disney combined, in their times, to do a great deal of harm to the world. People are animals, but animals are not people. Fortunately, I had a mother who was wise enough to remind me of that way back when *Bambi* was new. Alas, not everybody did. Tennyson got it right," concluded Haar. "Nature is red in tooth and claw."

The Tennyson reference comes from "In Memoriam A. H. H.," an elegy the poet wrote in 1850 in honor of his friend Arthur Henry Hallam, and a poem he wrote to try to come to terms with the survival of the fittest. The complete stanza reads:

Who trusted God was love indeed
And love Creation's final law—
Tho' Nature, red in tooth and claw
With raving, shriek'd against his creed.[73]

From my nephew, the lawyer Alex Roth, I received a reply that's a typical example of his wry humor. "Obviously he just ran out of patience with the flight attendants who kept getting confused about which specialty meal he had ordered," is how he explained the VEGAN tattoo.

"He looks like a gentle sort, maybe once even an intellectual type (glasses, high forehead, curly hair) and he's decorated himself," mused my friend, Tom Steinberg, a botanist, as he considered "people going off the rails in acts of folly and/or violence around strongly held matters of principle, but with dead-end results. The half-facial tattoo, startling touch. Do you see that a lot?" he asked me.

Well, no.

Word of Walter Bond's arrest resulted in an entertaining blitz of Internet commentary. My favorite was posted by one Vixen13, who wrote, "Shame on some of you! I love how people always believe what they read in the news. Oh it was on TV so it must be true! SHEEP, SHEEP, SHEEP! As for the comments about Walter not really being Vegan or Vegetarian. This is a completely UNTRUE statement. The people that were there while Walter was arrested didn't even know him that well. They made up lies to add fuel to fire. Walter would never eat meat because it disgusts him to even think of eating the flesh of an animal. Walter is a decent and loving person. The other article about him being 'Unlikeable' is also a lie. Walter has many friends. Let's keep one thing in mind here. Just because someone looks different from you and may not fit in to your 'Perfect' mold, doesn't mean they are guilty. Please keep this in mind. INNOCENT UNTIL PROVEN GUILTY."[74] *Fuel to the fire* and *sheep, sheep, sheep?* If credibility was Vixen13's goal, then she should have considered her choice of metaphors in defense of a guy charged with arson at a sheepskin outlet.

From the Jefferson County jail I ride back to Denver, past the Foothills Animal Center, thinking about this thoughtful, articulate, demented man. My taxi takes me back to Capitol

Hill where a bronze memorial on the Capitol grounds—called the *Closing Era Statue*—plays to my assignments in Denver. It depicts a Native American, stereotypical feather jutting up out of a headband, posed with one foot on a dead bison he presumably just killed. Quaker slavery abolitionist John Greenleaf Whittier was commissioned by the statue's sculptor, Preston Powers (the son of Hiram Powers and dean of the University of Denver art department), to draft this poem for the base of the statue:

The mountain eagle from his snow-locked peaks
For the wild hunter and the bison seeks,
In the chang'd world below; and find alone
Their graven semblance, in the eternal stone.

The pose and poem made me think of Lord Curzon with the Maharaja of Gwalior, feet on the tiger corpses.

—◦—

The day after I talk with Walter Bond in jail I'm at the make-shift south Denver headquarters of the Sheepskin Factory where I meet the owner, Louis Livaditis, amid the chaos of renovation. The new outlet is just around the corner from the empty lot on Colorado Boulevard where the store used to stand. Customers come in looking puzzled by the disorder and offer their condolences.

"So sorry for the loss," says one.

"Thank you," responds Livaditis's daughter. It's a family business and she's busy at the front desk answering the phone, often giving directions to callers with the explanation, "It doesn't look like a store." Indeed, it looks as if its last incarnation was office suites with a front reception area, and that area is being turned into a showroom by laborers who are working around piles of sheepskins. Livaditis comes out of one of those offices, looking haggard and disheveled. His hair is silver; he's wearing shorts and a sports shirt with several buttons undone down the front. It's a hot summer afternoon and cooling thunderstorms darkening the sky have yet to roll across the city. His eyeglasses hang from a lanyard around his neck.

An immigrant, Livaditis speaks English with a Greek accent that I find charming and compelling. He ushers me into a cubicle equipped with a desk and a chair. Sheepskins cover the floor.

"Let me get you a chair," he says.

I don't want to impose more than I already am on this family in crisis. "I'll just stand," I suggest.

He rejects the idea. "I want to be a good host," and he goes off in search of a chair, returning with one equipped with a cozy sheepskin seat cover.

When his store burned to the ground three months before, he did not know the cause of the fire. Until Bond was arrested, investigators kept mum to him about any arson suspicions they may have had, a silence which added to his family's distress following their loss.

"We didn't know anything until the very end." The family was in limbo. "We've been questioning ourselves: Who did it? Why? It's been on your mind and you're going crazy." The distress shows on his face. "A lot of people have been accusing us of doing it." Not much of a motive existed for that. The business was uninsured, and Livaditis and his family lost, he says, half a million dollars worth of machinery, raw materials, and finished products.

I'm stunned that he was uninsured.

"Why did I have no insurance?" he responds to my question by repeating it. The rates were high and the family was trying to save some money. Business was booming before the fire. "It was our mistake," he says about the lack of insurance. But he was convinced that the equipment inside the building wasn't flammable so he figured the fire risk was minimal. "Knowing our machinery and knowing what we do, there's no way in the world that this thing's going to catch fire. But," he shrugs with dismay, "this proves me wrong. Insurance is a must; this made a believer out of me." Nothing was salvageable; the entire building was destroyed. Thirty years work lost in a matter of hours.

I ask him what went through his mind when he learned that it was a "militant animal rights activist" who is charged with the crime.

"As far as I'm concerned, they don't know what they're talking about." He reflects on animal rights organizers as "very powerful people. They can do most anything they want."

"What do you mean they can do most anything they want?" I'm thinking about his statement from my point of view. The animal rights lobby is growing, but I hardly see it as omnipotent.

"They burned my place down," he says with obvious simplicity. Of course. From his point of view at least one animal rights activist apparently did what he wanted to do.

"They have an association." He's referring to the Animal Liberation Front. "I cannot touch them. I cannot sue them. They call this guy a hero. Can they do whatever they want? Of course they can."

But if Walter Bond is guilty, he's going to pay for his crime.

Louis Livaditis sees a problem bigger than just the criminal who torched his business. "He's governed by other people." He's referring to the A.L.F. "This is my opinion. Everything I'm telling you is my opinion," he emphasizes. "I would feel much better if the law can go against them, for me to be able to sue them and get the products that I lost." He compares Walter Bond to suicide bombers—foot soldiers following the dictates of bosses they chose to obey.

He throws up his hands.

"We lost everything. Everything that we had is lost. It's devastating, absolutely devastating."

It has to be, I agree, as I look into his sad and tired eyes. The family lost twenty-five years' worth of patterns. All their computers were destroyed, as were all their company records. They lost walk-in traffic. They lost regulars who figured they were out of business. But they didn't lose the good will established over the years. Longtime customers come by the new place or call and sympathize with the family.

"You look both strong and weary," I tell him. "You look like you're ready to roll up your sleeves and build your business back."

"Oh, definitely. We will; it will be better than before."

"That's great to hear," I tell him. "That's the spirit that keeps our society strong." I mean it. I'm moved by the spectacle I see: a family roiled by unexpected and unnecessary trauma, fomented by a misguided criminal, a family making a fine line of high-quality products. I enjoy keeping warm wearing a fine sheepskin coat I inherited from my father.

"And this guy said he was going to burn this building, too," Livaditis says about his new operation. "That worries me. That really worries me. What's going to happen, we'll see."

"For now he's locked up," I point out, "if Walter Bond did, in fact burn your place. I know he's locked up because yesterday I went down to the Jefferson County jail and interviewed him."

Livaditis's tired eyes flash with surprise.

"I'm wondering, what did he tell you?"

"He told me that any tactic is acceptable to him in his effort to protect animals and to change what he considers our culture of animal abuse."

"They know their story very well," Livaditis says. "They know how to answer," he pauses, "not intelligently, because I don't think that's intelligent. To answer the way society will accept it."

I object. "I don't think society accepts burning down your business as a political tactic. Do you?"

He says he means that Bond's answer is a rationalization— an attempted excuse for arson. He knows what he would have told the accused arsonist if he had been with me at the jailhouse interview.

"This animal that we used right here," he holds up a sheepskin from a pile next to his chair, "is for food consumption. We don't kill the animal for the leather, for the fur, for the skin. Fifty years ago they used to throw the skins away, and it would be wasted. Now we have so many uses for it, phenomenal uses for it." He offers a dramatic example. For those who are wheelchair bound or confined to their beds, resting on sheepskin mitigates pressure ulcers and other bedsore-related irritation, both because the sheepskin is so soft and minimizes friction and pressure, and because of the soothing effects of its lanolin. Livaditis shows me a skin prepared for such medical use. His wife stops by the office and politely interrupts, telling the story of special arm protection the company designed and fabricated for a skin cancer patient that provided relief from painful irritation. "There are so many examples," Livaditis says. I saw another in the parking lot in front of his store. Two motorcyclists from Texas were checking out sheepskin saddle covers, to ease the burn of their cross-country ride—Christian motorcyclists, it was hard not to notice, who sported crosses on their colors, along with a patch that read, "Damn is not God's last name."

Louis Livaditis acts invigorated from talking about the benefits of his products; his arms wave and he's enthusiastic. "People don't understand another thing. We live in America, and we eat beef. The rest of the world eats lamb. We slaughter the lamb for food consumption." What a waste not to use the entire animal, he insists.

Why was the Sheepskin Factory targeted, then, of all the businesses that deal with animals? Livaditis theorizes that he was a victim of convenience; he's been told that Bond was working nearby on the south side of Denver. But he's nonetheless puzzled. "I don't know. I have no idea. I saw him at the court, and I wanted to ask him. He looks so threatening."

"He looks bizarre more than threatening," I suggest. In addition to the VEGAN tattoo across the front of his neck, there are images of wrenches, probable references to Edward Abbey and his *The Monkey Wrench Gang*, an inspirational book I devoured years before with great enthusiasm, one that influences many environmental activists, and likely fueled at least a few of the activists who choose tactics such as arson in their attempts to foment social change.

"I wasn't allowed to ask him anyway," he says. Marshals guarding Bond prevented an exchange between the two. "We were devastated. We went for two months not knowing what we were going to do, and we rented this place," his voice turns soft and determined, "and we're going to start all over again."

"An admirable choice." I am impressed with the family's stoicism. "It's really great that you're not allowing the arsonist to win."

"No, he's not going to win," the voice turns strong again. "I'm not going to let him win. He's going to lose. He gives us another side to the story." The origin of the fire is no longer a mystery. "He gives us energy to start all over again. We're not going to kneel down because of that. He, or anybody else, will not stop us." He points to the ongoing remodeling and says he expects the showroom to be finished in a week or so, "and it will be just like it was before."

I get up from my comfortable sheepskin cushion and thank him for allowing me to interrupt his busy schedule. But he wants to offer specific advice to others before we part. Insure yourself, back up your computers, and keep a copy of all your important papers. "We lost everything."

I sympathize, of course, but Louis Livaditis surprises me as we say good-bye.

"I'm not going to argue with him," he says about Walter Bond, "because his causes to me, they're nonsense. But to him, it's not. To me, our causes, and what happened to us, is reality. To him, it's not reality. But maybe he knows something that I don't know," he shrugs philosophically surrounded by his family laboring to rebuild the business, stacks of animal pelts, ringing telephones, and a steady stream of customers offering him both condolences and credit cards for enthusiastic purchases. "Or these people," he means the arsonist's apologists, "know something I don't know. But I doubt it very much."

"It's very big of you to say that, but I doubt it very much, too."

"How else can I do it?" he asks. "Should I wish him the worst? Should I wish that something terrible happens to him?" He quickly answers his own question. "No. No, I will not do that. I will let the law prevail."

"You have too much positive work ahead of you to be vindictive."

"Absolutely. In our religion, which is Greek Orthodox, we're supposed to forgive." He pauses. "We'll see. It's very hard to forgive. So this is the story, my friend."

We shake hands. "I wish you the best, and I will say *yasou*."

My minimal Greek brings a bright smile to his troubled face. He laughs at my pronunciation, but says, "That's pretty good."

CHAPTER TWENTY-SIX
Humane Meat

I'M SITTING IN THE BREAKFAST ROOM AT THE BURNSLEY, SCANNING THE *Denver Post*. A headline catches my eye: LOOKING OUT FOR CATTLE BUT LOVING THE BEEF. It's in the "Lifestyle" section of the paper, one of those q and a sessions over lunch during which a local notable breaks bread with a reporter and engages in mostly small talk. The subject looks like someone I want to meet; he's in a business that relates directly to the point where animal use becomes animal abuse. Tim Amlaw is the director of American Humane Certified, an offshoot of the American Humane Association, an organization that gives a Good Housekeeping–like seal of approval to farming and ranching operations that meet their criteria for not abusing the animals that ranchers and farmers use.[75]

"What's an overrated virtue?" the *Post*'s Bill Husted asked Amlaw.

"Exercise," is his answer.

"What's your favorite thing to do?"

"Go out to dinner and have cocktails."

"What would you change about yourself?"

"I would have been wiser earlier."

But along with the platitudes, a wiser Amlaw is portrayed, a former farmer working to make life more humane for American livestock.

The American Humane Association was founded in 1877, dedicated to the welfare of children and animals, at a time when there was rampant abuse of both (think child labor and bison slaughter). The not-for-profit is alive and well these many years later, and its certification program allows those engaged in livestock commerce to apply for their stamp of approval. "Humane treatment of farm animals is not only the right thing to do," the association says in its pitch to growers, "it's a powerful way to differentiate your business by showing consumers you share their priorities and values when it comes to food choices."[76] Approved farms must meet a long list of compliance standards including basics that seem obvious, but too often are dismissed in the pursuit of short-term profits. Limit the amount of stress on the animals, for example. Provide them with fresh water, food, and sufficient space.

A few days after my jailhouse meeting with Walter Bond, Tim Amlaw joins me at Burnsley for another q and a.

"There's nothing pretty about the death of anyone," he allows when I ask him to define the humane slaughtering techniques he approves. "You can't make it a pretty scenario." But he and his organization do not promote what he calls a "food agenda" other than to support an abundant food supply made humanely by growers with a social conscience who act as responsible caretakers of the environment. His staff audits the womb-to-tomb—or womb-to-marketplace—existence of farm animals. Ranches lose points for what may seem like minor violations. Take, for instance, the pitch of a ramp used to load cattle onto a truck. If the ramp is too steep, cows may stumble and injure themselves and each other. His group employs experts—Temple Grandin is a scientific advisor—not just to check on compliance by growers who seek ongoing certification, but also to draw up the specifications that must be met.

—⚬—

Dr. Grandin is a professor of animal science at Colorado State University in nearby Fort Collins. She is also an expert on autism (she is autistic), and her studies include trying to understand how animals think and feel. Autism, she says, can offer us a window on how animals respond to human behavior. "Animals are like autistic savants," she writes in her book *Animals in Translation*. "The reason we've managed to live with animals all these years without noticing their special talents is simple: We can't see those talents. Normal people never have the special talents animals have, so normal people don't know what to look for."[77] This sense of understanding how animals think and feel led Grandin to a career that includes working with organizations like American Humane Certified. She's identified aspects of husbandry that farmers and ranchers never realized were injurious to their animals' welfare, and she helped devise alternative approaches to farming and ranching, which results in a better quality of life for animals, right to the moment of slaughter. Take fans, for instance. "What drives an animal crazy is when the fan is turned off, but the blades are rotating slowly in the breeze. You have to put up big pieces of plywood or metal so the animals can't see the fan," she advises. "Otherwise, forget it. They're going to balk."[78]

Tim Amlaw is relaxed talking about animals at the Burnsley. It's Saturday and he's dressed for the weekend. But his face takes on a serious cast as he balances the pragmatic and the ideal: It costs more for a farmer to meet his organization's standards than to ignore them, costs that inevitably get passed along to consumers. A Whole Foods chicken that may have died happy probably costs more than its Wal-Mart cousin, a chicken that may well have lived a crowded and troubled existence. Chicken eaters must decide with their pocketbooks the value of a humane chicken life. "It's a growing number," he says about chicken raisers who are signing up for his stamp; about a third of the outfits doing business in America are on board with him. "It tells me that the industry itself is focused on doing best practice." Still he says he respects outside pressure like that which comes from animal rights lobbyists. "Just like BP is certainly more focused today on what kind of equipment to buy and not to shortcut." (We're talking while the cleanup of the Gulf of Mexico oil spill was still a major operation.) Amlaw is convinced humane treatment of animals ultimately means a better return on investment for growers because society is changing, embracing not just the practice itself but the better quality meat that often comes from humane producers.

I described what I saw at the chicken-processing plant near my home in Sonoma County: the electric stun, the quick automated neck slice, the backup blood-splattered attendant standing by ready to slice any neck missed by the machine before the chicken wakes from its electroshock anesthesia. I asked Amlaw if all that trouble is necessary; does he really believe that a chicken suffers pain? "If I stab you with this knife," I pick up a piece of cutlery from the breakfast table, "I've got a pretty good idea about what kind of pain you're going to suffer because you're one of us. But a chicken, with all due respect to it—and I don't eat them—it just doesn't look like its suffering pain is that big a deal for us to consider." I know I'm leading the witness again, and even as I make the point I'm not convincing myself. I certainly don't convince Amlaw.

"Oh, it is," he insists. "It is in any animal." But there is a pragmatic business issue at stake in humane slaughter. If an animal dies a painful death, the quality of its meat deteriorates. "You have tightening of muscle fibers. That creates bad product." He picks pork as a good example. "You stress a pig prior to slaughter, that meat is just dark and it won't sell. You get no premium for it." He's convinced that if care is not taken, trauma results. "We know they feel pain. So you do want to avoid that pain."

"Just because we should be good people?"

"Because we should be good people," he agrees. "Because it is the humane thing to do."

Tim Amlaw speaks from experience. On his family's farm back in Massachusetts, he says he raised (and killed) every farm animal I can list.

"I always had a strong connection to all my animals. I was always proud of their growth, their physical attributes, what they looked like. The most beautiful thing is the birth of anything. You are there, and then you are responsible." He recalls sleeping in the barn to monitor births and newborns, checking nests for chicks, and sleepless nights in the middle of blizzards sheltering cattle.

"You're there with this pig you helped during its birth," I suggest as an example. "You raised it. A pig is a relatively smart animal so you know him and maybe even named him. And now it's time for him to become ham and bacon."

Amlaw is sipping his coffee and nodding his head, smiling. "That's perfect," he agrees with the scenario. "It was a complete understanding that that was the process. And I was proud, although maybe it was a little sadistic." He laughs remembering serving his pigs for dinner and identifying them. He would announce, "Here, have a little piece of whatever his name was." Amlaw raised animals for slaughter from his early teens on, "and I was pretty happy because somebody would take it home to feed their family. I had done a good job of rearing that animal to the point that it was now going to be food at somebody else's table and grow their family. This was something that sustained life as a whole. It wasn't that life ended at one stage; it continued and went on into somebody else's life."

A nice explanation or a nice rationalization, depending on your prejudice. But we don't need meat to survive. Why then raise animals to be killed?

"I'm all about everybody choosing," he says quickly, making it clear he's not pushing meat down anyone's throat.

"As am I," I agree, "but why—if the animals feel pain— should we be killing them if we don't need to eat them?"

Tim Amlaw points to the vegetable garden he tended. "At the same time I was growing animals for food, I was growing corn and tomatoes and peppers. I sold them and they were gone. And I killed them. They were killed," he says with precision, "every year."

"One could argue the corn and tomatoes and peppers were not in pain when you pulled them off the vines and stalks."

"You could," he says, and then takes a different tack. "We know there is electrical stimulation," he says about growing vegetables, "and once you stop it, when you yank it out of the ground, it changes." But he's not much worried about the poor dead vegetables, or the pig, in part because he does see us humans as number one on the food chain.

"I do believe, I guess," he smiles again, "that we're somewhere at the top of the chain." But he doesn't view that role with arrogance. "That creates a great amount of responsibility. How to use our talents in the best way."

The American Humane Certified organization obviously endorses the use of animals for food, and it does not oppose the use of animals for entertainment—as long as that entertainment is created using humane techniques. The week Tim Amlaw and I talk a Mexican rodeo in Jefferson County agreed to cancel an event called *coleadero* from its planned schedule. *Cola* means tail in Spanish, and *coleadero* is steer wrangling without a rope. "All you need are two parallel walls to form a bull run, a river of Tecate beer to maintain the machismo, and a *Norteño* band to wail *corridos* as you charge after a shell-shocked cow at maximum velocity," suggests writer Dominic Bonuccelli in a Lonely Planet guide to Chihuahua state in Mexico, where *coleaderos* are popular. Bonuccelli took a turn at a *coleadero* himself and rated the experience a treasured rite of passage. "You chase down the steer, seize its tail, loop it around your leg, and veer your horse left to sweep the cow's legs out from under it and bring it down. Points are awarded for flair, time, and roll of said steer."[79]

Not in Jefferson County they're not, where sheriff's deputies said that steers used in a *coleadero* the month before were injured and not properly tended to after they were hurt. A search of the promoter's property revealed seven steers suffering from skin pulled from the tails, two were found lame, one suffered from a broken pelvis, and another with a broken leg. Animal control officers euthanized the two with broken bones.[80]

But the rodeo went on with traditional North American steer-roping events, and that's just fine with Tim Amlaw.

"When you're down in the brush in Texas and you're trying to get an animal in and they've been out there for two or three years and they haven't seen you for two," Amlaw laughs the laugh of experience, "it's not like you can call them. There are some methods you have to use. Those are tried and true, and you can do them correctly, without abuse." To replicate those techniques at a rodeo for the amusement of the crowd, or to do it to educate, is okay with him. "It's just like 'No animals were harmed' at the end of a movie," he tells me. Depending on how the lions are trained and how they are kept between Hungarian State Circus show times, Amlaw can even see how Vladislav Goncharov's act could pass muster as a humane use of animals.

He draws a line, however, at animal fights. "The whole impetus of a cockfight, like a dogfight, is to turn two animals against each other. You incite within those animals their most base nature and you create an environment that is artificial so that they attack each other."

I tell Amlaw about my interview with Walter Bond, and he's not surprised by Bond's philosophy. "We go through these cycles where poorly informed or fanatical activity surfaces." Amlaw—just as Walter Bond did—cites the Holocaust, but he equates the Animal Liberation Front–type activities with Nazism while Bond calls those who traffic in animal products the murderers. Not that there isn't aberrant and irresponsible behavior in the animal business. Amlaw has seen evidence of it and strives to end it. In Ohio he worked with an animal shelter that used such evidence—several hours of video collected by the animal rights organization Mercy for Animals—to help make the arrest of an abusive dairy worker. "It shows the most obscene, indefensible abuse. Stomping on calves' heads, pitchforking dairy cows when they're in the stanchions. Just this macho, bravado bullshit." Another animal metaphor, this one cattle specific.

The worker pictured beating the cows went to jail, Amlaw tells me. I notice that soft piano jazz is tinkling from the Burnsley Hotel speakers as we say good-bye, providing a discordant soundtrack to the conversation Amlaw and I have just had about animal abuse.

CHAPTER TWENTY-SEVEN

Dairy Cow Abuse

THE GHASTLY VIDEO OF ATTACKS ON DAIRY COWS WAS POSTED ON YouTube by Mercy for Animals, which preaches vegetarianism and advocates against what it calls rampant mistreatment of animals on farms. "Over 99 percent of cruelty to animals in the United States occurs at the hands of the meat, dairy, and egg industries," the group claims, "which confine, mutilate, and slaughter over 9 billion animals each year." Mercy for Animals sent an undercover operative to Conklin Dairy Farms on Route 42 near Plain City, Ohio, and their agent came back to the office with footage that is extraordinarily difficult to watch, even for a hardened journalist like me.

The three minutes of video that whipped around the Internet had been downloaded by more than a half-million users by the time I watched it in mid-summer 2010. It depicts events that occurred during the spring of that year and starts with images of a calf being kicked and stomped on. A cow is tethered to a corral and beaten with a pipe while the soundtrack offers commentary by an assailant. "You're mine, motherfucker," he says. A worker jams a pitchfork into the udders and heads of cows in their stalls, unable to escape. An abuser straddles a calf to immobilize it and punches it in the head, demanding, "Stand the fuck still, fucker." On the soundtrack a voice further explains, "I get going it's just like, oh this feels good. I want to keep fucking hitting them."[81]

Billy Joe Gregg was arrested and charged with twelve counts of animal cruelty, all misdemeanors. In Ohio, no matter how abhorrent the abuse, mistreating animals warrants only a misdemeanor charge. Gregg told the judge as he pleaded for release pending his trial that he served in the army, was wounded in Iraq, and hoped to become an Ohio policeman.[82]

"Undoubtedly they should be felonies," Steffen Baldwin, the executive director of the Union County Humane Society, told me while Billy Joe Gregg was in the Tri-County Jail awaiting his next court date. "He put a newborn calf in a headlock and viciously punched it," Baldwin says about Gregg. "I think that should be a felony."

But Baldwin, despite the rising number of animal cruelty cases he sees in his rural jurisdiction, does not worry that such overt abuse as is pictured on the famous videotape is rampant in the dairy and other farming businesses. "If you're systematically beating the heck out of your cows and then trying to sell them, people aren't going to buy from you." It benefits no farmer, he says, to abuse his animals.

But abuse can be the result of the best of motivations. An example of not thinking things through came via the website of another animal rights organization, Negotiation Is Over (their motto is "Words without action are meaningless"). Soon after the hideous Conklin Farms video became notorious, a notice was posted from Gary Yourofsky—an animal rights activist with a long rap sheet of arrests while protesting animal abuse—on the Negotiation Is Over website:

> Even if the system follows through with cruelty charges and convicts every reprobate who punched, kicked, used metal bars and pitchforks to stab cows and calves, we cannot let that slave-owner Gary Conklin operate his dairy imprisonment camp with impunity any longer. He—and every other torturer and murderer of animals—needs to know that we—as a movement—are fed up with passively ASKING people to stop torturing, enslaving and murdering animals. THE TIME IS NOW!!!
>
> So, in honor of every imprisoned cow and calf at Conklin's camp, for each innocent being who was punched and kicked repeatedly, and for every other imprisoned animal on this planet, we need to gather on MEMORIAL DAY, this Monday

May 31 at noon, for a massive demonstration at the Conklin Concentration Camp located at 12939 US Hwy. Route 42 North in Plain City, Ohio. AND TOGETHER WE WILL DISASSEMBLE THE FARM PIECE BY PIECE AND SHUT DOWN THIS PLACE OF TORTURE!!![83]

That Monday the police protected the Conklin farm with a show of men and matériel that reminded me of my undergraduate days at the University of California at Berkeley in the late 1960s. A few protesters showed up with picket signs that read: SHUTDOWN CONKLIN'S FARM OF ANIMAL TORTURE.[84]

On the Negotiation Is Over site, Yourofsky wrote, "I, personally, will be going INTO the farm to confront Conklin and the workers and—if possible—OPENLY liberate at least ONE calf. I hope others will do the same. If you have a van, bring it. Maybe we will take a cow, too. If you know how to operate a semi trailer, and you can get a hold of one to liberate dozens of cows, please come on down. The Conklin camp is HELL. THIS is a CONCENTRATION CAMP! Anywhere else we can take the animals is better. I don't care if we drop them off in an obscure field somewhere in Ohio. Again, anywhere else is heaven!"

Really? Exactly how would liberated cows fare wandering around an obscure field all by their lonesome? In fact, in the midst of an animal cruelty investigation, it's hard to imagine there would have been a better farm for a cow to reside in than Conklin's dairy under worldwide scrutiny.

Animal shelter director Steffen Baldwin dismisses the tactics suggested by Yourofsky and his colleagues. He laughs at the idea of the "liberation of these 1,300-pound cows," as he points out that Route 42 bisects the farm. "Semis are careening down at sixty miles an hour, and they want to liberate these cattle onto this highway?"

Not that Baldwin exhibits any sympathy toward Billy Joe Gregg, whom he calls not the brightest bulb.

"My mom was the victim of domestic violence. I know that there are people who have mental disorders who are prone to being abusive by nature. I have a theory," and it is one shared by other students of abuse, "that it starts with animals and progresses from there. There could probably be a million different reasons for what gets them to the point that they become abusive by nature. I have this suspicion that they start with things that are smaller and easier to control and move on to things that are bigger and harder to control." He extrapolates from his theory to the accused Gregg now locked in jail. "This guy was a veteran. Of course, I was too." Baldwin resigned his West Point commission in protest of U.S. military policies following the attacks of September 11, 2001, and left the army with an honorable discharge. "This guy apparently was going to classes for post-traumatic stress disorder." Although Gregg claimed to be a combat veteran in Iraq, at the time of Gregg's arrest the Union County prosecutor was unable to locate records confirming such duty.

No matter Gregg's history, Baldwin was disgusted with what he saw on the Mercy for Animals video. "He really seemed to enjoy it. He was getting a kick out of it. He was also angry. If you've ever worked around cattle, they can be very stubborn. They don't necessarily do what you want them to do. And they weigh about a thousand pounds, give or take. You could see a lot of frustration," he says about Gregg's actions on camera. "But a normal, rational person would not respond so violently." For the investigation, Baldwin watched some twenty hours of similar behavior. "It wasn't always provoked. Sometimes he walked up to one [cow] and just stabbed it and laughed."

I ask Steffen Baldwin to add to my survey of when animal use becomes animal abuse. In the Conklin Farms case, the animals in question are dairy cows, so they obviously are being used even when they are not abused. What marks that point for him?

"That's a good question," he agrees. He reiterates that cows don't necessarily do what you want them to do. Baldwin relies on the expertise of veterinarians to help him determine the line between use and abuse. Yet sometimes he worries that vets give advice that favors the business interests of farmers and ranchers over their animals' health and safety. I suggest that the question of what constitutes animal abuse is somewhat like Supreme Court justice Potter Stewart's statement about pornography. "I know it when I see it," Stewart said in the 1964 case, *Jacobellis v. Ohio*.

"Yeah," Baldwin agrees, and he worries that such a definition adds to the ambiguity he faces as a humane society official. "Cruel and unnecessary" is the wording used in Ohio law to define animal cruelty, but of course those terms can be defined differently by anyone asked. "What is cruel and unnecessary?" asks Baldwin, and then immediately asks the natural follow up question, "What is *not* cruel and necessary?"

CHAPTER TWENTY-EIGHT
The Animal Lawyer

LAWYER JENNIFER REBA EDWARDS AND I MEET AT THE METROPOLIS coffeehouse in Denver. She brings her son, Vincent, to the meeting and beams with delighted motherhood. Only a few weeks old, he's a quiet baby as we talk, dropping his pacifier only once. Pragmatic farm girl that she once was, she picks it up off the floor, sucks it clean herself, pronounces it sanitized, and sticks it back in Vincent's waiting mouth.

Growing up around animals, Edwards knew she wanted to work with them and initially was conflicted: Should she be a veterinarian or a lawyer? She decided that dealing with sick and injured animals would be too depressing, and chose instead to practice what she calls "animal law," a specialty she's quick to inform me does not mean that she is an animal rights lawyer. Her work is mainstream law, she says, and she strives not to take sides. Gratuitous brutality charges repel her and she won't add them to her caseload—perhaps this is understandable given that she chose to avoid the traumas that face veterinarians.

"After looking at that video," she says about the abuse documented at Conklin Farms, "I don't think I would have it in my heart to represent those guys," referring to the farmer and Gregg. "I do have some moral objectives in running this firm."

I had alerted her to the Ohio case and directed her to the YouTube video. "After watching that video, I actually cried," she says. "There's no way I could represent that person neutrally. I care too much about animals. What happened, from what I saw, was just so egregious and so disgusting, that while I believe everybody deserves a legal defense, I would have a very hard time not to want to string that person up."

Amazing the emotions other animals bring out in us humans. Here is this demure new mother, cradling her infant, sworn to uphold the law, blithely articulating her own savage response to animal abuse with a vindictive desire to inflict similar pain. I empathize with her Wild West response and find it disconcerting at the same time. Edwards's work is motivated by her love of animals, and her conviction that she can, at least at times, understand their needs and emotions. She uses her horse as a prime example; she tells me she knows he's happy when the two of them go riding.

"But how can you be sure?" I ask. "Maybe it is abuse to mount your horse and direct it where and how you want to go. You go riding for *your* entertainment. Perhaps that's not much different than training a bear to dance for a circus audience."

"I think there's a bond when you go out and ride your horse," she counters, "and go and explore together. Horses like to be out and about. I really do get the sense that he enjoys going out on the trail ride just as much as I do, taking in the scene and looking at nature, finding a stream to play in." But she draws a distinct line between what she considers the mutual entertainment she and her horse enjoy together and the abuse of horses in a rodeo, where the animals are forced to perform stunts to amuse paying customers. "When you're riding a horse in the rodeo and you're beating the crap out of these animals," she sighs, "it starts to become more just pure entertainment to the point of cruelty."

"But how do you know," I persist, "that your horse really wants to go on those trail rides with you on his back? Maybe he feels as coerced and miserable as his rodeo cousins." How do we ascertain across species, I want to know, that the horse is enjoying himself?

"My horse for one," she says with great confidence in her assessment, "would probably throw you off if he wasn't enjoying himself. He's known to do that." Good point. "But the connection you make with an animal," she continues to try to explain what she feels in her gut, "you can feel it. You can feel when the two of you are connecting. Animals let you know if they're not happy. They make it quite evident."

I ask her for examples.

She laughs, because the list is long and obvious. "A dog will bite," she starts with what's common. "A dog will growl. A horse will kick. A horse will bite. They cannot use words," she says about the animals we routinely encounter, "but they will use alternative forms of communication. A dog will stare you down if it's challenging you." She believes that the thousands of years that so-called domesticated animals have lived with humans has established relationships in which the animals prefer opportunities to work with people rather than being left alone. "My horse is not a wild mustang from the prairie lands; he's an Oldenburg who's been bred to be great at hunter, jumper activities. It's bred into them, the utility that they serve us."

Maybe that is another form of abuse—that we have bred animals to serve us. Perhaps even the most benign or constructive uses for animals are forms of abuse, because we are forcing animals to do what they would not otherwise choose to do.

Nope, says Jennifer Edwards. "I think they rather enjoy it. You can see it when my Rottweiler goes to training, how excited he becomes. He's doing something that he wouldn't normally do if he were wild and living in the woods somewhere." She gushes with enthusiasm for what she sees as his happiness. "But just the look in his eyes, the excitement, and the wagging tail, the way he looks at me like he is saying, 'This is exactly what I want to be doing. Thank you so much!' You can absolutely tell," she concludes her analysis with certainty.

The lawyer in Jennifer Reba Edwards is proud of the work she's accomplished in terms of changing police practices in some Colorado cities. She cites Brighton, Colorado, as an example. Her client's dog was shot during a police investigation. The dog owner said that what occurred was an unnecessary escalation of force. Edwards filed a federal lawsuit and the ultimate settlement with the city mandated that police training include specific techniques in non-lethal animal control, something lacking in many police jurisdictions. She hopes the Brighton model spreads so that police officers confronted by potentially dangerous animals are equipped with tactics besides shoot first and ask questions later. "These guys are afraid," she understands, "and end up shooting first to protect themselves. It's just a lack of know-how." Throwing a hat would distract many dogs, she offers as an easy alternative to a bullet. "Most dogs will not bite, even if very strongly provoked." Tell that to the five million dog bite victims that the Centers for Disease Control and Prevention document each year.[85]

Animals cannot speak in court, of course. They cannot write their own legal complaints. But lawyer Edwards believes the day may well come in the not-too-distant future when animals will obtain legal standing in courts of law.

"Isn't that somewhat absurd?" I challenge her. "The courts are there for us. Shouldn't any animal involved in a case be subservient to what occurred with that animal in relation to a human being?"

"We put injured ships and commercial entities on an equal playing field with standing in court," is her reply, "and that's not a living thing. I think there is a little more equality between two living things than there is between an inanimate object and a person." She sounds a tad exasperated by my suggestion that Rover and Tabby don't belong in the courtroom.

"And yet you eat meat," is my response. We're not being combative. I'm impressed with what Edwards does with animal law, particularly her lack of knee-jerk animal rights dogmatism (so to speak). "How does eating meat factor into your animal-loving life?"

It's natural, she says, echoing what I remember my mother telling us as she dished out the pork chops for dinner. "People die," Edwards reminds me, "and animals are part of the food chain. We're all part of the same food chain, and they just happen to be lower on that food chain than we are."

Until the maggots eat into our caskets.

But we're not always at the top of the food chain, she agrees, noting Colorado mountain lions periodically eat unfortunate hikers. "We're all part of the circle of life, and that's how I justify eating meat. It's a matter of utility. Why else would there be cows and pigs? They're not going to just run wild in the street. They're in farms for our use."

An intriguing ontological question for humans and animals alike. Why are we here? What is our purpose? As far as those pigs and cows go, is their only raison d'être pork chops and hamburger? Was the five-hundred-pound cow that snuck out of a New York slaughterhouse and ran up 109th Avenue in Queens knowingly trying to escape its fate? The animal control officials from the city who finally corralled the cow, named her Molly, and promised to find her a farm animal sanctuary where she could live out her life without hamburger nightmares.[86]

Baby Vincent is crying out for Edwards's attention, but I want to pose one more question before she returns to her maternal duties. What about the ongoing destruction of fighting cocks after cockfight raids?

"That happens a lot," she laments. "In an attempt to stop cruel treatment of animals, animals are taken and then they're euthanized." She cites other examples: dogfighting, mistreatment of livestock. "It really doesn't make much sense, does it?"

"Some of those birds would survive a fight," I suggest, "but when they raid a cockfight, often all the birds are killed by the authorities."

"Cockfighting is pretty cruel," is her tempered specific response. "They tear each other apart. It's not like at the end of the day the handlers are going to render veterinary care to the injured animals. They'll just kill them. If I were a chicken," she muses, "and I were going to be used for cockfighting, I think I'd rather die." She's obviously able to stretch herself to identify with her clients.

"But some of those roosters win," I protest, "and live out their days in retirement as studs."

"Is that what they do?" I've made her laugh. "They have chicken retirement?"

I tell her about the magnificent rooster I held at Paul Huln's coop in Louisiana, a healthy survivor.

"That would be the rare occasion," Edwards surmises about the cockfights, but then offers a depressing case study from the cattle industry. "They confiscated hundreds of cattle on thousands of acres," she says about the authorities. "Because of the hard winter the Department of Ag comes in and says, 'These cows are too skinny, we need to take them off this grazing land,' where they'll eventually fatten up and nature will take its course." She doesn't try to hide her disgust and sarcasm as she again assumes the voice of government agriculture officials. "'We're going to take these cattle, cram them into a sale barn where they're one on top of the other.' It's a place for disease. 'We'll keep them there for a couple of weeks and then we'll just sell them off for beef.' It absolutely doesn't make any sense."

Killing animals to save them from abuse indeed makes no sense.

CHAPTER TWENTY-NINE
Vivisection Dissected

In a park next to the natural history museum in Milan, I'm listening to the melodious Italian flowing from Alessandra Chierici. She works with the Hans Ruesch Centre for Scientific Information on Vivisection—its mission is to keep alive the works and philosophies of the race car driver, author, screenplay writer, and antivivisectionist who founded the center.

Ruesch raced Alfa Romeos and won on the Grand Prix circuit until he crashed into the onlookers at a race in Bolzano, Italy. He next steered his talents to writing and quickly achieved the same successes with books that he had enjoyed with race cars. One novel, *The Racer*, was based on his driving experiences and was made into a film starring Kirk Douglas. In the 1970s, while working as a medical textbook editor, his opposition to medical experimentation on live animals developed into the cause to which he would dedicate the rest of his life. He founded the Centre for Scientific Information on Vivisection (its acronym CIVIS suggests, through its Latin roots, civic responsibility) and he published thoughtful and well-documented books and articles assailing the morality of vivisection and its scientific value. The pharmaceutical industry was a gross villain in his works. Ruesch died in 2007 at the age of ninety-four, still active on the front lines of the antivivisection movement.

Alessandra Chierici tells me stories of Swiss Big Pharma conspiring to impugn Ruesch's early antivivisection work, and how the early work of Peter Singer and other bioethicists helped counter the attacks on Ruesch.

"Bioethics is exactly what you said," she tells me referring to the quandary I've been pondering while researching this book. Handing me a stack of Ruesch's books and books about him, she says, "What's the limit between use and abuse?" She credits Ruesch's works with instigating the contemporary antivivisection movement. He claimed his research showed that the results of medical experimentation on live animals are not applicable to human needs.

"It's even worse," Chierici tells me, imploring me to read the pile of books. She herself became an antivivisectionist, she says, when she lost her pet cat and heard that suppliers of live animals for medical experimentation collect stray animals and sell them to researchers. "If you lose your cat," she leans toward me from her chair in the Milan Public Gardens, her eyes imploring me to understand, "it's likely to become a victim of the vivisection business even though it is against the law to collect stray animals and sell them to laboratories."

"It seems from what little I've already learned about him, that Hans Ruesch was an amazing guy," I say about the man whose archives she is responsible for as the foundation's secretary. She swoons at my characterization of him—her eyes brighten and I watch her smile broaden. "Ah," she exudes, "he was a real man, a real fighter. He had an incredible mind. His enemies couldn't cope with him because he was so clear. They avoided discussions with him because of his logic and the strength of his scientific arguments. It was marvelous to listen to him. He really made sense and he could prove it."

Ruesch considered his efforts to stop medical experiments on live animals his most important work, despite his successes on the racetrack and with his novels. "He always used to tell me," and Alessandra Chierici smiles at the memory, "before you are sixty years old you can't do anything serious with your life." Sixty was the age when he first learned about vivisection.

My own first exposure to the vivisection controversy dates from the early 1980s when I was working as an NBC News correspondent in the network's Washington bureau. My family and I lived in Bethesda, Maryland, near the headquarters campus of the National Institutes of Health. Demonstrators associated with the then-nascent People for the Ethical Treatment of Animals were stationed at the NIH, loudly protesting experimentation on live monkeys, calling on passing motorists to honk their horns to show support for a ban on such work. (My wife would blast her Oldsmobile horn, which confused our very young niece whenever she was in the car with Sheila since the NIH was where her father worked as a researcher.)

A PETA co-founder, Alex Pacheco, managed to get a job in an NIH-funded lab where behavioral neuroscientist Edward Taub was researching rehabilitation possibilities for stroke and spinal cord injury victims. Dr. Taub's team operated on monkeys to surgically create conditions that replicated the human injuries he studied. Pacheco used his access as a lab worker to document the conditions of the monkeys in the lab—what he considered to be an unacceptable environment for the animals.

The treatment technique being developed at Taub's lab was labeled constraint-induced movement therapy. The theory was that the brain could be retrained to compensate for loss of normal control. The photographs distributed by PETA of a restrained ape crying out in what looks like pained anguish are quite disturbing to view.

Pacheo's written chronicle of what he witnessed rivals the pictures he took. "Many of the monkeys were neurotic," he reports, "particularly Chester, Sarah and Domitian. Like a maniac, Sarah would attack her foot and spin around incessantly, calling out like an infant. Domitian attacked his arm mercilessly and masturbated constantly. Chester saw himself as the troop leader, powerless to defend his fellows, enraged at the world. It was astounding that Taub and the other researchers expected to gain any reproducible, let alone reliable, data from these animals, considering the condition of the animals themselves and of the colony and surgery rooms."[87]

PETA went to the police with their claims of abuse and Montgomery County authorities raided the lab September 11,

1981—the first time American cops ever broke down the door of a bona fide research facility seeking evidence of animal abuse. Dr. Taub eventually was found guilty of misdemeanor cruelty to animals, a conviction later reduced to one that cited him for inadequate veterinary care—and he finally was exonerated by the Maryland Court of Appeals after years of court fights.[88] PETA, meanwhile, found the publicity it garnered in Maryland of great value, publicity that fueled its growth toward becoming an international powerhouse in the animal rights movement.

Edward Taub continued his distinguished career, developing therapies for the treatment of neurological injuries.[89] The University of Alabama's official Taub biography—he is a professor in its psychology department and he heads the Taub Therapy Clinic for stroke victims at its Birmingham Center for Psychiatric Medicine—applauds his work as effective for patients who suffer loss of movement because of strokes. And the summary of his results does not shy from his research processes. "This work is derived from basic research he carried out with deafferented monkeys whose upper extremities had been surgically deprived of sensation," explains the university.[90]

"In contrast to their adversaries," wrote Hans Ruesch, "the antivivisectionists want the truth out—and that's an enormous advantage. It's the vivisectors who want secrecy; who hire lobbyists to buy politicians, and pay journalists to blow smoke in the public eye; who barricade themselves in their laboratories and devocalize their victims. So others must cry out what the mutilated animals can no longer voice."[91]

No question this Renaissance man knew exactly what he considered to be a use for animals that constitutes abuse, just as Dr. Taub labored against Maryland prosecutors and a barrage of negative publicity to continue using animals for what he considered a greater good than a few monkeys' health and welfare.

CHAPTER THIRTY

What's Right and What's Wrong?

I'M DRIVING DOWN U.S. HIGHWAY 101 FROM SONOMA COUNTY TO Sausalito for a high school reunion. I stop at a cafe for some caffeine for the road and pick up the *New York Times*. A headline on the front page is impossible to ignore: HARVARD FINDS SCIENTIST GUILTY OF MISCONDUCT. The researcher in question, Marc Hauser, called "prominent" by the *Times*, is quoted as acknowledging "significant mistakes" and expressing that he is "deeply sorry for the problems this case has caused my students, my colleagues, and my university."[92] What grabs my attention is Dr. Hauser's specialty. He's the author of *Moral Minds: How Nature Designed Our Universal Sense of Right and Wrong*, and his studies deal with trying to determine what monkeys think based on their reactions to sights and sounds. I get to Sausalito early and sit on the deck of the old barge that is the Sausalito Cruising Club, reading the *Times* story and waiting for my high school chums to assemble.

Dr. Hauser's studies and troubles are fodder for my own thoughts about animal use and abuse. If there is, as Hauser theorizes, a "universal sense of right and wrong" that most of us can agree upon, then it ought to be possible to come to some sort of consensus about when use becomes abuse. I muse about his experiments that interpret monkey thoughts triggered by sound. How can we know for certain what an animal is thinking? The animal can communicate a reaction, but that doesn't really tell us what it is thinking, does it? I put a harness on my cat Schrödinger recently because I'm thinking of taking him on a road trip and I want him to be able to exercise without running off. He does not like being tampered with and it was obvious that the harness irritated him. When I tried to detach it, he hissed at me and gave me a look of sheer hate. But what was his cat brain thinking? Was it, "I hate you for putting this harness on me?" Or was it, "Please, dear housemate whom I love, would you take this hateful harness off me already?" Is it possible to know what a cat is thinking? Most people agree it's hard enough knowing what another person is thinking. Isn't it often difficult sometimes to know what we ourselves are thinking?

My reverie is interrupted by a hello from Margie Finney, the first classmate to show up for the party. Of course we ask each other for updates and I tell her about this book.

"Oh, I hope you're not writing about the same old controversies regarding lab animals," she says.

I disabuse her of that worry. Lab animal use and abuse is well-trod territory. I tell her about my new pal in Budapest sticking his head in the lion's mouth as an example of my research, and she nods with approval.

"So you're not dealing with dogfighting?"

"Not much," I say, "that's obviously abuse, isn't it? In the dog business, I'm more interested in service dogs. Is it abuse to train them to guide people? Is that what they want to do; is it fair to train them to serve us; are they happy?"

She's nodding again in agreement with the questions. "Reject service dogs don't know how to play."

It's a new term for me, "reject service dogs," but it makes sense: Not all dogs that go into a training program graduate and succeed.

"They're officially called career change dogs," she informs me and proceeds to tell me about friends of hers who keep rejects as pets.

As the evening festivities continue, the husband of another classmate suggests I would enjoy fly-fishing. Maybe simply because he enjoys it.

"Barbless hooks," he proclaims as an example of what a fine sport he practices, adding, "catch and release!"

I think: Barbless hooks, catch and release, use or abuse? Two gin and tonics into my reunion, an invitation to go fishing, and still I can't avoid the question.

CHAPTER THIRTY-ONE
Sit, Stay, Roll Over

FREDDIE JACKSON TRAINS DOGS FOR A LIVING. WE MEET ON A SUNNY summer day in Palo Alto, California, at a park where she teaches her clients' pets how to sit and stay, heel, and come—she's been doing business for some twenty-five years as a Top Dog dog trainer.

"Why is it okay to tell a dog what to do, to force it to sit?" I ask her after we've been talking just a few minutes, after she's told me about dogs she's trained to sit with the sick and help rehabilitate the injured (just brushing a dog's coat, for example, provides both companionship and motor skills training for stroke victims).

"We want our dogs to be part of our lives," she explains. "In order to be part of our lives, there has to be a structure. They have to have certain manners to live in our world. It's just like training kids." Plenty of parents only wish their children were as obedient as their dogs.

"You bribe the dogs with treats to do your bidding?" I ask, trying not to appear antagonistic.

"We don't call it a bribe," she says, laughing. "We call it luring." She compares her role as trainer to the puppy's mother and to the leader of the puppy's pack, and says she never hits—all the training is reward based; it's all positive reinforcement. There's no hitting, but Jackson employs physical force when she yanks on the leash connected to a dog's collar.

"Isn't that abuse?" I ask. "Yanking on the collar means you're yanking on the dog's neck."

"To control the dog, you control the head," is her answer. "It's not abuse; it's correction." When a dog makes what Jackson considers a wrong choice, it must be encouraged to make a different choice. Hence the yank. Or she may take a dog reticent to obey a lie down command and show it what she wants by placing it into the "down" position.

"But I'm not willy-nilly asking him to do something without a reason," she says. She's convinced that dogs learn to appreciate the importance of following basic commands, and that they don't accept her training just to avoid the yank or gain the treat. The ideal dog-human relationship, she believes, is a partnership.

"If the leash yank is not abuse and Michael Vick beating his fighting dogs senseless is abuse," I'm looking for her studied opinion, "at what point does use become abuse?"

"I respect their boundaries," is her answer. "Dogs are all about space, just like we are. You want to talk about abuse, that's where we abuse them. We invade their space and we don't think about it. That's abuse."

"Invade their space how?"

She uses a human analogy to explain. "If you and I didn't know each other and I ran up and threw my arms around you, you would tense up."

Maybe. Probably.

"You'd think, 'Wow, that's weird.' It would be inappropriate. Think about it. We do that all the time to dogs when we stand over them and rub their heads. Rule number one: going face-to-face with a dog over the top of its head is pure dominance. It's not fair and it's rude. It's disrespectful."

Don't invade a dog's space, Freddie Jackson teaches. Watch how dogs greet each other side-to-side. Don't stare at a dog. "I've had more people get bitten because they just stare at the dog." Jackson's been around animals all her life, and not just dogs. Cats and birds and snakes and an alligator have made up her menagerie over the years.

"When I was growing up we had a pet alligator, but that was a mistake," she laughs at the memory.

"What happened to the pet alligator?"

"It did not end well."

"What happened to him?" I don't know why I assumed it was a guy.

She sighs. "It fell out of a fraternity house window at the University of Southern California."

"And didn't survive the fall?"

"It did not survive the fall," she confirms.

CHAPTER THIRTY-TWO
Fighting Cocks Rescued and Euthanized

NOT ALL GAMECOCKS RESCUED FROM THE COCKPIT BY A RAID END UP being killed by their rescuers. An exception to the usual euthanizing occurred in Shelby County, Indiana, in autumn 2010. Upwards of two hundred birds were confiscated from a breeder and all but about ten were resettled in new homes, adopted by the type of animal lovers who promise the chickens a world as bucolic as the one enjoyed by *The Little Red Hen*.

"They're so happy they just cluck all the time," Dawna Clearwater said after adopting some of the chickens. "I think it's neat that they can have a great life, just like us." She readily identified with her new charges as they paraded around her farm while a local television crew documented the happy scene.[93]

The Humane Society of the United States (HSUS) orchestrated the raid that freed Dawna Clearwater's flock. The Society's John Goodwin roams across America, looking for cockfights to bust and legislators to lobby. I caught up with him at his Washington, DC, office just after he returned home from Ohio, where he was working to bump cockfight violations up from misdemeanors to felonies.

"Why dedicate so much of your life to saving chickens?" I ask.

"Cockfighting is extremely cruel," is his simple answer. "It has no socially redeemable value at all."

Goodwin tells me he's only been to cockfights when he's crashed into the pits tagging along with the law during a raid; he's never participated as part of the audience. "But I have a team of people that go into these things on a regular basis, wearing hidden cameras. I've probably watched well over a hundred hours of cockfights." He's studied cockfighting magazines, monitored cockfighters' websites, helped police with investigations, and documented their raids. He is the Humane Society's cock-fight expert. "It's captivating," he says about the subculture.

I find that an intriguing word. "Are you drawn to that world at all, now that you know so much about it? Do you ever day-dream about being on the other side, rooting for your favorite chicken, a wad of gambling cash in your hand?"

He rejects the premise. "I don't have any romantic notions of it." He cites not just animal cruelty as a problem, but also corruption. It's impossible to hide rural cockfights that draw several hundred people every weekend from the local sheriff, he says. Goodwin is convinced it's not just the gambling and the socializing that bring out the crowds. Some people in the crowd, he says, "just like watching the animals tear each other to pieces. That's their idea of competition and sport."

Goodwin and his crews accompany police raiders for a couple of purposes. Some rural counties don't have animal control officers and the HSUS takes responsibility for mopping up the chickens. They also help police identify incriminating evidence. "For example, the layperson would look at wax string and a couple strips of moleskin and not think anything of it. But we can go in there and say, 'Hey, look at that moleskin—the little strips that they put on their leg underneath the knife provide cushioning between the weapon and the bird's leg. And the wax string is what they tie it on with. We need to seize that. Or that vitamin K right there, that's a blood-clotting agent, we need to take that.' But if you don't know anything about cockfighting you wouldn't think anything of wax string and vitamin K."

I query Goodwin about the "destroy the village in order to save it" analogy. How does he rationalize supervising the euthanizing of the roosters he's saved from the cockpit?

He's ready with an answer and an example. During a raid in Lewis County, Tennessee, he tells me, he found two dead birds thrown under a trailer. "The intestines of one was hanging out and wrapped around the feet of the other. I can only imagine what that felt like. When gamecocks are euthanized and it's done right, it's painless. One is so different than the other," he says about the deaths, "there's no comparison." He says he's all for finding new homes for birds captured during raids, but accepts that such adoptions are the exception, not the norm. "We're not going to let the cycle of violence continue just because there's a fear of euthanasia. If we let the cycle of violence continue," he sounds like a preacher, "and these places are not shut down but just continue to operate, you're actually going to have far more animals being killed than if you just shut it down right now."

John Goodwin isn't some city slicker unaware of the realities of farm life. When he was growing up he kept ornamental roosters and hens as pets. "They're more complex beings than most people think or realize. They're sweet birds. They don't deserve to be hurt." He rhapsodizes about their beauty, the rich colors and patterns of their feathers, and he recounts a raid where he looked into the eyes of spooked gamecocks and spoke to them "in a gentle tone. Some of them still pecked at me. Some of them still went a little ballistic. But a lot of them calmed down and were easier to deal with and handle. You can really see the personalities and the difference in attitudes and outlook that these birds have from one another."

A few days after the British Petroleum well blew in the Gulf of Mexico I'm at the offices of Offshore Cleaning Systems in Abbeville, Louisiana. Offshore Cleaning employees were on the drilling ship; there's a note on the door expressing gratitude that they all survived. Before I turn off Interstate 10, I pass a pickup truck towing a trailer, the driver chewing on a stalk of wheat. The trailer is painted circus colors and boasts "six exhibits," one of them the unexpected "two-headed turtles."

My appointment this day is with a couple of cockfighters who claim their Louisiana derby days are behind them. Mark Borque, a baseball cap pushed up on his head, tells me he bred, raised, and fought roosters until the Louisiana law changed. In his mid-forties, Borque speaks with a sharp Cajun accent about a lifetime of cockfighting. "I got rid of everything. It was very hard to do that. Roosters that I believed in, like a horse. It's a bloodline. A horse is raised to run. Cockfighting roosters are raised and bred to fight."

He refers to his pastime as a lot of hard work, but hard work that kept him out of trouble. He smiles and laughs. "It kept me home in the afternoon instead of hanging out in a bar. My kids and my wife knew where I was." Borque makes the standard argument I've heard from aficionados time and time again—that cockfighting is a wholesome family sport.

"But to win means to kill the other guy," I protest.

"Not really," he says. "Some roosters stop fighting and the other rooster wins even though the rooster who stops fighting isn't dead. It's a win, just like anything else. You win a horse race, you win at football. You've got to win to be happy and to stay in the game."

"But in cockfights the loser usually dies."

"Most of the time," he acknowledges the harsh reality. He tells me about the two years he invested in each bird, raising it and training it. "I enjoyed it. They were friendly, nice pets until you showed them another rooster."

When his birds lost, he mourned those who put up a good fight, but quickly wrote off those who didn't.

"If he didn't fight, and he ran around and lost, well he deserved it." His laugh is a cackle as he drawls. "I was attached to most of my roosters. I raised my own. I trained my own. They all had names. I really fell in love with them roosters, every one I raised."

"What did you think," I ask Borque, "when the legislature outlawed cockfighting?"

"Terrible." The lilt is out of his voice, and he sounds sad. "Never could stop 'em from shutting it down."

The two of us are joined in the company kitchen by Farrell Desormeaux, the father of the Offshore Cleaning owner. He's a dapper gentleman, looking sharp in a Ralph Lauren polo shirt and chino pants, and he reminisces about going to cockfights every Saturday night.

"It's those—what do you call those people?—animal lovers. They're the ones that stopped us. It doesn't make sense what they did. We were only enjoying ourselves. We wouldn't hurt nobody." He quit when the law was signed, he tells me. "I didn't want to go to jail for some chickens." But he's convinced the law didn't stop the fights. "They're fighting in the backyards right now."

Mark Borque says he spent over $50 a week on feed for his roosters, and he spent more money on medicine and vitamins.

"Oh, those chickens were healthy," interjects Desormeaux.

But Borque tells me all that care meant he spent more than he won, "because I took too good care." Another laugh. "When we had 'em in training I'd touch 'em every night, work 'em on a bench, wipe their face, wipe their legs, their toenails, their ears, their mouth. It was like a horse or baby. I'd like my roosters to look like a photograph, you know? Beautiful. But fight hard, too, at the same time."

It's about winning, they both tell me, not killing. Desormeaux asks me what the difference is between grabbing a chicken and breaking its neck to eat it, and using it in a cockfight where it may be killed. He quickly answers it himself: "There's no difference. It don't make sense what they did," he says about Senator Lentini and the other state legislators who voted to outlaw the fights. "They're a bunch of idiots, I tell you. It don't make sense."

"Which had a better life," I ask Borque, "your chickens or the chickens over at Tyson's?"

"Mine," is his immediate answer. "Most of mine live four or five years. I've had some that were seven years old, nine. Those over there," he says about the factory farm, "only live a few months."

"Yeah, yeah!" chimes in Desormeaux.

I report to them Lentini's point that over at the slaughterhouse the chicken is killed for use as food, not so an audience can gleefully enjoy one killing another.

Farrell Desormeaux has a message for the senator. "He's full of shit, that bastard. If you see him again, tell him I said he's full of shit."

Euthanizing roosters seized in raids is another thing that makes no sense to the two of them.

"Let them kill each other," says Borque, "that's what they're bred for."

"And a lot of people eat 'em, too," Desormeaux says, "after they fight. Some people pick 'em up and they clean 'em up and they eat 'em."

"Gumbo time!" sings out Borque.

The two of them are laughing now and it's impossible to ascertain if they're teasing me.

"You guys didn't eat them," I suggest.

"No, we didn't eat 'em," says Desormeaux. "We didn't need to eat 'em."

"Anybody that I ever brought to a chicken fight that had never been, they had a blast," Mark Borque says when I tell him that the friend of a friend suggested Borque might hook me up with a cockfight across the border in Mississippi, where the penalties were less severe than Louisiana and old-style fight nights were still common. The answer is, "Sure can," and we exchange mobile phone numbers. It sounds like a sure thing, but I can't help thinking of Sherry and Paul Huln and their initial promise of entrée to a fight.

When I call Mark Borque back a couple of weeks later, as we arranged, he apologizes, explaining that his contact felt uncomfortable transporting a journalist he didn't know to an illegal cockfight.

CHAPTER THIRTY-THREE
The Case for a Kill-It-Yourself Dinner

MY SON MICHAEL IS QUITE THE CHEF. AND HE TEASES ME RELENT-lessly about my eating habits, reducing the lack of animal products in my diet to an absurdity: "You don't eat anything." I've taunted him back, telling him that when he least expects it I will surprise him and eat a mouthful of flesh just for sport. Instead, he offered to prepare a gourmet dinner for his mother and me as an anniversary present, and I promised to break my animal products fast that evening and at least taste every course.

That night, Michael invaded the Greenwich Village brownstone kitchen of family friends and shanghaied one of their sons into acting the role of sous chef. We feasted on a five-course meal. I ate the salmon and the tuna and ostrich (after a few glasses of wine), and I transcended my prejudices. The flesh tasted great. But eating the meat did not convince me to change my habits. I felt no draw the next day toward a hamburger and fries, or even another fancy fish dish.

Later, talking with Michael about eating meat, I asked him if he would slaughter a farm animal for the table, and if he would hunt and kill and clean a wild animal for the same purpose. The ingredients for the anniversary meal came from his favorite New York purveyors, all nicely packaged, looking nothing like the animals they once were.

"No," he told me without much hesitation, he would not slaughter a farm animal. He was less emphatic about a hunting trip. He didn't want to go out with a rifle in search of deer, but he didn't rule it out. Hunted animals may survive an encounter with the hunter, was his rationale. The farm animal is led astray to the slaughterhouse with no chance for survival.

How, I wanted to know, could he reconcile cooking and eating meat but not being prepared to hunt and slaughter it? His blunt and candid answer caught me by surprise.

"I don't reconcile it. I can bypass having to reconcile it because the killing is done by proxy, and I am removed from it."

I asked him how he rationalized deputizing others to do the dirty work.

"It's morally bankrupt and unconscionable," Michael said about his use of meat, and he offered what seemed to me like a disparate comparison. "It is no different or worse than buying the cheap T-shirts that are killing people overseas," he said, referring to the sweatshops where the shirts are made. "Children are sold into servitude and are working in unsafe conditions so that they don't live very long. This silver was most likely mined in Bolivia," he waved one of his rings at me, "most likely by a child."

So why are you wearing the ring and T-shirt, I asked him. Maybe you're wrong. Why don't you learn the provenance of the ring; perhaps the silver wasn't mined by a child.

"I work to strike a balance," he said, "to be conscious of everything I purchase and, when my rich First Worldliness allows, I purchase something that has less impact and that I see as less negative than something else."

I wasn't convinced by the comparison. I asked him how he could rationalize eating meat when he didn't need it for sustenance. His answer left the burden on him.

"Every so often I allow myself a luxury that bears some karma."

I was back to my initial question, which I repeated. How can you rationalize that?

"I don't," Michael said. "You can't. I make that decision knowing what it entails, and that's maybe a little bit better than doing it in ignorance."

Writing this book is interfering with my life. It's about midnight. I'm sitting in the Carter House, an uptown hotel in Eureka, California. My wife and I are en route to Eugene, Oregon, where I've taken a post at the University of Oregon. We're meandering up the Pacific coastline from our longtime home in Bodega Bay. Last night we stayed in Fort Bragg and ate brunch in Mendocino. She enjoyed the fresh-caught petrale sole, blackened Cajun style. I tolerated yet another roadside veggie burger. I'm finding I'm reconsidering my vegan lifestyle, now several months old. In fact, I'm reconsidering my vegetarian lifestyle, now some thirty years old. And yet, if in the midst of writing this book, I return to the ranks of meat eaters, what does this do to my thesis? How can I rationalize being indignant about the dolphin killers pictured in *The Cove* if tomorrow, when we arrive for the evening in Florence, Oregon, where the king salmon season is flourishing, I dismiss the pasta primavera and order a fat slab of grilled salmon steak?

It's too late this night to characterize the changes that seem to be swirling through my vegan brain these last several days, and how they may result in using animals in the near future to again fuel my human body. But I realize now, before I crawl into the overstuffed bed in this overpriced room, that I cannot allow writing this book to dictate my diet. If my dinner tomorrow night makes it seem to some readers that I've abnegated a responsibility to other animals, so be it. My obligation to my readers is not to avoid a juicy salmon dinner, but to explain why I decide to change my own rules, if, in fact, I do. Maybe I'll get lucky and the decision will be made for me—the restaurants there will be sold out of this local delicacy when we arrive.

Florence, Oregon, looks like a dreamy oasis, especially after passing through some of the desolate backwaters on the northern California and southern Oregon coast. The main drag in Brookings, for example, is a forlorn mish-mash of strip malls, and poor Crescent City never recovered from the tsunami that devastated it in 1964, although it tries to pull visitors off Highway 101 with its aquarium, where the billboards promise, you can PET A LIVE SHARK! Those live sharks, I learned during a quick stop at the Ocean World Aquarium, are sequestered in their own little tank for roadside diversion. Up the road from Brookings, in Bandon, travelers can augment their shark petting at Game Park Safari and be, as their brochure screams, "amazed, entertained, and astonished by the original and innovative way of meeting, mingling, petting, and seeing wildlife, offering an unsurpassed adventure." We humans are drawn toward wild animals, especially when they seem to pose no threat to us.

The old town section of Florence, rebuilt to capture the tourist trade, manages to maintain the atmosphere of a working harbor city while offering sophisticated store window displays and menus along the Siuslaw River. After unpacking our bags we chose the Bridgewater Ocean Fresh Fish House for dinner, and I suggested we split the charbroiled salmon. Sheila said nothing about my decision, and I offered no explanation, although we were philosophizing all day about the morality of animal eating. The meal arrived, and it was cooked to perfection. Nothing like enjoying the fresh catch of the day, we thought. The next morning I stopped by the Bridgewater and met the owner.

"Dinner was delicious last night," I told her, and she beamed.

"What did you have?"

"The salmon," I answered, and queried, "what type was it?" I figured I ought to document with specificity what led to my fall off the vegan wagon.

"Atlantic king salmon from Canada," was her devastating reply. Atlantic salmon, by definition, is farmed salmon. But I double checked.

"Was it farmed?" I asked.

She nodded. I forced a smile and waved a good-bye.

Later that morning Sheila and I split a tuna wrap at a lunch counter in Florence and headed for Eugene.

I've become a vegan backslider. I'm back to "vegish," and I made the change that day back in Florence. Since then I've chowed down on baked wild halibut and halibut burgers, roasted *wild* salmon and salmon burgers, baked Petrale sole, lox, smoked trout, and cans of Moroccan sardines for quick hits of protein (not to mention those trendy omega-3s).

I'm still not completely comfortable eating fish, and not only because of the ghastly scenes in *The Cove* that are seared into my memory. I anthropomorphize the fish. But I've allowed Sheila's rationalizations, and others whose opinions I respect, to sway my routine. The fish, I'm led to accept, are not sentient. I'm starting to think of them as carrots. Of course there are some strict food maniacs who wouldn't consider brutally yanking a carrot out of its home in the earth and instead feast only on windfalls from trees and other plants that they figure have lived out their plant lives. What's left of them—fruit lying on the ground in an orchard for example—goes this radical theory, is fair game (so to speak) for human gatherers. But the fish and other animals preach to me that I should observe nature. Animals eat animals and we're top dog. Or at least one of the top dogs.

Then I start wondering about all that highly processed textured vegetable protein I've been ingesting while practicing veganism (and during all those vegetarian years). Who wants to eat TVP? And where does it come from? I was finding it difficult to get enough lentils or split peas or quinoa or almond butter (or pick your vegan alternative) into me to keep me energized without feeling bloated and stuffed. Do I want to be a fat vegan or a svelte fish murderer? As I suggested to Walter Bond, how many butterflies lost their habitat to factory soybean farms plowing fence line to fence line? And what about the negative estrogen-like properties supposedly spilling out of soy products, according to the critics of a tofu-heavy diet? In a paean to Spam that I stumbled upon in the *North Coast Journal*, food critic Joseph Byrd attacked TVP and quoted a Spam-lover's poem: "Pink tender temptress/I can no longer remain/Vegetarian."[94] I'm not ready for Spam, but I'm certainly thinking about what personal, social, and environmental calamities might result if we all relied on TVP and other vegan alternatives for our sustenance. These thoughts were all conspiring to create a rationalization for eating still more fish, a lifestyle change assuaged by the fact that I'm not closing my eyes to the reality of where those salmon steaks and halibut filets originate. It's not as if I am one of those barbarians who think fish come from the cold case at Safeway, wrapped by God in cellophane.

Who the heck are we to decide what to do with animals anyway? Of course there are those who thump religious tracts and claim God or gods gave us that right (or even so ordered us). And others who claim that as long as we can make animals do our bidding, we should. But when we can't manage to tame ourselves (read: Iraq, Israel and Palestine, street crime, domestic violence, child abuse, etc.), exactly how do we rationalize deciding we're in charge of lions and tigers, monkeys and chimpanzees, pythons and boa constrictors—let alone sheep and cattle?

Is an animal ever content to share a home with humans who demand the companionship? The best answer I can come up with so far reminds me of our human laws about things like sexual contact or slavery or indentured servitude or child soldiers. If the sexual relationship isn't mutual, isn't it rape? If we shanghai boys into armies, isn't that robbing them of their childhood? If we force non-human animals to do our bidding, how does that differ from forcing people to act against their self-interests and desires? Is a sheep on your farm waiting to be mutton stew or a winter coat happier than one who manages to get under your fence and forage on its own (until it's slaughtered by a wolf!)? You can only answer yes to that last question, I believe, if you sign on to the idea that animals are here on Earth to be exploited by us for our own nourishment, entertainment, and profit. My mother explained meat eating with a simple, "The animals are here for us to eat." I'm no longer convinced, with all due respect to my late mother, that hers was the correct answer. Meanwhile, I remain happily conflicted when I sit down to a fine dinner of pan-seared, fresh-caught, wild Pacific king salmon.

Once we moved from California to Oregon, our poor old house cat, Schrödinger, went from being a free-to-roam outdoor cat to a confined indoor cat, cowering at strange noises and afraid of the barking dogs next door. After living his entire cat life (and probably eight out of his nine lives) wandering around wherever he wished to go in Bodega Bay, we locked him in the new house. All the experts—from veterinarians to hard-core cat lovers with scores of their own felines—advised us to lock him up for a few weeks until he realized the Eugene house was his new home. Otherwise we risked him wandering off and getting lost. Getting lost may have been a better option both for him and for us. He knows this is where he lives now, and he seems miserable. He won't venture out for more than a few minutes at a time, and he rarely leaves the front porch. I look into his crazed or fearful eyes and wonder where he ought to be and what my responsibilities are to him.

Wild turkeys haunt my new neighborhood, roosting in trees and waking me with their incessant cackling and cawing. They probably scare Schrödinger, too. I can confess to fantasizing periodically about turning my old Volvo toward them and gunning the engine. They're not cute, are probably too tough to eat (we cannot, legally, try—they're within the city limits and protected, plus I don't eat fowl), and their only worthwhile attribute seems to be the oddity of their dinosaur-like appearance and the strangeness of turkey flocks invading city streets.

Most of us, I believe, are conflicted regarding our relationships with non-human animals. But it's important to consider our own feelings. If it is okay to squash an annoying mosquito (I'll do that mercilessly), why do I attempt to remove spiders from my house without hurting them? And if it is okay to squash the spider if it keeps escaping my attempt to corral it (I will kill them if I can't remove them), is it game to run down an annoying turkey? Or is it not okay just because the turkey roosts higher on the (arbitrary?) pecking order we humans created for ourselves regarding the animal kingdom (and isn't "kingdom" an interesting choice of word for such a list, a list that is hierarchical by definition). If we give ourselves license to off the turkeys, where do we stop?

Not that the turkeys are pacifists. I watch from my new kitchen window a natural version of Louisiana cockfights. Two huge wild toms start pecking at each other; the ugly fowl prance in a circle making jabs with their beaks, apparently contesting a plain-looking female turkey. She nonchalantly walks around the perimeter of their ad hoc fighting pit, not showing much interest in the contest. Eventually they, too, seem to lose interest. The fight stops and they wander through the yard, now pecking at the ground, searching for whatever it is they find to eat on the forest floor.

If we're reduced to observing most of the animals we encounter when they're confined in zoos or maintained in homes as captive pets (an appropriate term I learned from Craig Redmond at the Captive Animals' Protection Society in the UK), it reinforces our (false) sense of control and our (mistaken) belief that we're at the top of the food chain. We're not.

CHAPTER THIRTY-FOUR
Las Vegas Epiphany

IT'S AUTUMN ON THE LAS VEGAS STRIP. AT THE RECOMMENDATION of friends who stayed there in the past, I've booked a room at the Imperial Palace, a shopworn second-tier casino and hotel surrounded by the glitz of the Bellagio, Treasure Island, Caesar's Palace, et al.

"It's a bargain!" my friend advised with thrifty enthusiasm.

You get what you pay for. Early afternoon I try to check in. Dozens of victims are ahead of me, waiting for the few harried clerks. I watch the progress of the line and figure it will be over an hour, easy, before I get my room key. I hate lines. I refuse to wait for restaurants or shows or barber chairs. I figure I'll come back later, after the rush. Were the room not already paid for, I'd just go looking for accommodations elsewhere.

I don't like Las Vegas much more than I like lines. When I lived in Nevada, I lived in the old mining camp Silver City, hundreds of miles north of Vegas, in the high desert on what was the Comstock Lode. Silver and gold from the Comstock financed the Union side of the Civil War (hence Nevada's motto: "Battle Born"). During the boom years, ten thousand fortune seekers populated Silver City; when I lived there the population approximated 125. When friends would come visit and ask what Sheila and I did there, I took to saying, "We watch the sagebrush grow." No lines, no crowds, no noise, and miles of view across the Dayton Valley to Mount Como. Back then, we called Las Vegas—with dismissal—Las Vegas, California.

I leave the Imperial Palace and join the throngs on the Strip. My destination is the Bellagio; I've always wanted to see the casino's fountain and its water ballet. The sidewalk is as crowded as Times Square or Oxford Street—it's an effort to keep from bashing into the other creatures meandering around this desert. I'm accosted by a lineup of Latina women—all well past the age and physique that would make them candidates for a Strip show-girl chorus line—silently foisting cards on passersby that offer, "Girls, girls, girls!" Cannons blast from faux pirate ships at Trea-sure Island, one ship staffed by women who look like those pic-tured on the "Girls, girls, girls!" cards. The opposing crews yell back and forth at each other, their voices amplified so those of us on the sidewalk can't help but hear their innuendo-laced dia-logue. Next door to the pirates, the fake volcano at the Mirage erupts with deafening explosions and flashes of fire. The cacoph-ony is impossible to ignore. The crowd jostles along. I slalom through it, secure a railing waterside at the Bellagio, and wait for the next fountain show to begin.

Earlier in the day I stopped off to visit Zuzana Kukol and Scott Shoemaker at their compound in the Nevada desert outside of Pahrump. We first met when I was researching my book *For-bidden Creatures*. The two of them live with Bam-Bam the lion along with an assortment of other big cats and a pack of wolf/dog mixes. Sheila and I were invited to come meet the newest mem-ber of their pride: Princess, the three-year-old tiger. The Great Dane–size cat was a beauty. I kept my distance, but—with Kukol holding a short chain leash—Sheila bottle-fed the kitty. Kukol is an ardent advocate of what she calls her right to own such ani-mals. She considers the continuing attempts to outlaw exotic pet ownership a blatant example of unnecessary government intru-sion into her life as a law-abiding citizen, and she rants on the couple's website about the inequities she perceives in animal con-trol laws. Her commentaries often are laden with newsroom-like gallows humor and arrogant sarcasm, such as her reaction to the death of fellow lion owner Terry Brumfield.

The story is complicated and requires some background. Brumfield kept his cat at home in Pike County, Ohio, aware that not all observers were infatuated with his pet. "To me," he said when the five-hundred-plus–pound cat escaped his enclosure in 2007 and wandered down U.S. Highway 23, "he's a big, old house cat. A big, old teddy bear. But to anyone else, he's a wild animal."[95] Brumfield figured in the 2010 film *The Elephant in the Living Room*, a documentary about exotic pet ownership. Not long after the film debuted, Brumfield was driving across the Norfolk Southern tracks near his home. A train hit his 2001 Ford truck and the impact killed him.[96] At about the same time, southwest of Cleveland, Brent Kandra was mauled to death during feeding time for a four-hundred-some–pound black bear named Iroquois at a private compound housing a variety of animals not usually found in suburban Cleveland. The owner of Iroquois, Sam Mazzola, said Kandra and the bear often played with each other.

"This was his choice," Mazzola said about his dead worker's job. "If we get injured, it's no different than an airline pilot getting injured. The food was already there. He was interested in playing with Brent, and when it was time for him to leave, the bear didn't want him to go and just grabbed him."[97]

Sam Mazzola was a longtime target for animal rights activists prior to the attack. He promoted bear wrestling and had pleaded guilty a year before Brent Kandra was killed to transporting a black bear and selling a skunk. "It's a concern to all of us," Mazzola's neighbor and retired Cleveland cop Raymond O'Leary told reporters about the private zoo after Kandra was mauled. "We can hear animals in the evening at feeding time roaring over there."[98] Animal ownership is all but unrestricted in Ohio, and lobbyists for the Humane Society of the United States and other organizations that oppose private exotic animal ownership used the two deaths to call attention to their cause. On what would have been Brent Kandra's twenty-fifth birthday, a Cleveland Heights showing of *The Elephant in the Living Room* was dedicated to his memory.

Zuzana Kukol responded to the film—featuring the late Terry Brumfield and the show dedicated to the late Brent Kandra—in typical form. "Now this is as idiotic, pathetic, self-serving as it gets," she wrote. "This is pure propaganda to help HSUS in Ohio ban exotics, playing on heart strings, OMG. I am grossed out. One of the main 'stars' of this movie, the lion owner, Terry Brumfield, just died recently after being hit by a train in his truck. How ironic," her tirade continues. "How real life—TRAIN DEATH—even though he owned lions, truck on train tracks got him. NOT HIS LIONS! How about," her rant doesn't stop yet, "honoring all the train fatality victims from now on to keep with the theme, and ban trains and trucks, too, so people like Terry Brumfield don't have to die that way ever again . . . ???" She adds a parenthetical, "Yeah, insert my usual sarcasm," and then after signing her name, notes, "Still holding my barf bag."

Mahatma Gandhi is often quoted as preaching, "The greatness of a nation and its moral progress can be judged by the way its animals are treated." It's a compelling line, but I've been unable to verify that the quote originated with him, unable to find its source in his writings or speeches. The International Vegetarian Union notes that Gandhi wrote in his autobiography that he read *The Ethics of Diet—A Catena of Authorities Deprecatory of the Practice of Flesh-Eating*, a collection published in 1883 by Howard Williams. In it Williams quotes the German theologian David Strauss as writing, "The manner in which a nation, in aggregate, treats the other species, is one chief measure of its real civilization."[99] No matter the origin of the sentiment, it's become a mantra of animal rights organizations.

But perhaps that fine line requires an antecedent; maybe before we cite the other animals we ought to consider the likelihood that the greatness of a nation and its moral progress can be judged by the way it treats its people and the way each person treats herself or himself. How can we expect to care for other species if we don't care for ourselves?

These questions bring to mind the commentary of one of Gandhi's contemporaries, Mark Twain. In his 1906 essay "The Lowest Animal," Twain takes issue with Darwin's theory of the ascent of man from the so-called lower animals and announces that his research proves the opposite, what he calls the Descent of Man from the Higher Animals. He cites a long list of examples: greed, revenge, slavery, nationalism, and religion. In typical Twain fashion, he concludes that "we have reached the bottom stage of development—nameable as the Human Being. Below us—nothing. Nothing but the Frenchman."[100]

I'm thinking about these contradictions as the Bellagio fountain performance begins. It is an amazing and delightful spectacle—if a tad schmaltzy. Andrea Bocelli and Sarah Brightman belt out their hot hit "Time to Say Goodbye" over massive loudspeakers, as the precious water dances in the urban desert. The jets push the cascading water ever higher. It pulses and undulates, explodes with surprise, and lies down after an exuberant crescendo.

I fight the crowd back to the Imperial Palace. The check-in line has decreased and I wait only a few minutes before a cheerful clerk informs me that I've been "upgraded" to a penthouse. Minutes later Sheila and I open the door to suite number 1935, a slightly tattered throwback to the Strip's 1960s heyday, complete with colonnaded Jacuzzi in the vast bedroom, a huge plasma TV in the living room where the fireplace ought to be, a sprawling bar, and a mirrored dining room equipped with a sprawling glass-topped table. I check out the unobstructed view from high above the swirling masses on the Strip, looking far beyond the Vegas sprawl deep into the endless desert alive, I know from my days in Silver City, with all sorts of wildlife.

The Strip noise, the revelers wandering from casino to casino drinking from their huge tequila go cups, the "Girls, girls, girls!" cards, the mind-numbing assault that I always feel when I'm subjected to Vegas—including the bizarre luxury of the penthouse—conspire to remind me that we humans don't just abuse other animals. We abuse ourselves all the time. Las Vegas strikes me as twisted self-flagellation.

My visceral reaction to Vegas reminds me that while we continue abusing one another we're in a poor position to judge what is or is not animal abuse. As long as we're cruel to each other overtly, or by doing things like ignoring our countries' leaders as they torture and kill others in our names (while we enjoy a lack of proximity to the crimes and wrap them in the pseudo-sanctuary of legality), we're all abusing animals. As long as we continue allowing our neighbors to starve while we luxuriate in excess, our moral authority is in serious jeopardy. But I don't suggest we must wallow in despair at the human condition. Hope flourishes with continuing examples of selfless individual acts of human sensitivity and kindness. I remind myself of the Velvet Revolution I was surrounded by when I was reporting from the joyous streets of Prague in 1989, and of the outpouring of international aid to a Haiti overwhelmed by earthquake in 2010. As I'm finishing this book, a Tunisian dictator was just chased from his lavish lair by a mostly peaceful populace moved to action because an impoverished vegetable peddler became a symbol of basic human dignity and decency. And there was animal abuse in the Tunisian story: U.S. ambassador Robert Godec reported in one of the secret State Department cables released by Wikileaks that the dictator's son-in-law kept a "pet" tiger in a cage at the family's compound, feeding it four chickens a day. The diplomat's descriptions of the opulence he observed during a visit with the ruling family fueled the Jasmine Revolution.[101]

Yet for me, the Las Vegas Strip continues to epitomize human abuse—an assault on self-esteem, a pandering to all that is base—all wrapped up in a package tour of escapism. The day before I arrived in Las Vegas I was wandering in the peace and quiet and solitude of Death Valley. Now I was surrounded by mind-numbing self-indulgence as the city consumed water in the thirsty Southwest and electricity generated by power plants that spewed smog into the desert sky. We abuse ourselves. We abuse the Earth. Is it any wonder that dogs get kicked?

Shortly after I left Las Vegas, the Smithsonian yanked the short film "Fire In My Belly" by David Wojnarowic out of the National Portrait Gallery. Objections to the film came from House Speaker John Boehner, who announced that he wanted the exhibition "cancelled" as he threatened the Smithsonian's federal funding.[102] Speaker Boehner heard about the film not because he frequents Washington's museums but because William Donohue, the president of a far right-wing organization called The Catholic League (which enjoys no official connection with the Catholic Church[103]), complained to the congressman's office about a brief sequence in the film that shows ants crawling on a crucifix. Not mentioned during the assault on the film (which is easy to view from the comfort of your La-Z-Boy via YouTube) are the close-ups of cockfighting and bullfighting scenes in the original, interspersed with human-on-human fights. One rooster kills another, leaving it a mess of gory feathers. The matador attacks the bull.

A taxpayer-supported gallery caved in to self-promoting complainers who claimed the film in question shows ants abusing an image of a crucified Jesus and/or is an example of an artist abusing a religious symbol. Even a cursory study of Wojnarowic's work suggests nothing of the sort—not that the meaning of or motivation for the work should matter once it was chosen for exhibition by the Smithsonian's curators. Animal abuse: the animals in this case being us, the body politic, abusing each other.

I returned to Eugene, the seemingly quiet college city that is now my new hometown, and encountered a crime scene just down the street from my house. During what police said was an attempted robbery, the clerk at a drive-through coffee kiosk shot and killed another man—the one he identified as the bandit. I wrote an op-ed for our local newspaper suggesting vulnerable drive-up businesses adopt a credit and debit card only policy to eliminate the lure of late night cash in a lonely till. The mindless ravings that choked the comment page on the newspaper's website over the next few days were sobering.

"Give 'em all a gun," wrote one commentator. "No paperwork, no court costs. No more robberies."

"Give the guy who shot the low-life thief a medal and a reward," said another.

"Shoot 'em!" agreed a third.

"I am proud of the employee who saved us taxpayers the price of garbage being housed in a jail with free health care, education opportunities, free meals, bed, and entertainment," preached another anonymous correspondent. "The only housing they should ever have is that of eternity-in-a-box."[104]

Nothing about due process from these new neighbors of mine, just mob rule shrouded in anonymity.

At about the same time of the coffee kiosk shooting, I was asked to comment on the Great Ape Project, an idea traced to an anthology edited by philosopher Peter Singer and Palola Cavalieri. Essays in the book argue that other primates express human-like emotions and intelligence.[105] What did I think, I was asked by a couple of students at the University of Oregon, about proposals by anthropologists, bio-ethicists, lawyers, philosophers, and other such experts who organized the global project in the mid-1990s to extend to our close primate cousins the right to life, the protection of individual liberty, and the prohibition of torture?

An idea worth considering, perhaps, was my answer, but shouldn't we take care of each other first? Humans continue to fail miserably when they attempt to provide such rights to other humans. Our priorities should be to guarantee humans dignity and respect, and if we do that perhaps we will be in a position to consider extending them to other species. Or might it be easier for us to start the experiment with the non-humans, animals that exhibit innocence and don't talk back. In a perfect world we could do that work simultaneously, but given our obscene failures at extending the rights the Great Ape Project advocates to our fellow human apes, we're in a weak position to expect we can offer it to the other apes. We engage in capital punishment, confine others without due process, and we torture—and that's the government of the United States, considered (at least by many of us here in the States) to be an epitome of democratic regimes. Can we be expected to treat other animals better than we treat ourselves?

"You have just dined," Ralph Waldo Emerson wrote in his essay on fate, "and, however scrupulously the slaughter-house is concealed in the graceful distance of miles, there is complicity."[106]

EPILOGUE

Of course plenty of animals—despite the wishful thinking behind the title of this book—were harmed during its writing. Impossible to avoid, dear reader, from the bugs squashed on my car windshield during countless miles of research trips to the gamecocks I watched assault each other when I finally encountered a cockfight in Puerto Rico.

The passengers applauded as our plane touched down late on a Sunday night at the San Juan airport, depositing me into one of America's lingering colonies, and one of the places under the Stars and Stripes where cockfighting is still legal. Just after seven the next morning I take a stroll on my local tropical paradise beach. I've moved into a hotel in the supposedly swanky Condado Beach neighborhood. Cartier is on the corner and Gucci a block down. But nestled around them are vacant lots used for parking and trash, and old hotels and apartments that have seen better days. Much better days. Paint is peeling; air conditioners and window bars are rusting. A diamond's throw from Cartier are fast-food joints, tattoo parlors, and condom retailers. Five-star resorts line the beach side of the street. The ocean is that seductive deep tropical blue that matches the sky and contrasts with glistening vibrancy behind the greens of the palm fronds and the whites of the billowing clouds lolling eastbound toward the Virgin Islands (another U.S. territory where cockfighting is legal).

From Condado, it's just minutes east to an exclusive beach community, Isla Verde, home of my Puerto Rico quest, the Club Gallistíco. The route offers more examples of Puerto Rico's extremes. Glorious wide sandy beaches mix with decaying housing projects and debris-strewn vacant lots.

But I was there for the cockfights.

Club Gallistíco del Puerto Rico operates out of a nondescript two-story concrete building, nondescript except that over the entrance it features a low-key plastic sign on its facade announcing:

COCKFIGHTS. The club sits in the middle of a parking lot across the street from exclusive resorts and their perfect beaches, just a cock's crow from more rundown public housing projects, more junk-filled vacant lots, and uninspiring strip malls offering rum-soaked tourists more tattoos and condoms.

I walked around an unmanned metal detector up steep steps to the box office and paid my twenty bucks (plus tax) for one of the best seats in the house.

"¿*Qué cerca?*" I asked the guy at the box office. How close would I be to the chickens?

"¡*Muy cerca!*" was his answer, and he offered a knowing smile.

I wade into a cacophony of roosters crowing, a Phil Spector–like wall of sound literally coming from a wall of fowl. The birds scheduled to fight this day are waiting their turns sequestered in ventilated clear plastic boxes arranged so that we spectators can study them before the fights, assessing their "gameness," as my Cajun cockfighting informant Paul Huln would say. They do look chopped and channeled to me, reminiscent of a 1951 Ford Victoria coupe I owned years ago.

I notice that their natural spurs have been removed, so attack spears can be attached instead. Their underfeathers are plucked to the skin so I can see their breasts and drumsticks on display like the meat they are, looking ready for the frying pan. Their wing feathers are left intact, but their backs are bare. All this customizing is designed to lighten their load so that they can maneuver with agility once they're let loose to fight in the pit. The effect makes them look as if they lost their pants, as if they're naked from the waist—if they had one—down to their feet. The contrast of the brilliant plumage that's left in place with the naked legs suggests burlesque strippers on stage.

I find myself thinking of Winston Churchill again. Legend, perhaps apocryphal, claims he asked for chicken breast at a fancy dinner party in Virginia and was told by a woman sitting next to him that his language was inappropriate, that he should have asked for white meat. The next day, goes the tale, Churchill dispatched a corsage to his tablemate along with a note that read, "Pin this on your white meat."[107]

The remaining fowl feathers are gorgeous: from solid whites to vibrant reds and blacks and browns, some dabbled and some striated. Their tail plumage is groomed to local standards of pre-battle perfection, waving proud and high.

I'm early. Bird breeders and their helpers are busy strapping weapons on the fowl. Here in Puerto Rico the spears are plastic and a club monitor carefully measures them to ensure that they don't exceed the legal limit. They're far shorter than the gaffs and knives my neighbor Lanny showed off to me in Nevada or the ones Bob Garcia keeps on display at his Sonoma County animal control office. *Deporte Cultural de Puerto Rico* reads a sign. A poster on the wall praises *San Andres Patron de los Galleros*, and shows the good saint in monkish garb appearing to bless a pair of fighting cocks about to do battle.

My seat is in the second row from the pit. There is no formal opening ceremony and I watch as a clear plastic box is lowered on a cable from the ceiling. It's the transport vehicle from the death row of soon-to-be-fighting cocks the other spectators and I had been studying. A Rube Goldberg apparatus scoots the transport box from the preparation room to high above the pit and then it drops slowly. In its two compartments are the combatants, separated by an opaque wall so that they cannot see each other, but the chickens are on dramatic view to the audience. Once the transit box reaches the pit, handlers grab the birds and stuff them into large bags. They hang the bags on a balance to ensure a fair weight match. Then they place them far apart on the Astroturf-covered pit and antagonize them with a dummy rooster, slapping them across the face (do roosters have faces?). A handler grabs each fighter and they swat their heads at each other.

The ready-to-fight birds are transferred into still another partitioned clear plastic box. They face each other, tail feathers high, and the bottomless box rises. Without a pause they attack, leaping into the air and at each other. They peck at each other. Most of the action is pecking. Of course roosters engage in this type of behavior without human provocation. That's how the ubiquitous cliché "pecking order" entered our vernacular.

I watch a dominating rooster stomping on its opponent, continuing to peck at it. Blood is smearing ringside on the vinyl-covered barrier that marks its perimeter. Feathers fly down and stick to the fake grass. Between bouts the blood is wiped off the vinyl and one of the handlers grabs a Dustbuster to suck up the lost feathers.

A routine sets in. The bird-filled box drops. The handlers tease the birds and release them to fight. The birds attack each other. They jump and the scene literally is a flurry of feathers. They land and peck at each other. The loser falters, stumbles, and often lies motionless on the Astroturf and yet often rises with amazing vigor to make a few more desperate pecks at his attacker before resigning in total collapse. Some matches are decided on points, both birds still standing and pecking when the buzzer announces time is up, but bloody and ruffled.

The bird-filled box drops again. A feisty bird jumps at a harassing handler. He runs from the cock, spectators laugh, and the handler checks his jeans for an embarrassing tear.

The crowd is mostly middle-aged and older, and all *hombres*. Plenty of beer bellies. Casual clothes: slacks and sports shirts. They chat like pals relaxing on a park bench, telling stories. This Tuesday afternoon it's not much of a crowd, just a few dozen. But as soon as a new fight starts, they turn their attention to the pit and come alive and start pointing at each other, waving wads of cash, shouting numbers, and nodding acknowledgments. The wagering obviously is the primary draw here, not the repetitious rooster pecking, the chaotic ballet of blood and feathers. The fights can't be the main attraction; they're much too similar and predictable. The wagering is the draw along with the ritual: the care and feeding of the animals, the breeding and the training, the meticulous preparations for combat, and the camaraderie. The handlers return a wet-with-blood winner back to his owner, an envelope of winning cash placed on the rooster's soaked feathers. I don't see much blood lust exhibited by the audience when the victors show their dominance. The faces in the crowd often express a bored-looking reaction to what is commonplace for them, what you might see in the stands at a ballpark in the bottom of the ninth with a lopsided score. Of course there are exceptions. One fellow cheers his rooster on, yelling instructions at him with great passion and amusing the crowd with his cheerleader antics.

That initial jump—when the two birds first engage—can look quite dramatic. It's a flash of colorful plumage in flight that's even pretty, coming as it does before the carnage.

I look at the sodden white feathers of a fighter sopped with blood as he attacks over and over again. His bloody opponent no longer responds and falls, looking quite dead. *Blanco* kicks the downed bird a few times, steps on him, and the buzzer sounds. Out comes the Dustbuster. Bills change hands as the Plexiglas box drops with another couple of birds prepared for show time.

A waitress walks around the cockpit chewing gum. Her jet-black hair is pulled back, and she's sporting distressed jeans, a bare midriff, and her "white meat" is spilling out of the top of her blouse. She catches the eyes of the *hombres*, distracting them momentarily from their rooster studies as she seeks drink orders.

After several fights I realize I am finding the bouts tedious: two more chickens, flying feathers, blood, the buzzer, and the cash exchange. It's no fun for me to watch: two healthy birds reduced in minutes to battered, bleeding, and maybe dead things.

But is it animal abuse? I consider the words of the Cajun cockfighter who tutored me in Louisiana: "They're not animals, Peter. They're just chickens." The birds could just walk away from each other, couldn't they? They don't, of course. They fight. But the chickens electroshocked before their necks get slit at the California slaughterhouse I visited don't even get a fighting chance. One after another I watch as the roosters fight each other. It's disgusting to watch them make chopped meat of each other, the brutality almost nauseating at times. No question it's not my sport. But I'm no football fan either.

Another box, two more birds. And a surprise! One of the birds *does* run out of the pit. The other bird chases the escapee, who keeps running and leaps into the stands. But his liberty is short lived. A referee jumps up and grabs them both. He carries them to the center of the pit, spots them on the fake grass, and restarts the match. It's not much of a battle. The escapee is no street fighter and is fast lying in a heap, then carried out of the pit by a handler. Now this act is starting to feel like animal abuse to me. A runaway would not be forced to fight if *I* ran Club Gallistíco.

I keep watching. A pair of particularly aggressive fighters takes center stage. They jump and fly at each other repeatedly. Their animated behavior excites the crowd; bets are yelled along with encouragement for a favored rooster. For a moment it appears that both birds are dead. They're laying prone in the pit. But they get up again phoenix-like and stumble toward each other. Finally the buzzer sounds and the human interest no longer is directed at the birds, it's focused on the cash changing hands.

Enough. I've been watching this spectacle for over an hour. My journalistic duty is done. I leave my ringside seat and walk out into the warm Puerto Rican evening. When the door closes behind me, the bizarre activity I just witnessed stays in its nondescript building, sequestered behind the simple sign that announces COCKFIGHTS. My experiences as a reporter covering wars and pestilence, natural disasters, and crime must inure me from being debilitated by what my radio colleague David McQueen calls "the dismal details of the daily downer," cockfights included. I'm hungry and ready for dinner. Next door is the Metropol restaurant, and it gets an acceptable review in my San Juan guidebook.

A clipping from the *New York Times* is posted at the restaurant's front door headlined, WHAT'S DOING IN SAN JUAN. The article features the Metropol's Cornish game hen stuffed with black beans and rice, and sure enough the menu is as alive with poultry as is the Club Gallistíco next door. One-half *pollo grille* goes for $10.95. For the kiddies, Metropol offers chicken wings and chicken nuggets. Listed under House Specialties I find the *Times* favorite and $13.95 buys the stuffed Cornish game hen.

Tell that to the roosters next door.

ACKNOWLEDGMENTS

As I finish this third book of my animal trilogy, I cannot help but think of the late Jane Foulds, the Butterfly Lady of Granada, who invited me to her butterfly reserve in Nicaragua. Her paradise was the first stop in what became my worldwide quest to gain a better understanding of the relationship between us humans and the rest of the animal kingdom. A Coca-Cola toast to you, Jane.

For *No Animals Were Harmed*, University of Oregon School of Journalism and Communication graduate teaching fellow Lisa Rummler provided valuable research assistance and was a delight to work with. Thanks to Charles Reeve, professor at the Ontario College of Art and Design, for arranging the liaison with the elusive Adel Abdessemed. Translations from the original French were handled with panache by poet André Spears and University of Oregon French professor Barbara Altmann. Journalist Terry Phillips was in charge of the Russian. *Merci* and *spasibo*.

My wife and I enjoyed a week-long passage across the Atlantic on the *Queen Mary 2* in exchange for me talking about butterflies and exotic pets (a fair trade!). So a doff of the bowler to Cunard Line. Getting there (to Staines, Milan, and Budapest for animal interviews in this book) really is at least half the fun, and it was grand to experience the reality of posh: port outbound, starboard home. Here's to my mentors at Leeds Metropolitan University, Neil Washbourne and Lance Pettitt, and what they taught me about my cultural studies. *Grazie* to Jutta and Professor Stephan Ruß-Mohl, at the Università della Svizzera italiana, for their hospitality in Lugano. And a hearty *köszönöm* to Eleni and Markos Kounalakis for their welcome at the Embassy Suites in my father's hometown, Budapest.

Of course I appreciate the gracious hospitality I was afforded during my journeys from the sources I encountered during this investigation. Their candor was crucial for my attempts at understanding us animals.

Thanks to my creative and supportive editor at Lyons Press, Holly Rubino, and to the entire Globe Pequot Press team for joining me on this unexpected adventure.

As always, I owe a perpetual debt of gratitude to my wife, Sheila Swan Laufer, for her skillful and patient first editing of the manuscript, and for her personal patience with yours truly.

NOTES

1 "Autopsy on Sea World Trainer," Associated Press dispatch published in the Santa Rosa *Press-Democrat*, April 1, 2010.
2 http://blogs.phoenixnewtimes.com/valleyfever/2009/09/former _maricopa_county_inmate.php.
3 http://abcnews.go.com/US/LegalCenter/story?id=4824123&page=1.
4 http://blogs.houstonpress.com/hairballs/2010/03/spring_man_accused _of_sodomizi.php.
5 http://articles.orlandosentinel.com/2006-01-09/news/orl-seaworld -trainer-killed-dawn-brancheau_1_killer-whales-trainer-shamu-stadium.
6 www.youtube.com/watch?v=sbegU5x_c8s&feature=player_embedded.
7 Mike Schneider, "Killer Whale Attacks, Kills Trainer at Orlando SeaWorld as Horrified Spectators Watch," Associated Press dispatch, February 25, 2010.
8 www.telegraph.co.uk/news/worldnews/northamerica/usa/7322889/The -story-behind-Tilikum-the-killer-whale.html.
9 www.csmonitor.com/USA/2010/0225/Sea-World-tragedy-How -common-are-killer-whale-attacks.
10 Ibid.
11 http://abclocal.go.com/kabc/story?section=news/local/los_angeles &id=7322036.
12 www.thehump.biz/.
13 www.tednugent.com/sunrize/sunrize_details.aspx?album Id=f8266815-fe17-458a-b217-03d73058cbab.
14 www.tednugent.com/sunrize/sunrize_details.aspx?album Id=01e04c6b-ef04-4c96-9d38-68277ae33956.
15 C'mere Deer's creator, Ivan Hawthorne, calls his product his dream come true. "I learned to love deer hunting, at a young age," he writes on the company's website, "more than a kid loves ice cream and candy. I later took my own sons to kill their first deer. I'll never forget my oldest son Adam sitting in my lap at six years old helping daddy hold the gun as I harvested a doe."
16 www.theunion.com/article/20100818/BREAKINGNEWS/ 100819746/0/FRONTPAGE.
17 http://latimesblogs.latimes.com/outposts/2010/08/ted-nugent-hunting -deer-baiting-no-contest.html.
18 www.tednugent.com/news/newsDetails.aspx?PostID=1072790#topNav.
19 Thomas Gilbert, "Hunters Are Just 'Hiders' Now," letter to *Register-Guard* (Eugene, Oregon), December 18, 2010.
20 www.newsweek.com/id/128842.
21 www.salon.com/news/feature/2000/05/12/Edwards.
22 http://daltondailycitizen.com/murray/x1897238227/More-arrests -possible-from-cockfighting-raid.
23 www.times-standard.com/localnews/ci_11204159.
24 Clifford Geertz, "Deep Play: Notes on the Balinese Cockfight," *Daedalus* 101, no. 1 (1972): 1–37.
25 www.nytimes.com/2003/12/23/science/from-the-head-of-a-rooster-to -a-smiling-face-near-you.html?pagewanted=1.
26 Shane K. Bernard, *The Cajuns: Americanization of a People* (Jackson: University of Mississippi Press, 2003), 97.
27 www.angelfire.com/mi4/cajunsue/CajunJokes.htm.

28 http://vegetariancuisine.suite101.com/article.cfm/how_many_people _are_vegetarian.

29 www.haynieandassociates.com/.

30 www.hsus.org/acf/fighting/cockfight/state_cockfighting_laws_ranked .html#Alabama.

31 www.hsus.org/press_and_publications/press_releases/louisiana_cockfighting _rais_031709.html.

32 "Major Describes Move," *New York Times*, February 8, 1968.

33 www.nola.com/news/t-p/capital/index.ssf?/base/news-6/ 1237353742170370.xml&coll=1.

34 www.nlm.nih.gov/hmd/greek/greek_oath.html.

35 www.startribune.com/entertainment/music/105781818.html.

36 http://montgomerygentry.com/news/troy-gentry-statement.

37 *Newport Miner*, August 19, 2009.

38 http://sports.espn.go.com/outdoors/general/news/story?page=g_fea_bear _pet_OR_new-CA-home05_M.Freeman.

39 Mark Freeman, "Once a Pet, Bear Adjusts to Zoo," *Register-Guard* (Eugene, Oregon), December 29, 2010.

40 www.hsus.org/acf/fighting/cockfight/state_cockfighting_laws_ranked .html#Kentucky.

41 www.news-expressky.com/articles/2010/05/01/top_story/01cock.txt.

42 www.hsus.org/acf/fighting/cockfight/state_cockfighting_laws_ranked .html#Kentucky.

43 http://articles.sfgate.com/2008-03-30/bay-area/17169017 _1_animal-rights-rights-groups-public-forum.

44 www.waltermcbean.com/past_adel.shtml.

45 www.ktvu.com/video/15667485/index.html.

46 Abdessemed's agent and I did enjoy a convivial correspondence over the months of negotiations. In one note, along with her latest rejection, she added, "I enjoyed watching your interview on 'The Daily Show.' Quite interesting. Made me order the book."

47 *New York Magazine*, May 6, 1968, 48–49.

48 Cynthia Carr, *On Edge: Performance at the End of the Twentieth Century* (Hanover, NH: Wesleyan University Press, 1993), 181.

49 Jim Abrams, "Congress Passes Bill to Stop 'Crush Videos,'" Associated Press dispatch, November 19, 2010.

50 David Cannadine, *Ornamentalism: How the British Saw Their Empire* (London: Penguin Books, 2001), 115.

51 www.telegraph.co.uk/news/uknews/1556808/Ministers-eye-Her -Majestys-swans.html.

52 Ernest Hemingway, *Death in the Afternoon* (New York: Scribner, 1999), 61.

53 *The Early Show*, CBS, October 4, 2010.

54 Read more: www.nydailynews.com/news/world/2010/06/15/2010-06 -15_bullfighter_christian_hernandez_runs_out_of_ring_in_mexico _arrested_for_breach_o.html#ixzz0r4sUkhY3.

55 http://blog.peta.org/archives/2010/06/peta_pays_fine.php.

56 www.dailymail.co.uk/news/article-1313480/Spains-blood-fiestas-make -bullfights-tame-youre-paying-them.html.

57 www.guardian.co.uk/world/2006/may/26/animalwelfare.uk.

58 www.pressdemocrat.com/article/20100512/ARTICLES/ 100519834/1036?Title=Fulton-plan-closing-to-cost-123-jobs-.

59 Shirley Jackson, "The Lottery," in *200 Years of Great American Short Stories* (Boston: Houghton Mifflin, 1975), 782–783.

60 www.newsweek.com/2007/09/24/tradition-or-cruelty.html.

61 http://articles.latimes.com/2010/apr/19/local/la-me-0420-bear-hunting-20100420.

62 Stewart Breck et al., "Selective Foraging for Anthropogenic Resources by Black Bears: Minivans in Yosemite National Park," *Journal of Mammalogy* 90, no. 5 (2009): 1041–1044.

63 X.-B. Jin and A. L. Yen, "Conservation and the Cricket Culture in China," *Journal of Insect Conservation* 2 (1998), 211–216.

64 http://online.wsj.com/article/SB125935631852667013.html.

65 Hugh Raffles, "Cricket Fighting," *Granta* 98 (Summer 2007), 132.

66 http://blog.nola.com/judywalker/2008/06/biting_back_fried_dragonfly_an.html.

67 www.harvardsquarelibrary.org/poets/bates.php.

68 www.sheepskinfactory.com/babycare.cfm.

69 www.denverpost.com/ci_15590722.

70 www.animalliberationpressoffice.org/news_articles.htm.

71 www.noisecreep.com/2010/08/05/earth-crisis-arson-alf-lone-wolf/.

72 www.9news.com/rss/article.aspx?storyid=147068.

73 Alfred Lord Tennyson, *In Memoriam A. H. H.* (London: The Bankside Press, 1900), 60.

74 www.huffingtonpost.com/social/Vixen13/walter-bond-denver-arson-_n_657767_54911537.html.

75 As of the date of publication, Tim Amlaw is no longer employed by the American Humane Association or affiliated with its farm animal certification program.

76 "The Humane Touch," American Humane Association pamphlet, Englewood, Colorado.

77 Temple Grandin and Catherine Johnson, *Animals in Translation: Using the Mysteries of Autism to Decode Animal Behavior* (New York: Simon & Schuster, 2005), 8.

78 *Ibid.*, 37.

79 www.lonelyplanet.com/mexico/travel-tips-and-articles/42/15617.

80 "Mexican Rodeo Cancels 'Steer-tailing,'" *Denver Post*, August 7, 2010.

81 www.youtube.com/watch?v=gYTkM1OHFQg.

82 www.dispatch.com/live/content/local_news/stories/2010/05/28/100000-bond-set-in-dairy-cruelty-case.html.

83 www.negotiationisover.com/2010/05/28/conklin-dairy-the-time-for-a-monumental-action-is-now/.

84 www.10tv.com/live/content/local/stories/2010/05/31/story-plain-city-dairy-farm-protest.html?sid-102.

85 www.cdc.gov/HomeandRecreationalSafety/Dog-Bites/dogbite-factsheet.html.

86 www.nydailynews.com/ny_local/2009/05/06/2009-05-06_cow_hoofs_it_from_qns_butcher.html.

87 Alex Pacheco (with Anna Francoine), "The Silver Spring Monkeys," in *In Defense of Animals*, Peter Singer, ed. (New York: Basil Blackwell, 1995), 135.

88 Alston Chase, *In a Dark Wood* (New Brunswick, NJ: Transaction Publishers, 2009), 194–195.

89 Leland Shapiro, *Applied Animal Ethics* (Simi Valley, CA: Ari Farms, 2007), 114–117.

90 www.psy.uab.edu/taub.htm.

91 Hans Ruesch, *Slaughter of the Innocent*, CIVITAS Publication, Klosters (Switzerland), 1983, 410.

92 Nicholas Wade, "Harvard Finds Scientist Guilty of Misconduct," *New York Times*, August 21, 2010.

93 www.fox59.com/news/wxin-cock-fighting-folo-092410,0,1548661.story.

94 Joseph Byrd, "In Defense of SPAM," *North Coast Journal*, August 26, 2010, 17.

95 www.dispatch.com/live/content/local_news/stories/2007/11/24/pikelion.ART_ART_11-24-07_B1_N38IOUR.html.

96 www.portsmouth-dailytimes.com/view/full_story/9641908/article-1-killed-another-injured-in-train-collision?instance=secondary_news_left_column.

97 http://abcnews.go.com/WN/fatal-bear-mauling-questions-private-menageries/story?id-11452990&page-1.

98 www.dispatch.com/live/content/local_news/stories/2010/08/20/0820-exhibitor-owned-bear-kills-man.html.

99 www.ivu.org/history/gandhi/.

100 Mark Twain, "The Lowest Animal," in *Past to Present: Ideas that Changed Our World*, Stuart Hirschberg and Terry Hirschberg, eds. (Upper Saddle River, NJ: Prentice Hall, 2003), 356–360.

101 www.guardian.co.uk/world/us-embassy-cables-documents/218324.

102 http://washingtonscene.thehill.com/in-the-know/36-news/7223-boehner-and-cantor-call-for-closing-of-smithsonian-exhibit.

103 www.nytimes.com/2010/12/12/opinion/12rich.html?_r-1&hp.

104 www.registerguard.com/csp/cms/sites/web/opinion/25634933-47/cash-coffee-bros-dutch-drive.csp.

106 www.greatapeproject.org/.

107 Ralph Waldo Emerson, *The Conduct of Life* (Boston: Ticknor and Fields, 1860), 5.

107 Ralph Keyes, *Euphemania: Our Love Affair with Euphemisms* (New York: Little, Brown and Company, 2010), 4.

INDEX